OCCUPATION DIARY

Philip Le Sauteur

Seeker
Publishing & Distribution
in the Channel Islands

Published in 2017 by
SEEKER PUBLISHING & DISTRIBUTION
Units 1 & 2 Elms Farm
La Route de la Hougue Mauger
St Mary
Jersey   JE3 3BA

www.seekerpublishing.com

Origination by
SEAFLOWER BOOKS
www.ex-librisbooks.co.uk

Printed by CPI Anthony Rowe
Chippenham, Wiltshire

ISBN 978-0-9955644-1-1

*Special thanks for help and support go to family, friends
and Paul Ronanye of CIOS*

CONTENTS

1940   6

1941   58

1942   118

1943   202

1944   232

1945   294

1940

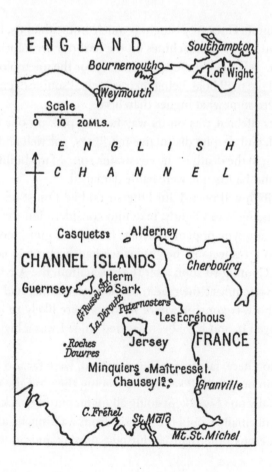

ENGLAND
Southampton
Bournemouth
I. of Wight
Weymouth

Scale
0   10   20 MLS.

E N G L I S H

C H A N N E L

Casquets   Alderney
CHANNEL ISLANDS
Cherbourg
Herm
Guernsey   Sark
Gt Russel Str.
La Déroute   Paternosters
Les Ecréhous
Roches
Douvres   Jersey   FRANCE
Minquiers   Maîtresse I.
Chausey Is.   Granville
C. Fréhel   St Malo
Mt. St. Michel

JULY 1940

July 4th 1940

So many things have happened during the last week or two, it seems like living in a nightmare; the panic during the awful time of June 19th – 21st, when the whole island resembled nothing so much as a huge lunatic asylum. Then there was the quiet settling down period of the next day or two, when we received the enquiry visitation of both Nazi and RAF planes but without excitement, until as reported on the radio, our little air raid on Friday evening – personally, I must admit I thoroughly enjoyed that little bit of excitement, and the motorbike got toured most unmercifully.

There were 29 small 'eggs' dropped, together with incendiaries and much machine gunning, and the casualties were 11 killed and about 30 injured. We received the attention of three Dorniers in three separate raids during the period 7.00 to 9.30 p.m.

From all accounts Guernsey caught it much worse than us, being treated to a concentrated attack by six machines on the harbour area during the time the mail boat was in. It is the practice in Guernsey for the unemployed population to gather around the mail boat, being their principal source of entertainment, so the casualties were somewhat higher than here.

The Guernsey lifeboat was on its way here to pick up our lifeboat to take both to England, and despite distinctive markings, got well and truly machine gunned, resulting in the death of the coxswain's son. Many buildings in the area of our harbour and La Rocque were badly damaged.

I suppose Britain will regard our little air raid as a most insignificant affair, but before dismissing it too lightly, take into consideration the fact we had no protection from any type of plane, barrage balloon or gun – not even a rifle to keep them up to a respectable height, as we had been most conscientious in our disarming. Coming so soon after the evacuation, the Air Raid Precaution (ARP) services were not at their best, as many personnel had evacuated, and no one knew who was gone or where wardens were likely to be on duty. I thoroughly enjoyed it, and have been assured since I was a bigger danger than the bombs.

The population here, far from being panicked, were far too inquisitive, and put a heavy strain on the ARP service in keeping them off the quays while the raiding was actually on. I was kept going all night, putting back enough cognac at intervals that normally would prevent me from walking, let alone riding.

We had numerous other alarms during Saturday and Sunday but a bit of machine gunning with negative results was all that happened.

Monday 1st July is a day that won't be quickly forgotten in Jersey. Early in the morning several copies of an ultimatum signed by the Commander of the German Air Forces were dropped, attached to small parachutes. Thus were we called upon to lay down our nonexistent arms, to display large white crosses in certain places, and to fly white flags on all houses and buildings as a sign we were willing to allow Occupation without resistance.

Failure to do all this before 7.00 a.m. on July 2nd was to result in heavy bombardments. In case of peaceful surrender, the lives, property and liberty of the inhabitants were solemnly guaranteed. Although the ultimatum did not expire until early on Tuesday morning, it is apparent the Germans knew full well the place was undefended for I myself saw German officers inspecting the Post Office at 5.00 p.m. on Monday afternoon. A force of some 100s, complete with equipment even to motor cycles, was brought by the huge Junker troop carrying planes, and the Occupation was carried out without incident.

One of the first (and expected) things to happen was a list of orders issued and posted. We were thus brought under Central European Summer time and a curfew of 11.00 p.m. to 5.00 a.m. imposed. This alteration of time makes us an hour in advance of Britain.

Spirits were banned and lethal weapons had to be surrendered. The use of all cars was banned, black out kept going and no boats are allowed to leave. We are not allowed to raise prices, and wireless transmission or reception from any except German controlled stations is also on the banned list. All of which seems to us to be pretty reasonable.

Now we are in course of getting ourselves used to the new conditions. I have had to come down again to a pushbike, in common with everyone else and, like them, I don't appreciate the change. The Germans have set up light AA guns in various places, and are doing their best to ingratiate themselves with the population. Fortunately billeting is being done in hotels and not private houses.

In order not to be tempted into listening to forbidden stations, I have disconnected our set – who wants to listen to the German version of war news at a time like this – and anyway the local press is now very much controlled. Just now, we are all feeling a little apathetic about it all, except those hardy optimists who expect another BEF to be here pushing them out again in three week's time. My own idea is we have at least 12 months of this Occupation to face before we can look for happier days.

Naturally there is a considerable amount of unemployment – the complete cut off from the mainland has automatically closed many businesses. As stocks diminish many other firms will have to follow suite, and so the employment problem will grow, I fear, to really big proportions.

The States have undertaken the repair of all air raid damage, which will keep the building trade moving a bit, and if people will spend their money and keep it circulating, we ought to rub along alright. Later on there may be a bit of bother with the food problem, but we will have to meet our troubles as we come to them. We adults can put up with quite a lot, and we can let the milk and so forth go to the youngsters. We will surely have to revise all our previous selfish ideas and help each other.

I am quite content if I can keep the doors of 'Pirouet' open – we are losing money every day, but even so I can see a year or more ahead if necessary.

In the circumstances, this firm is fortunate – many other places won't be able to stand the strain for long. We can manage to carry on, if not indefinitely, for a long time. We are lucky the losses incurred by evacuated customers' debts are comparatively small. Our expenses are reduced since one of my store hands was commandeered to run a chicken farm, the owner of which had evacuated and the youngster in the office elected to go fishing. Business just now may not mean a lot of work, but it does mean a whole lot of worry.

There has been panic buying of food, clothing, pushbikes, etc. which is a pity, as it means those with ready cash get a double share whilst those without get nothing. And it will result in the closing of shops before it would have otherwise been necessary. I had expected and hoped our States would have taken a firm hand in the matter and rationed everything from the time when it became apparent that nothing else would be coming from England. Up to date, this panic buying has not affected us – I will do all I can to deter it as building material looks like being a big factor in the employment market.

This place is as quiet as if we have gone back 50 years, and in a way it is nice not to be disturbed by noisy lorries and motorbikes. The roads are not congested, though we have to keep a sharp look out for our 'friends' who have been in the habit of driving on the right.

One of the worst enemies Jersey has at the moment is rumour, especially as the only news is German news and therefore even more unreliable than rumour.

July 6th 1940

A good dose of rain has made us all moan more than ever about this push biking racket, and also made us realise what marvellous weather we have had but not enjoyed these last few weeks.

I messed up one of my suits at a big fire the night of the air raid, and had another being altered in England, which won't be returned until the war ends, so I am not doing so well out of it.

So to the end of our first week of incarceration - it seems like a month. In that time we have got thoroughly used to seeing German Army and Air Force uniforms about and, with the exception of a few Irish, most people are accepting it philosophically as a fortune of war. I can see it sticking out a mile winter won't be very pleasant, for we will be going short of a whole lot of things. Already we are rationed down to 4 ounces sugar, 4 ounces butter or margarine, 4 ounces cooking fat and 12 ounces of meat. It seems we have a pretty good supply of tea available, which pleases me.

July 6th – 9th 1940

Jersey has been unlucky about all this, as since the evacuation from Dunkirk, there has been no shipping available to bring us anything except vital foodstuffs. On the other hand most firms anticipated some shipping difficulties, and stocked heavily against it – I did for one. Provision was made in the food line for some sort of visitor season, which we have, only it is the wrong sort of visitors. Naturally we find ourselves very short of certain items, and the prospects of getting more are, to say the least, remote. Even after it is over, it will be quite a while before things get back to normal again, though I reckon the British Government owes us some consideration. In many ways, we are feeling the pinch more than any other British place through no fault of ours.

I have heard, though I hardly dare believe it, we shall be able to write soon, in stereotyped phrases to England – through the International Red Cross.

Our local evening paper is much controlled, so there isn't much in the way of news. It is mostly taken up with adverts and titbits culled from old papers and books and the brief German official communiqués. There are some hardy souls who listen to the English news, but by the time it is passed on a few times, it is so distorted as to be even more unreliable than information we are given officially. There isn't much local news allowed to be published unless it has no bearing on the existing situation. Our chief conjecture and worry is how long it is going to last.

July 9th 1940

Today brings a new proclamation which allows us to pray for our King and Empire – I don't know whether to consider this a kindness or just biting causticness. There still will be King and Empire to pray for long after Adolf's moustache is eaten off by the worms. Also the rate of exchange is altered from

9 marks to the £, as first fixed, to 8. Which makes it buy 2\6d worth of our stuff, but the value in Germany itself is only about 1\-. It doesn't matter at all to us just now, except that it gives the troops greater purchasing power. Whether they call the Reichsmark 1d or £1, it will still only be a bit of waste paper when this is over. As usual, the proclamation ends with an 'or else'. We are getting into the habit of living from day to day, and don't see much sense in kicking against the pricks. Even if we did get really annoyed and chuck out the crowd here now, it would only mean a bigger and tougher crowd next time, and we can't destroy the whole German Army even bit by bit.

We hear reports people in England are rather perturbed about this Occupation. If so, and if it makes England more eager to get ready for the real show down, then our little troubles won't have been in vain.

Herr Kommandant has ordered ARP to be kept going, so maybe he is afraid of the RAF coming over – if they do come, I hope they can aim straighter than Jerry. In the last show with everything in their favour, they couldn't hit a single thing they tried for.

We had about 150 Jersey servicemen here on leave when the Occupation took place, and thanks to the pig headedness of one, the parole on which they were placed is ended, and they have been interned in a local holiday camp in which we had previously interned our 'dago' population. I don't think much of the British Government for allowing these men to come on leave when they knew we were likely to be occupied. Another item the British Government will have to explain is why they waited until after the raid before publicly declaring the place undefended – it had then been completely demilitarised for 10 days. I can understand the defence of these islands under the present circumstances wasn't practicable, but I do think we might have been accorded a little more sympathy and understanding.

A fortnight ago we rushed out every time we heard a plane. It doesn't cause excitement now, and we are starting to distinguish each type by sound. The RAF seems to pass fairly regularly, but mostly stay up good and high, and can only be recognised by the even note – and by the height they fly. German planes are running around all day and night, but they usually stay very close to the ground – too close for most peoples' nerves. They love hedge hopping and only just clear houses, sometimes using roads and gardens rather than go above the houses. This may be a petrol saving dodge, or more likely a safety measure – but it doesn't appear safe to us poor mortals on the ground. The worst offenders are the huge Junkers, 52 troop carriers, which fly so low over the beach one can easily see the top of them from the sea wall.

Quite a few lorries, motorbikes and cars have been commandeered for military use, and some have been taken away. I am hoping my motorbike will remain safely in my care. They seem to be after the bigger cars, V8 Fords being favourites. It looks as though it is intended to skin the island dry of everything that is of use to them – this, we hope, being a preliminary to an early departure. As far as I can see, they have had all the propaganda value out of the place. It will now start to be a bit of a casualty.

I have certainly had to eat my words about Jersey being the safest place in the British Isles. Anyone who had forecast a few weeks ago we should be living under the swastika would have been considered fully qualified for an asylum place.

Unfortunately, in view of stricter rationing now in force, the extra exercise of cycling and walking has given me a very healthy appetite. I am eating and sleeping like an animal and to date I am in better health than I have been for years. I expect the winter to bring a further tightening of the belt. We are disturbed at the prospect for heating and lighting this winter, as coal and oil fuel for electricity supply are definitely limited. If the worst comes, we shall have to go to bed as soon as it is dark to keep warm and save light.

Keeping this diary going seems to help relieve the absence of getting letters. We go out plenty while we can – if this continues through the winter, we almost certainly won't be allowed out until 11.00 p.m. and, having to walk, it won't be possible to go far.

15th July 1940

St. Swithins Day marks the end of two weeks incarceration by Jerry.

We have a less pleasant type of soldier here now (they change all the time and seem to be regarding this as a sort of rest camp). I believe there are a number of storm troopers here, but I haven't seen any yet. The ordinary soldiers about are younger, tougher looking and less polite – they expect everyone to get out of their way, and, until it was stopped, developed a habit of pinching peoples' bikes. The farmers wanted to pull out their crops of tomatoes, which had been grown as usual in large quantities for export, in order to plant other vegetables. But our friends won't have that – they want our tomatoes. They must be in a bad way to come taking the small quantities which can be squeezed out of a place this size.

The German Reichsmark is now 7 to the £, making it worth 2/10d. One bloke to whom I have just spoken describes it most aptly as legalised robbery.

I reckon after this is over, there is going to be a complete shake up in Jersey. There have been many big blunders. I believe it was originally intended to carry out a complete evacuation, as was done in Alderney, but instead we had two days of panic and then just sat back and did nothing. Properly organised, it could have been done in the time available, for there was a full fortnight between the time when it became apparent we would be occupied and the actual day it was carried out. Now there is the prospect of a serious food shortage and growing unemployment, besides other snags which even I foresaw a month ago. After the great panic, they just carried on with two mail boats a week, instead of at least one a day. There were many who could not just drop things and go at an hour's notice on the evacuation boats, but who wanted to go, and would have if there had been ships. If you ever want to recommend muckers, think of the Jersey States. The Germans have done more in the way of organising in the last two weeks than our States did in the previous 100 years, though there is no denying the Germans can beat anyone at the organising racket. We have surely had an eye opener at the efficient way in which they brought troops and full equipment here while we were still hanging white flags out of our houses and painting white crosses as specified.

I have been amazed at how calmly people have taken this Occupation – all except the younger female section who are thrilled to bits. It is blasted shameful to see brats of 15 and 16, as well as older (and who should be more sensible) females offering themselves to German soldiers. And there is more than one British soldier's wife going out to dances with them.

The so nice Kommandant has given us back permission to listen to any programme we like. The first few days we mostly felt too apathetic to want to listen, and we had a healthy fear of the consequences. But during the last day or two, most people have been having a quiet 'hark', and last night we were thrilled to hear, in addition to Churchill's speech, the running commentary on the air battle over a convoy in the Straits of Dover. We won't have to keep the volume so low and be stationed near the window now we are no longer breaking the law. It is rather funny, and more than a little difficult, to pick up the threads of the news once again, especially as it is some three weeks since we saw an English paper.

I don't quite know what the reason is for this much appreciated concession – it may be a reward for being good, or calculated to keep us good, or it may be our 'friends' want us to hear firsthand the news of the fall of England – they think.

We are getting German pictures here now as a special treat – talking is in German, but with captions underneath in misspelt English. I must really go once, while I have the opportunity of seeing for myself just how subtle the propaganda really is. Got to try everything once, though I fancy the experiment won't be repeated.

The RAF are most unpopular around this end of the world, and as soon as even the buzz is heard, usually very high up, down comes the swastika on the signal hut at the end of the pier, and the blokes who are supposed to be using the machine gun there make a dive for the coal cellar underneath. Maybe it is because they are wearing out so many ropes raising their lousy flag that they have stripped the lifeboat of all her fittings, ropes, sails, binnacles and instruments – an act which does not increase Jerrys' popularity.

17th July 1940

The air activity around here today is so great I am wondering whether the blitz on England has really started – it would fit in well with their kind permission to listen into the BBC, as I am sure they wouldn't like us to miss that threat. If it be so, may God give courage to the people of England, for if they cannot hold out, our hope of relief is gone. Yet I cannot conceive British people will ever knuckle under to the Nazi regime. Even we here in little Jersey would have preferred to fight rather than lose our traditional freedom had we been allowed equipment for the job. It was not without a good deal of bitterness we put discretion first, and as a reward, we now have to play the ignoble part of feeding and helping the enemy ready for his widely advertised defeat of Britain. The Germans here are supremely confident, although they realise the first troops to land will never come out alive. Yet they are ready and willing to go. We have seen enough of the Germans to know they won't attempt it without some diabolically thorough and well organised plan which will, at the least, try the resources of Britain to the full.

July 19th 1940

Our local authorities have made one awful muck up – apparently the Kommandant never intended to take cars and motorbikes of people still here – only those deserted. But our honorary police, probably to save themselves the bother of pumping types and filling with water, have just been ordering people to bring their cars in. Most of the cars have already been painted a dirty grey and some have been shipped away. A motor car at the moment is no asset but we don't want to lose them. It is dammed annoying though, to see German ex housemaids running around in taxis while we have to leg it.

July 23rd 1940

This is the start of our 4th week of isolation. Not much of a week either, for Pluvius is weeping hard over Jersey's misfortunes and to crown it the States want a complete list of the amounts owed by evacuated people – presumably to try and avoid argument when the great attempt to straighten out the tangle is made. Whatever the reason I have about 40 customers whom I have not seen through this, so I must find out within the next few days whether or not they evacuated. As they are nicely spread around the country, most in inaccessible spots, poor old muggins has to go out every evening routing them out. I started last night, and after cycling more than 20 miles in the pouring rain, got home nearly half dead.

My days have been taken up getting various people to sign various papers in connection with ARP. The Kommandant wants it kept going, but he surely doesn't give one much encouragement. I have to use my own bike and my own petrol and I have spent hours filling in application forms for permits – one from ARP to be out after curfew, one from the Kommandant for the same thing, a German driving licence and a German permit for the bike. Each application has to be made separately and signed by the ARP chief, the Transport Controller and the Kommandant himself – all difficult people to contact. I would resign, but I am not allowed to – you don't do as you like when the swastika is around. Actually I started on this round of accumulating permits in the hope of getting the motorbike on the road all the time, but my hopes are rapidly vanishing. As most of the Germans can't speak or read English, it is as well to have one's papers in order, or one might become unpleasantly unpopular. I don't know what would happen if the RAF paid us a visit before I had all these many papers – they have had an occasional peep at us, but only from a long way up. I did hear one came down very low over the airport and had a saucy look around.

There were a whole lot of troop carriers about yesterday, looking heavily laden, so I don't quite know what was afoot. There don't seem to be any army or parachute troops about these last few days – only air force. We also see German sailors from the barges. No one is allowed on the piers now, so we don't know much about what is happening.

I do know there was a very healthy 'crump' the other night, and the following morning the beach was covered with charred cases. Good old RAF. I wish they would seal up our harbour and airport. The Germans still fly very low – seldom over 100 feet – in order to avoid attracting attention from upstairs. We find it trying on the nerves to have huge planes missing chimneys by inches, and one in particular seems to take a delight in doing close turns around the steeple of the Catholic Church. I like to see it, for it proves the wholesome respect they have for our boys – and one of these 'skimmers' is going to come such a 'purler' one of these days – may it be someplace where there aren't too many people about.

I reckon it is time we heard more about this writing business – it will take quite a few weeks to reach friends in England, going via Geneva and Spain, and a few more weeks before I get a reply.

There is only about 200 vehicles on the roads here – a big change from 12,000. Quite a few business men are using ponies and traps, but most use pushbikes, so there is a run on cycles, and decent second hands are fetching up to £15, while the oldest crock is worth £2.

A good many shops have already closed and even Woolworths have started sacking their staff. They reckon to close in about seven weeks. According to the German theory, it will be all over by then, but we know better.

Our authorities have just woken up to the fact available building material will govern work – and received an unpleasant shock at the amount of cement and other essentials. Up to date, I have sold to whoever wanted to buy, having no orders to the contrary – after all the States won't compensate me for whatever goes hard on my hands.

24th July 1940

At last I have made my last visit to the Kommandant, my permits now being in order. The possession of a German driving licence will be rather unique and worth having, and I am hoping I will have occasion to use it. They wouldn't give me a label for the bike – that is to prevent me from using it except for air raids. All cars on the road are decorated with a be-swastiked paper, together with a label indicating why they are allowed. Doctors, for instance, carry a 'Doctor' sign as well as a red cross, but even then only have petrol doled out at ½ a gallon a time – whilst German airmen are running around all over the place in taxis and commandeered cars. What petrol I had in my various tanks I have passed onto one of the doctors – we are pals for life.

Paraffin is even scarcer than petrol, there being only three weeks ordinary supply in the island. It is being doled out at ½ a gallon a week only to people who have no other means of cooking and the prospects of getting more are remote.

29th July 1940

This starts the 5th week of Occupation and for a few days I have had neither time nor inclination to write. It all started Thursday when the police came along to collect the boss's car, and I had to go out with them and drive it in. Now I have the pleasure of seeing German Air Force officers sporting around in it. They seem to want to go as fast on the roads as they do in the air. I managed to have a few minutes alone with the car and, combined with their heavy handed driving methods, it shouldn't last them long.

On Friday came the news the service men who had been interned here were being taken away. There is rumour some tried to get away and got hurt in the process, but we don't get told things like that. It left a cloud over the whole island.

Then Saturday brought its little packet of bother. The Kommandant, who had been enquiring into the stocks of boots, clothing and other things which didn't interest me, suddenly evinced an interest in cement and had to be told within an hour what stocks were available. I don't know what prompted the enquiry, but I didn't want my cement being used for German gun mountings, so I thought it as well to get rid of as much as possible. I had a busy time arranging for deliveries today (Monday). Then I am informed by our authorities I am breaking a new law now being prepared, making cement an essential commodity. I, of course, had been told nothing about it, though I happened to hold the biggest stock. I didn't try, but I might as well have tried to stop Niagara as to stop the panic I had started. I can only sell it once, and I would rather do so before it gets hard. Our worthy States have taken seven weeks to decide to do anything at all, even though it was obviously an essential commodity in handling the labour problem, so there is now comparatively little left. I am afraid I have annoyed some of our officials, but I can hardly be expected to thought read their lousy laws. The net result of this is that we have been working like steam all day. When you add these troubles to about 200 miles push biking in the rain, you can imagine I have not enjoyed life these last few days.

July 31st 1940

Yesterday morning I was told by one erstwhile-annoyed official the interest displayed in our stock of cement was not just idle, and would I please dispose of it immediately to certain specified jobs. We did, and as a day's work for two of us, we thought an output of 54 tons wasn't too bad. It left us tired and stiff, but I was happy my stocks were safely dispersed on various jobs all over the island, and happy too I was a bit more of a blue eyed boy than I was on Monday.

I have been fortunate in that the only chap I have left with me, of whom I had previously had some doubts, is really pulling his weight. I wouldn't have liked any dissension in the camp at a difficult time like this. He appreciates it is thanks to me he is still working – even if he had got another job, which is doubtful now, all building and relief work is being paid at 36/- per week plus small family allowances. The single chaps get 30/-, which doesn't get them far. They have been put to work straightening up air raid damage, widening roads, and clearing waste ground for cultivation.

At long last I have managed to get in my long promised visit to the flicks. It seems few local people go, for the place was nearly empty despite the presence of some troops. As the troops don't pay, there must be a pretty loss attached to running it. As expected, that is my first and last visit while the Germans are here. It is rather difficult to follow the German pictures – despite the peculiar captions. The English spoken news commentary made one writhe. We were, apparently, expected to accept it as evidence we cannot possibly win, which is all they know. I must say the troops do behave themselves in the pictures, as elsewhere, at least as well as British troops. A certain section of the community started making rude noises at last Sunday's pictures, which, in the circumstances, was not a very sensible thing to do. The Kommandant has made some pointed remarks on the matter, and I fancy it won't be repeated. He also laid in about jay-walking and jay cycling – says his men drive with discipline and the civilian population must follow suit. His idea of discipline doesn't coincide with mine, for I have never seen worse driving manners, combined with which, our protectors, not being able to read English, ignore one way traffic signs, and being used to continental methods, often drive on the right of the road. They haven't got much idea of reasonable speed either, and seem to regard our narrow roads as autobahns, hence many crashes.

Quite a lot of biggish barges leave here every week taking spuds and other stuff – I wish the RAF would seal up our pier heads and so prevent this general exodus of our goods. A good many cars have been shipped away. I was under the impression at first the Jaguar was going, but apparently the Kommandant's 2nd in command fell for it and took it for his own use.

We have had Jerry with us for a month now – it seems like years. We have to admit they behave extremely well, and the only case I have heard of, of one getting fresh resulted in a month's bread and water for him. There is no reason why they should get fresh with decent girls when there are so many not so decent ones just dying to oblige. Whether he wants blonde or brunette, married or single, fat or thin, young or old – Jerry can always get a good selection. Some of this latest edition of Jersey cows is the wives of men serving in the British forces. We have had our beliefs confirmed the propaganda atrocity tales are rather highly coloured.

I gather that, in comparison with Guernsey, we have a rather good Kommandant, and so must be duly grateful. On the other hand, if rumour is right, Guernsey didn't take the matter as philosophically as us and so invited harsher treatment. The German authorities certainly expect their orders carried out, and, if they are thorough, they are at least just. Alderney was completely evacuated, even to the cattle, three days before we were even told about it. The same could and should have been done here.

Up to now there is plenty to eat although lots of things are off the menu. There is a big difference between a dearth of certain foodstuffs and starvation, and if we are left with the stocks we had when it started, we should be alright for quite a while. Eggs, onions and salt are amongst the moments 'unobtainables'.

The RAF have been having fun and games around here, getting a bomber down off the Ecrehous on Tuesday and yesterday (Friday) mother had the thrill of her life to see two RAF fighters quite low on the tail of a whistling ME109 chasing it seawards. It can't have been a very healthy business for Fritz. Also, two Jerry machines are tails up at St. Ouens, apparently not being able to reach the airport. The raid reported this week at Cherbourg was no exaggeration, for we could hear it down here, 40 miles away. It pleases us to have evidence the RAF still exists and that we are not forgotten.

AUGUST 1940

8th August 1940

During the first week, one or two Irish were inclined to be obstreperous, but after one had been before the local Court, and warned any further offence would be dealt with by the military authorities, they subsided completely.

In Guernsey it is an offence to say anything at all nasty or suggestive about the Germans – such a law here is, of course, unnecessary as we love them far too much to think or say anything nasty.

According to the Germans here, IF Germany wins, they intend to make a show place of this. They seem to have fallen for the place and many photographs of our beauty spots have appeared in German newspapers. They talk of clearing the Esplanade of stores and making a casino at Elizabeth Castle. There is no denying a lot could be done with a little imagination and a lot of money, but of course Jerry wouldn't have to worry over the cash side of the problem. He need only print a few thousand bits of papers and that would be that.

We have a German air force band here to entertain us and they are playing in The Parade – more propaganda, as there are any numbers of fools down there looking pleased.

There was a wireless announcement last night about writing to occupied territories. I noted with disappointment, but without surprise, they couldn't guarantee delivery to the Channel Islands and it would take a long time.

The States are at long last controlling building material – a bit of a pest and looks like losing me a nice order for which I had been angling – I have an idea the permit won't be issued, which is a pity from my point of view, as it would have been a profitable job.

The other day in Halkett Place, the loud speaker van had gathered a nice little crowd with its music (playing 'Roll out the Barrel' of all things) when one of the officers asked all those who couldn't speak German to put up their hands. And so, Jerry had an unsolicited testimonial for Nazism from the fools of Jersey – of course, the results were duly photographed.

One of the terms of surrender was that every house show a white flag – rumour has it photographs have appeared in the German press of streets so degradingly decorated – but each flag has a swastika superimposed on it, proving the welcome we gave to our German protectors. It is true photographs of a store they wrecked here were published describing it as an aircraft factory put out of action by German bombs and superimposed on that photograph was a plane burning on the ground with the British markings so clear as to be unnatural.

I am always wishing the RAF would appear out of the clouds when there are a few aircraft knocking around – if they only knew the amount of air traffic about here, I know they won't miss the opportunity. I should say at least 100, probably more, German aircraft come and go from here every day. I don't think I am exaggerating when I say it is as nerve wracking as having air raids.

We still dash out hopefully every time in the fading hope we will be rewarded by the sight of an RAF fighter in action. We thought we were in for some fun on Wednesday, but the supposed machine gunning was only engine misfiring after one of the mad fools had been trying to loop low over the town. No, he didn't crash unfortunately. I wish one of them would and then maybe they might allow a little more clearance. Yesterday I got on the roof at home to watch them doing close turns around the lighthouse, zooming down to within five feet of the beach and then up to just clear the sea wall whilst still going under the electric wires. A 90' troop carrier passed so close with his hedge hopping act I was staggered by the wind and nearly came unstuck. There may be some reason for this low flying racket, but it doesn't suit us. Judging by the amount of coming and going, the British propaganda tale of oil shortage doesn't apply – if it did, Jerry with his usual attention to detail, would not allow the low circling over town which is a feature of every arrival and departure, unless he thinks it worth using the petrol to impress us with his might. At night too, they disturb us quite regularly on their way to blitzes over the South West.

9th – 12th August 1940

Air activity here is always followed by news of trouble over some place west of Portland, which seems to be the area covered by Jersey's own Luftwaffe.

For the past three days, since the States insisted on permits for building material, I haven't sold a single thing. Although they have been so long thinking about it, they haven't yet found out how or why to issue permits.

Our Kommandant, Captain Gussek, is no longer our sole boss. He is only Military Chief now, whilst Colonel Schumacher has been brought in as Governor of the Islands. I only hope and trust he will deal with us in as fair a manner as Gussek has. This change will, I suppose, bring a spate of new orders and contradictions of old ones. Up to date, we have carried on with very little interference except the 11 o'clock curfew. There is no maybe about the curfew – five minutes over time brings you a night in the cells, a fine and a telling off in the morning by the Kommandant. Black out is continued, but everyone is ultra careful about it, so we don't know how they will deal with offenders.

Yesterday, (Friday) afternoon we were once again treated to the sound of the drone of many planes and the regular crump of heavy stuff, and once again we were waiting news of what has happened where. We could feel as well as hear the explosions and it pleased us greatly to know the RAF were active around the district.

Later news proves the foregoing is no exaggeration and every place around caught it except Jersey. I could have cheered about what they did in Guernsey, and am now anxiously awaiting our turn. Well, that is what I call a happy ending to this 6th week. Our existence hasn't been forgotten, and we feel we must be of some importance after all.

August 12th 1940

Necessity being the mother of invention, it is wonderful the ingenuity brought to light by lack of transport facilities. A lot of push bikes are towing trailers made from old prams or boxes on cycle wheels for carrying of goods or juvenile members of the family. Shortage of horse drawn vehicles is being overcome by making up bodies on motor wheels and axles taken from laid up cars.

Jersey won't delight in a 9d income tax after this – we are already heavily in debt, having to bear the whole cost of Occupation, as well as ever increasing unemployment, which is a too heavy burden on the almost non-existent tax payers. Our biggest source of tax revenue, the English tax dodging millionaires, have all departed – that sort never stay when there is any sign of trouble. The many thousands of pounds worth of stuff being bought by the troops is being paid for in special Occupation marks, which have no value even in Germany. Still, it may be worth getting heavily in debt, for, if the people of Jersey carry out their present intentions, we will have a very different government afterwards. The stresses of this difficult period have exposed many of the weaknesses of our present honorary system.

I have discovered why there aren't any prosecutions for black out offences – the Germans patrolling the streets use the rather less polite method of shooting out the lights, which proves quite effective. Just as well we don't live in town.

I am afraid when the RAF has come here to pay us a visit there will be a warm time for all as, warned by Guernsey's first packet, they are taking many precautions. The bulk of the troops still billet in hotels in town and elsewhere, but those stationed at the airport no longer stay in the neighbourhood, preferring the cover of the woods of St. Ouens Manor and AA guns are mounted all over the place.

We are a bit busier this last day or so – a certain amount of panic business, but I don't care much so long as the stuff gets sold. This States' permit racket is a dammed nuisance, but it has had the surprising effect of doing us a bit of good – I find people, instead of dividing their orders and going to our competitor for straightforward stuff and coming to us for junk, get the whole permit made out to us to save trouble – they know it is no use getting the permit made out to the other bloke whose stocks of sundries is big but useless.

The Germans have been warning people to evacuate from the airport area, but there is a rumour in town this morning of RAF leaflets warning people to clear. If this be true, methinks the fun isn't very far off.

It is amazing how news gets around – we heard full details of Guernsey's raid long before it was broadcast and hours before the boat from Guernsey arrived. I don't know how it happened, but what I regarded as a rumour was right in every detail. The Guernsey raid has been completely ignored by our evening paper – I am wondering what will be the reaction to our raid when we get it. The paper is carefully controlled, having a German censor permanently installed who issues a special edition for the troops. It will be a little difficult to ignore a raid on Jersey. I hope we haven't got long to wait for the answer to that question.

We can't get used to this Central European Time – I get annoyed with the BBC for telling me it is a 7.45 a.m. when I know quite well it is nearly nine and time I went to work. It makes news bulletins all cock eyed – if we want to hear the midnight news, we have to wait up till 1.00 a.m. It will be worse in the winter, when it will seem like we are getting up in the wee small hours. Or shall we be back on GMT time before that?

The shops are starting to feel the pinch. The only sweets obtainable are sticks of rock, and there is very little beer left, as we have not the wherewithal to brew it. The only eggs I have tasted since we got in this bad way are a few that my erstwhile store man smuggled out to me. Jerry has had the picking of all these things, and has a habit of commandeering millions of cigarettes at a time. I understand flour will hold out till Christmas, but don't know what happens after that. Anyway, that won't be the only thing we will be short of by then.

More than 50 planes have been circling the airport during the last few minutes. Everyone thought they were British, but they have now gone away. They may have been giving a final warning to people to clear from the district. The excitement in town was terrific and everyone seems to have got over their fear of getting hurt and would welcome a visit from our boys. So now we are all hoping they will be back for a more serious purpose in a few hours. They were too far away for us to recognise any types or markings, but I was surprised there was no fire, for the whole place is a nest of AA guns; unless our protectors don't want to give away the position of their guns. Maybe there will be something to report tomorrow.

August 14th 1940

Tomorrow, but we are still waiting. A couple of years ago we were all moaning about how much money the airport had cost – now we are just as annoyed it hasn't been smashed up. If only the RAF had come last night, they would have had a fine haul judging by numbers of planes which left here in batches at about 20 minute intervals throughout the night. At the speed Jerry is losing men and machines it can't last long, although there is no doubt he has a hell of a lot of planes. Poor old England is surely catching it. I am wondering what sort of mess they have made of poor old Pompy. Wonderful as are the efforts of our fighter pilots, it is on your common or garden people we here are relying on for our release – may God give them strength to hold the fort.

They have given up the pretence of buying with Reichsmarks, and are now only using Reisch Credit notes, which have no pretence of value except for exchange purposes.

If rumour is right, there were quite a few planes besides the official figure of 78 brought down yesterday – I have heard of 4 which landed rather prematurely last night. A couple of big barges have just left here, visibly loaded with cars and with Lord knows what under the hatches. At least 100 cars have been shipped away.

15th August 1940

The day when, according to 'that man' England ought to be 'Heiling'.

Out of a maelstrom of rumour I have collected the following facts.

Just after 5 o'clock last night, four RAF machines passed over town heading westwards and a few minutes later an urgent call came through for the fire brigade. I don't know if the two facts are connected, but I hope so.

This is getting quite an important place – I understand it has been chosen as the HQ for the big noises of the German Northern Army. They have taken College House of Victoria College for the purpose. If this be true, what a haul the Navy would have if they landed here while the RAF made sure there was no aerial back door. Maybe I am being optimistic but we all believe there is a transmitter working here – we don't know where and don't want to. Jerry thinks so too, and is constantly making searches. There is a death penalty in Guernsey for the offence but crimes and penalties here have not been published as the matter was dealt with by the States in camera.

Jerry is busy again this morning, so I suppose some place is catching it again. One of the civilian employees at the airport nearly got shot for sabotage this week – he drove his car into the hanger in his usual hell for leather way and found a plane parked in an unexpected place. He managed to knock off the tail, which was a most fortunate accident.

I am still bitterly disappointed the RAF hasn't come along. Our airport is being used as a fighter base and hundreds of bombers clock around here whilst their fighter escorts go up from the airport to join them. On Thursday we counted more than 200, before it became too dazzling to count. Apparently this airport is too small for heavy laden bombers to take off, but being closer to the English coast, is useful for the fighter escorts. We hear plenty of bombing going on around the neighbourhood, and are jealous we are never included in the itinerary. They seem to be pressing their attentions more in England's direction and, as I confidently expected, with expensive results.

ARP here is being rejuvenated – we have a German ARP officer here for the purpose, who fortunately seems a decent sort, quite different from the Harbour Kommandant who, it is generally agreed, is a bit of a pig. He seems to delight in making pettifogging regulations, mostly directed against attempts to get away. Boat fishing is once again allowed under permit, within 1½ miles offshore and subject to certain other restrictions.

Which is just as well, as during the period when fishing has been confined to onshore, one had to be a millionaire to buy any.

18th August 1940 & the 8th week

Things have been fairly quiet over the weekend except for a few waves of bombers passing over last night. England seems to have had a pretty nerve wracking weekend, for they seem to be concentrating on that end of the world. It is being more expensive for our friends than the enemy expected and that fact cannot be kept entirely from the air force personnel. By sending planes from any aerodromes, thus keeping their personnel divided up into groups, each group may know what its own losses are, but can get no true picture of the total losses. It is fact that of the 14 pilots who planned a celebration lunch on Thursday for when they returned from their blitz, only one appeared at the appointed time and place (Ommaroo Hotel) and he sat through the time with his head in his hands. I know life in England is a pretty average hell just now, but the Luftwaffe is not enjoying life much either. I look forward to the time when German pilots will become less and less skilled, as they are bound to do with these heavy losses. I have never lost faith in our ability to win, but I feel that faith to be even more justified in the light of recent events.

Things in Guernsey seem to be much worse than here – the latest ration is one ounce of soap per person per week. In everything their stocks were not as good as ours, although we too might be in the same plight as other occupied places but for the courage of private firms in foreseeing shipping difficulties and stocking accordingly.

We are having a quiet time this week but our friends have sent us another band – an army one this time. I haven't heard it yet, and don't want to.

We are having the privilege of supplying colour to camouflage the airport, which seems to be a waste of time, as many of the RAF know the place as well as their own backyard. Fortunately, I am not in direct contact over these transactions, or I might quite easily say something better left unsaid. I believe things are quiet out there these days – no planes sleep there at all, though quite a few come and go during the day. It may be a sign of jitters, but I hope the RAF will give them a chance to settle down again so as to get a good bag when they do come.

This week's speciality is lorries – more than 40 have been taken away and more expected to follow.

The good Winston still seems to include 1942 in his calculations – not very pleasing to look forward to two more years of Occupation. .

23rd August 1940

We are now allowed to write to German occupied and neutral places, and in consequence, mother is trying writing to an acquaintance in America, who will hopefully advise her sister in Portsmouth. Thence the news should reach brother Bill in Berkshire. All this is most complicated and relies on the good sense of everyone to pass along the news, for we can't detail in the letter the above plan. It will take such a long time to get through (if ever) that before family gets it, we might be in direct communication once again or maybe at least through the Red Cross as we have so long been promised. I would not feel happy unless I had taken every possible chance of letting family know things are well with us. Today being 23rd August they might get the news around Christmas.

As a finale to our 8th week of misery, the town is being decorated with notices printed in French and German promising dire penalties to anyone who should dare to say anything against the German state or who should repeat British propaganda, or pick up or pass on any leaflet containing propaganda. Dear me, we are expected to walk a chalk line – the poor souls have great faith in their threat system and yet the whole thing doesn't fit in with their allowing us to use our wireless sets.

The week has been notable only for its monotony. Their planes are coming and going all the time, but don't seem to be flying quite so low these days, or maybe we are getting so used to it as not to notice. It has become apparent they intend to stay, as they have even brought some of their own workmen to supervise the various look out posts being erected. Once again there are a number of parachute troops about, but not wearing their harnesses this time. We seem to average between 1,000 and 2,000 but men are coming and going all the time, so it is impossible to get any idea. They have taken over nearly every hotel, and nearly all bigger houses which are empty, and so are nicely divided up over the Island where they can't be touched without endangering the civil population.

There are persistent rumours the airport was bombed early on Sunday morning, but I can't make out why we heard no AA fire and why we weren't called out. It was announced last night that Dinard had been bombed and I am wondering whether people who heard the noise of that supplied the rest of the information from their imagination. If there is any truth in it, I am bitterly disappointed not to have been invited to join in the fun, for I have been so looking forward to it.

27th August 1940

Tuesday brings the news the reported raid was the result of one of our bombers returning from Dinard and getting annoyed with an AA squad who would insist on playing with their lights and pop gun. Our friend of the RAF did a lovely falling leaf and laid an egg right on the gun pit, splitting a big AA gun to atoms, which rather shut them up. It was such a tip and run affair it wasn't necessary to call out ARP – there were only a few bodies shrivelled up.

The coxswain of the lifeboat has to go to France tomorrow (28th) and has suggested to me it might be possible, and certainly worth trying, to get news through from there. There is no way of getting a reply back, and I am far from sure my note will ever reach its destination, but I am not going to miss a single opportunity of trying. I have always liked the good man who has offered to do me this good turn, and I like him still more for this. I know it will be understood why the note is so terse and non committal – I should rather get a short one through than a long one rejected. We saw a crowd of bombers and fighters leave here early on Sunday evening – about 100, which compares with a BBC report they crossed the Dorset coast during the evening. But though, according to them, they rule the whole sky, they must have found life exciting, for 43 of them didn't leave England. We don't see them all coming back, as they each go direct to their bases, so we can't form an opinion of how many get back – all part of German silence, as the crews themselves are left in equal ignorance.

Judging by some broadcast talks, the British seem to know quite a lot of what is happening in the occupied territories, though there still seems to be a lot of underestimating going on. I wish they wouldn't keep harping on about the food shortage – will agree that, most naturally, there isn't much picking and choosing to be done, but to date there is plenty. Luxuries are rapidly disappearing, cakes being the latest thing to come off the menu. Jerry brought a few onions from France last week – cost 10d each. Chickens are still obtainable for the wealthy, but I don't know what happens to the eggs, although I have heard tales from the various hotels of soldiers eating 5 and 6 at one meal. It would seem they hadn't much time for eating during their grand tour of France and since then they have been making up for lost time – they surely have good appetites. Despite this, it would be wrong to say they looked starved or under nourished when they came.

30th August 1940

We are being treated to a display of aerobatics by a crowd of 109s this morning – they wouldn't be quite so eager to show off if there was a squadron of Hurricanes anywhere about. They seem to have spasms with their planes. Yesterday it was Junker troop carriers, which being too big and awkward to stunt, do their impressing act by flying very low and scaring people.

One of their car drivers, who thinks he has planes to drive, managed to turn three somersaults in town yesterday after tipping another car – gives some idea of their driving methods.

The RAF were having some great fun around here last night, making the coast of France look like Brocks benefit night. We got quite thrilled to hear some loud bangs very close, but it turned out to be only flaming onions – not the long hoped for bombs. The searchlights here are weak affairs, but no weaker than their handling of them – it will be sheer luck if ever they catch a plane in their beam. I fancy the burst of AA was just a shot in the dark, but it annoyed the bomber, who came down to give them a burst of machine guns. As he passed over our way afterwards very high up, I said thank you very much. Once again I am disappointed they didn't make a big do of it, as a number of machines were parked out there. This morning there is great activity out that way, shifting guns and planes to different and (they hope) safe places.

They are so kindly showing the films of the Occupation of the Channel Islands this week, and, I understand, include pictures of their barges loading our cars, lorries and buses, sub-titling it 'The first spoils of British Occupation'.

We are starting to realise how utterly dependent we are on England. The latest snag is no wireless batteries, so those poor souls with battery sets are just unlucky. Recent news from Guernsey shows serious shortage of wheat, gas and electricity – and as their drainage and water supplies depend on electricity, it is a poor look out.

Yesterday afternoon, we were once again treated to the music of dull explosions – apparently some place between Cherbourg and St. Brieuc receiving attention. I should imagine the coast is a different shape by now.

During the very early days of the Occupation, before we were in touch with Guernsey, I was told of some weird happenings there in complete detail. My informant would not tell how he got the news, and in view of that and the unlikely nature of the tale, I put it down to rumour and told him so. Now I have to eat my words, and it seems to be proof positive in Guernsey at least there is a transmitter operating. It appears two naval officers and four men landed in Guernsey (believed from a submarine) for espionage purposes. The two officers apparently stayed a while to do their jobs and, being Guernsey men, stayed in their own homes. Now it has officially been published their two wives are being sent to France with orders to be kept at least nine miles from the coast and to report to the local Field Kommandant daily as a reward for sheltering the two officers. No mention is made of the two officers, but it is presumed they got away and their presence not discovered until too late. Maybe the women were so proud of their share in it they opened their mouths too wide. Since the news travelled to Jersey and was handed around here pretty quickly, it was obvious it was bound to come to the ears of the Germans.

SEPTEMBER 1940

2nd September 1940

The latest evidence of the ARP consciousness is an order our tin hats have to be painted white. Quite a sensible idea really and I look quite handsome in mine.

These last few evenings, every Jerry plane is responding to the searchlights with a Verey light – some nights are red and some white. It makes the sky quite pretty and amuses me no end – it would be the easiest thing in the world for one of our blokes to follow their example and so avoid unwanted attention while he carried out the job he wanted to do.

Henceforth by law, no cakes, rolls or currant bread are to be made. White bread is to be made with 20% of potatoes and must be at least 24 hours old before it is sold. It doesn't sound too good.

The RAF is ending our 9th week by giving the surrounding coastline merry Hades – hearty crumps. It is pretty hard on the nerves, but very soul satisfying.

The good Lord isn't helping our efforts at being self supporting very much, as it is weeks since we had any rain and fields and gardens on which we depend so much for the winter are suffering badly. Still, so long as it is happening all over the continent and brings Jerry nearer starvation level, we won't mind drawing in our belts.

The bombardment mentioned continued nonstop for 36 hours, though it didn't seem to come from the same place all the time. We had a few hours respite, when the silence almost hurt, but this morning they are at it again – south of us this time and further away.

I am hoping the family heard the little bit of news about us last night, about the lack of beer, coffee and whisky and the rate of exchange – not much news, but no doubt they will be relieved the shortage is only on such things – as we can well do without.

Jerry is quiet just now here and looks like he is concentrating all efforts on England. One of the standing rumours is the various number of days our protectors have been given to clear out, but last week's rumour the air force were going seems to be right enough. That doesn't mean the end of Occupation – we shall still have the civil administration ensconced in Victoria College House.

We have had an overdose of black out jitters lately and have been threatened about signalling to the enemy at nights. No lights of any sort are allowed, and it is quite an adventure cycling in the dark. I got stopped two or three weeks ago by a trio of tin hat soldiers and told to put out my light, but it has become general now, and there are traps all over the place to catch one. The funny part is no definite instructions have yet been issued, so one is liable to be run in by the Police for having no lights or by the Germans for having one. I always switch mine on as soon as I get out of sight of the patrols and plead ignorance next time I am stopped – anything to be a nuisance.

Pedestrians are not allowed torches, so in theory our black out is absolute. Before the Germans came, our black out did not include lighthouses but now black out means just what it says.

I have just been up to ARP HQ to start a row about this anomaly of lights. I learnt while I was there of a bloke who lit a cigarette on the coast road and got shot at (unsuccessfully) for it. Nice guests we have. Anyway, I have established the fact we are able to use lights if there is a raid – I wouldn't like to go careering at my usual ARP pace without any.

4th September 1940

My erstwhile poultry farmer is back on my hands – I had hoped the job would hold out longer, but owing to the shortage of chicken food, the farm had to be closed down. Anyway I have a certain amount of work for him at the store, which we are cleaning up and painting. Later on, as stocks get lower, I intend to reorganise them, so we will have something to keep us out of mischief.

I find this cycling with no lights is a bit too adventurous, as proved by a head on collision with another cyclist. There were bound to be accidents, and equally obviously I was bound to get one. I've got three very shaky front teeth, but I am hoping they won't have to come out and also a very beautiful lower lip but it might have been a whole lot worse.

Jerry has been taking away a whole lot of his goods and chattels – there is a strong rumour he is only leaving the Feldkommandant and staff and some 100 infantry – maybe so as he can flit in a hurry if necessary.

I don't know whether the BBC comments about the rate of exchange here have anything to do with it, but yesterday the rate of exchange was altered to 9.60 RM to the £, making a mark worth 2/1d instead of 2/0d. Not that it makes much difference to us, as the Reich credit notes used here are just so much waste paper.

After a period of encouraging dances by making them free, all dances are now banned. I think the idea was to give the officers the opportunity of meeting the local business people , but the locals didn't swallow the bait, even when specific invites, including free transport and drinks, were offered. The only ones who went were the undesirable female section, and the shows used to deteriorate to drunken furniture smashing brawls – hence the ban. The Germans have succeeded in getting to know the class of female who will oblige as and when necessary.

5th September 1940

Gas is now rationed on a quota basis, based on somewhat less than previous consumption. This potato flour bread as made by some bakers isn't too bad, but others have made an awful mess of it. I hope they will learn in time.

I have just received an order for which I was angling for a really big roof of slates – plum of the air raid damage jobs. I have already had almost all the rest of the air raid orders in which I was interested, but this one job makes it certain that I won't be able to avoid showing a profit on the year.

Something funny is happening here and I am wondering whether the following facts are in any way connected. About 10 people left from Rozel during the early part of last week and their safe arrival in England has been confirmed by news brought by carrier pigeon. There is reason to believe they took away some useful information. On Tuesday about midday some sky writing was done. I didn't see it until it was pretty windswept, but it has been variously interpreted – mostly as 'six OK'. Now we are informed tonight there is to be a really complete and super black out – and woe betide showers of light. Maybe we will know more soon.

Tuesday night, Mum and I were walking home along the coast road about 10.30 p.m. and I was smoking a cigarette, when we were treated to a rifle shot from somewhere close at hand. Probably it was aimed high, but, not being one of those brave souls, I quickly doused that cigarette. Jerry has a habit of hiding in corners at night to catch one out in any offence, but though we looked, we could see no-one. There is no doubt he is under the impression someone is signalling to the 'enemy' at nights, as proved by the many precautions and the dire threats of punishment for anyone caught at it. It is possible the super black out is a trap to catch the signaller if there really is one, and if he is willing to take the risk of being the only light about.

Nearly everyone has been buying up Union Jacks in the shops in readiness for 'Der Tag' when we can remove the nasty taste left by having to hang out white flags. One comes across amazingly few people who have lost faith in the future – and methinks they would be quite justified in the present black circumstances.

I am still feeling sorry for myself with shaky teeth and a misshapen face and a bruised hip – I wondered why the latter part of me hurt, till I discovered I had fallen on my bunch of keys and broken the ring and one of the keys.

We are having a bit of a heat wave – close to 90o in the shade most days, so I decided yesterday (Thursday) to treat myself to an afternoon down at low tide. I brought back a feed of prawns, but even down there one couldn't forget what was happening, with Jerry planes passing low overhead every few minutes and the constant vibrations of bombs and gunfire on adjacent coasts. This has gone on without ceasing for six days now and maybe the BBC will enlighten us one of these days as to what the Navy and RAF are doing.

The Manager of Wests Cinema has fallen out with the Germans. Apparently a German film was late in arriving, so an English film in stock was advertised and shown. The German one arrived a day late and our visitors wanted the English one taken off, but, as the Manager wasn't having any, the place has been closed – whether temporarily or not I don't know.

My previous favourable comments on potato bread were premature – owing to a lack of yeast, sour dough is used, which is quite alright until the bread is 36 hours old. As the bread isn't allowed to be sold until it is 24 hours old, for economy purposes, it only leaves a margin of 12 hours during which it is palatable. Palatable or not, we have to eat it and like it.

Last weekend's rumour we were to be left more or less in peace has once again proved to be unfounded. Certainly a lot of soldiers, airmen and equipment left here, but a whole lot more arrived, and there still seems to be more than 1,000 Germans too many in the Island. They drill every morning on the playing fields near home, and I fancy they find it beyond a joke handling heavy machine guns with a temperature of 90o in the shade. Makes us laugh to watch them.

Jerry is still pinching cars – the latest are under 14HP and we are ordered, under penalty, to keep our cars in working order – removal or breakage of parts is sabotage. They look like being unlucky about mine, as I started some weeks ago overhauling it ready for the happy day when I have it on the road again.

September 9th 1940

We have given up hope of getting a visit from the RAF for there isn't much point now all the Germans' energy is concentrated on London, as raids don't leave from here. We still see quite a few aircraft – a dozen ME110s have just gone past, but mostly we get the troop carriers and the few elderly reconnaissance machines which are permanently stationed. I think we have seen just about every type Jerry has, except the engine bomber, which doesn't seem to be available in any quantity. From what little we can see, I have formed the opinion the Luftwaffe, whilst being strong, is being much overestimated. Some of the specimens who dress up like pilots are weakly, bespectacled youths. Many of them wouldn't get into the RAF in any capacity. The age limit for ground staff and for the Army seems to be 15 – 65. Many of those we get here (I don't mean high up staff officers) are white haired and a big proportion, even the younger ones, wear glasses. The German Navy is here in force today, but haven't brought their fleet. They were brought overland to run the barges which are pirating our stuff. They too are a scruffy and ill assorted lot, and few, if any, of the services have been taught to square their shoulders and look like soldiers. Judging by the crowd here, Jerry hasn't got a big reserve to draw on.

Our heat wave has come to an end, with a drop of 25o, but it still doesn't to rain much. We at home are getting short of water, as it is eight weeks since we had rain, and things are dying for want of it.

September 11th 1940

I have to attend a funeral tomorrow of the Manager of one our best customers. It is bad enough having to go at all, but I wish the good man had elected to die and be buried somewhere closer than St. Ouens, with transport what it is.

September 13th 1940

You would have thought our funeral was a picnic if you hadn't been told. We went out to collect the body in the weirdest assortment of vehicles you could imagine, ranging from pony traps to farm wagons. I clicked for a front seat on a farm wagon, just where the horse could (and did) dirty my shoes. It took two hours to get there, after walking up hills and five hours for the whole show. We had a proper convoy, as some hundreds went and a thoroughly enjoyable time was had by all, including the corpse.

While we were out there, we saw a large convoy of heavily camouflaged ships in St. Ouens Bay. I thought of asking the Kommandant, Colonel Schumacher, please could I send a telegram to the RAF about it, but maybe he wouldn't see the joke. We also saw many guns hidden in the woods of St. Ouens Manor. Our pier is full of barges, but it is a good thing the British are not unaware of preparations afoot.

It is believed an earthquake earlier this week was a munitions dump in France exploding. Certainly the RAF was about at the time.

Monday 16th September 1940

It looks as though our guests are preparing to accept England's hospitality as a change from ours. Methinks they will have a very different reception when they arrive in England to what they had here. The white flags which we displayed so proudly will be noticeable by their absence. There are many lorry loads of fully equipped troops rushing about, and hoards of cyclists with shovels, rifles and full kit riding westwards (right term I hope) towards the airport. They weren't singing in their usual tuneful mechanical style, but were shouting and just making a noise. It sounded to me as if they had been primed for the adventure ahead of them. The cycles were ordinary heavy German ones, and not the collapsible sort parachute troops use, and they were ordinary troops, so it looks as though they hope to land troop carriers, possibly after parachute troops have landed and cleared the way. As you can imagine, it is most unpleasant to see these preparations going forward without being able to do anything. We can only hope the transmitter which we believed to be working in the early days is still operation and able to pass on the news so England's side of the ditch may not be unprepared. I still have infinite faith a cold is all they will get, but I won't deny a certain amount of trepidation least they should get a decent foothold. Well the RAF has done their stuff like Trojans and has shown they will give all that is asked of them in this part of the struggle. Now it will be the turn of the Army to show they are the same breed and for the civilians to show the harassing air raids haven't got them down. I can't settle to write or work today unless I know what's what, I shall be all jumpy.

September 17th 1940

It looks as though Jerry intends to have a roundup of all cars and motorbikes in the place, as we have to give full details, even to mileage, of all vehicles we own or have charge of.

I don't know whether the hefty and unexpected gale has upset Adolf's plans or whether it was just a bigger version of troop movements which is a regular feature now, but my fears yesterday things were going to happen have proved unfounded. I fancy the former is the case, for, although many thousands of troops have come and gone from here, I have never before had reason to suspect funny business. The power canal barges we have seen have a freeboard of only 2 to 3 feet, and would prove most uncomfortable in a gale.

Although they don't appear to be using Jersey as a raiding base now as they did at first, we still have to put up with the delightful music of Jerry plane engines all night – apparently on their way to and from the West Country and South Wales, and it is so pleasant and comforting to know we are hearing the before and after of a bombing raid which is wiping out families and causing the misery modern science has made possible. Can anyone wonder if I sometimes doubt my ability to come through this little lot sane?

Our friend Hauptmann Gussek, who came here as Civil and Military Kommandant on July 1st, and who since the arrival of the big noise Feldkommandant, has been in charge of the Military, is leaving us. We have a lot to thank him for, as taking it full and large, he has been fair and just in his dealings with us. If he were a fair sample of German, there would never have been war between us. Those who have met him are unanimous in considering him a gentleman. He has certainly kept his troops in wonderfully good order, and has avoided many possibilities of trouble by tact and understanding. I have honestly never heard anyone with a grudge or complaint against him. I wonder how many British officers, under like circumstances, would have left such an opinion behind.

A few Jersey men, who were serving in the French Army are trickling back home, and one who was a prisoner, and who saw a good deal on his way home through Germany and France says the food conditions are already very difficult. Well, if bad now, they surely won't improve as winter comes on. Many Germans here don't expect to win and I am sure, if they were certain of victory, we would be much more harshly treated. This last is second hand information, as I avoid contact as far as possible with the Germans. Many people meet them more than half way in their attempts at friendliness and quite a big proportion of the troops speak English.

11 people in Guernsey have received letters through the Red Cross and been able to send short stereotyped replies. Apparently no-one in Jersey has been lucky yet, but I am still hoping.

I have often wondered whether, in the short time we had to choose, I did right in electing to stay. Yet, if I had to choose again it seems to me I could not do other than I have done. It was the bitterest choice I have ever made or hope to be faced with again. Anyway, the choice was made, and there is now no opportunity to change my mind. Only, please God, it won't be for long.

Saturday 21st September 1940

I have just had the pleasure (?) of a visit from Jersey's most notorious young lady, a Miss L. Her claim to everlasting fame is, ever since Captain Gussek has been here, she has been ready and willing to oblige him. Well, I can't say I blame him, for she is quite a fine wench but you can imagine the wrath of all decent people here is directed against her as the representative of those females who give preference to Germanic methods of love. She is the sort of wench who seems to want everything in pants to be admiring her, but I was most abrupt, and mighty glad to get rid of her. Now I feel my office ought to be fumigated. According to last night's paper, a few enquiries have been received in Jersey through the Red Cross, but we are not amongst the favoured parties.

23rd September 1940

We had quite a shock to learn from the BBC Jersey was bombed on Friday night and it wasn't till today (Monday) I learned the statement had been corrected to Guernsey. Guernsey gets all the fun, for some of the ships coming from there are showing battle scars – so I am told, for we are not able to go on the piers to see.

Some amusement has been caused to all except the interested parties by the action of the wife of the ARP Chief. Apparently she got ogled by two German officers and she showed her disapproval in the good old cockney style with her five fingers. They promptly picked her up by the scruff of her neck and the ass of her pants and yanked her off before the Kommandant, where she was awarded 14 days and she is now busy scrubbing floors under the eye of German officers at the Palace Hotel. She is surely learning not to be so dammed silly in future. But it has rather upset my plans, as the ARP controller's deputy was only waiting to get the bloke in a good temper in order to get him to obtain the necessary permit for me to use my bike. I have a feeling now he won't be in a very good temper for some time to come. I have wasted many hours pulling every string I can find in my efforts to get back on the motorbike again.

We have run out of our stock of flour, but have managed to get, to date, one week's supply from France. They must be in a pretty bad way, as they are supplying us with the 1940 harvest, which is very moist and certainly not in a fit state to make bread – but beggars can't be choosers.

Meat rations are cut to 8 ounces and that won't be the last cut. Poor old Mick (dog) may have to go, as we can't buy any more dog biscuits, and bones are far from plentiful. We are eking out the little stock of biscuits with baked crusts, so as to keep him as long as we can. We are getting a little in the way of essential foodstuffs from France but I don't expect the barges will be able to run much in the winter, and unless we can build up a little stock, we will be in a bit of a mess. Still, we will meet those troubles as they come along, and meanwhile have to be grateful there were such good stocks of food in the island.

Many of the shops are only open a few hours a day, and others, including Woolworths, are closing down entirely. It is a struggle for any of us to keep open, and I have good reason to be thankful my governor wasn't extravagant and left the business in such a prosperous state. I am afraid it will be far from prosperous before this is over, but if we are still open, it will be worthwhile. The whole thing depends on the answer to that ever recurring question – how long will it last?

On Monday night (23rd), the RAF dropped leaflets here, and despite threats of 15 years gaol and worse for anyone spreading such propaganda, everyone in Jersey knew of it and the contents of the leaflet, before Tuesday afternoon. I haven't yet seen one, but believe it contains a photo of the King and Queen standing in front of one of the damaged portions of the Palace, as well as the usual guff about keeping ones pecker up. I suppose the Government think, as I first expected, we aren't allowed to listen to the BBC news, and so need that sort of thing. Anyway, we are pleased we are not entirely forgotten.

In order to prevent any more people getting away from here, all boats except some dinghies have to be brought and kept in the town harbour. You ought to hear the fishermen's remarks about that.

The local 'know alls' insisted in the early days to comply with International Law, Fritz could only stay 72 hours. This being disproved by events, the specified time became 7 days and then 28 days. Now, these fatuous and clever people insist 90 days is the time, and therefore we will shortly be left alone. If International Law did specify any time limit for the Occupation of an open town, which I doubt, it is evident there is no intention to get out. More hotels are being taken over – at 6 hours notice – this time only those with central heating, so it doesn't look like being over before winter. Many of the bigger garages have been commandeered at short notice, and a large number of really big trucks, lorries and armoured cars brought here and it looks as though Jersey is to be used as a repairing centre.

We have completed the first 3 months, and, if my most optimistic hopes are justified, the first quarter of our Occupation. If the next 9 months are no worse than the first 3, we won't have much to moan about, although I expect, when eventually he does leave, Jerry will give us a good hammering to remember him by.

We are told, and are grateful, the clocks are going to be put back an hour on

October 6th, which will bring us on a par with BST. It is darkish now at 8.00 a.m. so we shall appreciate the change.

A little bit of news about the Channel Islands was broadcasted last night (26th) on the overseas programme at 5.00 p.m. They said we were only allowed meat on 2 days a week; instead of 2 meatless days and we weren't allowed wireless. As they also mentioned the rate of exchange of 7RM to the £, I can only presume the news was a long time getting through, as this state of affairs stood during the first fortnight of Occupation only. They also said some people had managed to get away from here.

I have been living mostly on tomatoes for weeks now. They are plentiful and to be had for the picking, as it is better to eat what is available and save the too meagre reserves for worse times. But I am far from sorry they are coming to an end, as one gets fed up with the same thing meal after meal.

The meat ration is cut to 8 ounces – this was announced on the same day as Britain's increased ration, but I have been lucky enough to occasionally get hold of half dozen eggs from the good man who posted the letter in France for me. He brings some back when he can. The food shortage has made people go rabbit mad, and high prices are being paid for breeding rabbits. Methinks the bunnies will need even worse habits than usual to justify paying 25 to 30 shillings for a doe.

Yesterday afternoon (27th) Mr and Mrs Pirouet received a message from their son through the Red Cross. A German officer, interpreter and a policeman went to their house, and the message (in German) was read to them. It was merely an enquiry as to health and whereabouts, and took more than a month to arrive. They were able to give a verbal answer, taken down in German, all were well and carrying on. Even that bit of communication is well worth having. Unfortunately we at this end are not allowed to investigate these enquiries, or even to enquire as to whether one has been received for us. We just have to wait and hope.

Week the 13th ends with the news a purchasing commission has arrived to buy cars and lorries – apparently they intend to take everything worth having. One has to take cars to a centre in town for them to inspect and try. The 1939 models have to be there Monday, and as most of them haven't been started for 3 months the batteries are flat. I started putting mine together again – not that I think they will want anything so ancient, but it is a punishable offence not to keep a car in running order, even though one may not use it. Actually, I merely intended to overhaul it but the job got left half way through on the appeal of a neighbour whose old car developed rot in the body, so for the last week we have been making new door pillars – even now, Jerry will have a fit when he sees it without windscreen or windscreen pillars. There is great weeping, wailing and gnashing of teeth going on – everyone has developed a great affection for their cars. What is really hurting people is, even if they pay a fair price on today's standards, that money won't buy a car of equal value after the war. The worst aspect of all is our vehicles will be helping Germany's war effort. We presume they will help to create foreign credits for Germany.

Cigarettes are getting a problem as Jerry has had so many millions – we can only get two sorts now – both lousy. So I have gone back to a pipe to eke out the few hundred decent fags I managed to accumulate. It appears the day isn't far distant when we shall have to cut smoking out altogether.

During the spud season, a crowd of conchies were sent here to dig and a whole lot of Irish labourers didn't evacuate. Now we have to keep them employed and fed out of our limited resources. I had a fear Jerry might take men of military age to work in Germany and he may decide to take those.

I have just been having a look at the car buying (?) at the Old Town Station. I believe they are being generous as to price, as they can well afford to be out of our pockets. But it is pretty heart breaking to see the cars go to be valued and then straight down the pier for shipment – they don't waste time.

Blimey, they have brought some cakes from France and what a grab to get them. People are following the lorry which is distributing them to the shops, with no chance for shopkeepers to take them out of the box. We were on the top line, and managed to have buns with our tea for the first time in many weeks. One had to pay 2d for a ½d bun, but it was worth it. I have managed to get hold of a bottle of cognac through underground channels, despite the veto of Mein Fuhrer and his lousy men.

OCTOBER 1940

2nd October 1940

More proclamations were registered in Court this morning. One states employees must not be sacked or have their wages reduced. The second makes all shops open from 10.00 a.m. to 12.30 p.m. and from 2.00 p.m. to 4.00 p.m. This doesn't affect us, and is probably intended to save light and heat. The other is all clothing, shoe and textile shops are to close for a 10 day period - it is generally believed this is so as Jerry can stock take – and take stocks.

Escaping from Guernsey has become so popular amongst the inhabitants, and so unpopular with the lords of creation, a notice has been published threatening next time this happens the whole male population will be taken to France. I can't help thinking these escapees are a bit selfish. After all, they could have evacuated, and they can't argue conditions are worse than was reasonable to expect, so if they decided to stay during the evacuation period, why change their minds now, when their actions are liable to cause trouble to the whole of the remaining population.

The main fear against the Jersey people is apparently sabotage, for we get regaled quite regularly with details of offenders in France being 'fusillated' – a lovely term.

I imagine conditions in Guernsey are not as smooth as here – the latest ration is half a pint of skimmed milk only per day. Whole milk is only allowed for babies or against a doctor's certificate. The severe rationing of everything may be the result of sensible caution on the part of the authorities but I think it more likely to be caused by genuine shortage.

October 3rd 1940

The first of 10 days closing. It seems awful – just like coming to work on a Sunday. Especially as, when the news got around yesterday, everyone went panic buying and made the town look like Christmas Eve. These orders about closing and shop hours don't affect us, though we could quite comfortably do present trade in 4 hours a day – some days we could do it in 4 minutes. Ever since the evacuation I have shortened the hours from 8 till 5 instead of 7 till 6. Even so we do nothing most of the day. This last day or two we have been delivering the big slate order I mentioned, and so are able to keep ourselves comfortably amused. On the days when we have nothing else to do, I get the others on cleaning, painting and reorganizing the stocks while I amuse myself writing.

On Thursday I was given sight of No 1 RAF leaflet dropped last week, and since then I have been making copies for the benefit of those who haven't seen one. Even though the leaflet only measured 10" x 6", with photograph of the King and Queen and cartoons, each set of copies took me 2 hours, covering 5 closely typed sheets. Imagine the size of the print. Reading the leaflet, and especially the extracts from Churchill's speeches, made me feel like punching every German on the nose.

The week's great 'grab' has been soap, as it is rumoured Jerry intends to take most and ration the rest. So shops have been letting people have as much as they would take - anything to stop our friends getting it.

I have a feeling I should be rather unpopular if a German got hold of this little book, and at the very least should spend the remainder of the Occupation in gaol.

Jerry has disappointed us again by cancelling the arranged reversion to winter time. So we still have to get up in the wee small hours. They don't seem to look quite so cocky these days – methinks they don't like the idea of another winter. Whilst I can't vouch for it, there are rumours a barge went down last week with 350 men aboard. There is certainly another on the rocks at La Rocque, and St. Catherines is adorned with the wreckage of a couple of bombers. I also heard this morning yet another barge loaded with cars being taken from Guernsey sank in Guernsey harbour.

Well, Jerry isn't the only one who doesn't like the prospect of another winter. As far as I am concerned, it is like a long straight road with no turnings in sight – if one could see the end of the road, one could bear it so much easier.

October 10th 1940

A second batch of leaflets has been dropped, and once again I am busy making copies. But today is much more important because at long last we have been told we may make enquiries for our relations through the International Red Cross and I am not missing that chance. With luck I might know by Christmas how the family were in November, which would be most acceptable.

Jerry, with characteristic kindness, is allowing us to have bonfires between 10.00 a.m. and 4.00 p.m. on Wednesdays and Thursdays only. A bonfire near home still burning after 4.00 p.m. received a burst of machine gun fire from a patrolling plane as a hint it ought to be out.

Last night we got all excited hearing about a dozen bursts of machine gun fire, but it was only a fool with a flying pencil being pleased with himself and doing some shadow fighting – just out to sea, but quite close enough to be dangerous.

October 12th 1940

The end of week number 15. We have been issued with more official orders, making us officially under German rule, but, for all the lengthiness of the proclamation, it doesn't mean much. No public meetings are allowed, and one isn't allowed to ask people in to listen to any other broadcasts except German, or to discuss any news detrimental to the Reich – they hope. Also my little efforts in disseminating the propaganda brought by the RAF are punishable by death – if they catch me. It puts a spice of interest into an otherwise boring existence to do what one isn't supposed to.

Rationing of clothing and shoes starts on Monday with the reopening of shops, but we don't know yet how it will be worked.

Yesterday a plane dropped something at Grouville, assumed to be a time bomb. Later, when the Jerries plucked up courage to look closely, it proved to be part of the undercarriage of the machine. Rumour has it some of the barges taking cars from here have arrived safely in England, though that wants a lot of believing. These little alarms and excursions give our minds and tongues some exercise, but life generally is very boring. Roll on time.

October 14th 1940

One of the less considerate of our guests, finding himself in difficulties, celebrated the end of the 15th week by bailing out his bombs late on Saturday night, just outside the town between the Kommandant's residence at Government House and College House which is his office. One landed in a field and the other in the road, but houses in the neighbourhood were damaged. Don't know yet about casualties, but I bet the pilot will be on the sick list for doing it so close to the big noise. A section of ARP was called out and craters filled in quickly to hush the matter up – that, I suppose, is the last we will hear of that, as Jerry is not in the habit of doing much explaining – hence the wealth of rumours.

We find it advisable not to talk too much about things in general unless they are well known Jersey people, as the place is lousy with German men and women in plain clothes, many of whom speak perfect English, so one doesn't know who's who.

I am still amazed at our local girls. We have about 2,000 troops here now, and it is only on rare occasions one sees a German soldier just before curfew without one to keep him company.

Reports from my tame spies show Saturday night's affair was the result of a Jerry being hard pressed by one of our lads. He was in flames when he laid his eggs and just got to the airport in time to burn out (pilot and all) on the ground. Another one went into the sea west of the island about the same time, but the lifeboat found no wreckage or survivors. So the RAF can add two more to their Saturday's bag.

October 15th 1940

During the Great Panic, my chief fear in electing to stay here was Jerry might take it in his head to take men of military age for work in Germany. Time has nulled that fear, but now comes the order all men between the ages of 18 and 35 must report and state whether they have ever served in the British forces. It isn't much use trying to dodge it by lying about one's age, as they have full particulars in the recent census which we unthinkingly filled up in good faith. There seems no doubt; this is a preliminary to taking men for work in Germany or France. If I am called on to go, it will mean my sacrifice in staying to keep Pirouets open has been in vain, and I would have been better advised to chuck over what I conceived to be my duty. You can imagine the turmoil which this causes in my mind – my going will affect a good many people, not least my mother. I intend to appeal straight to the Bailiff if the need arises, as I fear it will, but I am not being too hopeful – Jerry doesn't take excuses. If the worst comes, I suppose we will have to make the best of it – there are others in the same boat as myself and who like it just as little, especially those who will be leaving their wives and families here. Believe me, being bombed every day and night is a picnic compared with the uncertainty of living as we are. If only one could see the end of it, one could face it with courage. It gets one down.

We don't let Jerry see it even if we are a bit down in the mouth. If we do have to go, he won't know when we feel utterly hopeless. We have to register tomorrow and then just sit back and wait (I hope).

October 16th 1940

A reaction to yesterday's pessimism has set in, and everybody seems to believe there will be no developments from the registration. I certainly hope not, but if that is the case, I can't quite see why they are having the registration – after all, we have just had a census which gives full details except about previous service with the Army, Navy or Air Force. No doubt all our hopes and fears will be set at rest soon, though it is possible the registration is a preliminary to taking us away later on before our friends leave us – seems to me they won't want to leave thousands of potential soldiers behind. What price the solemn guarantee of the German Reich the lives, property and liberty of the peaceful inhabitants will be respected, given in the original ultimatum?

October 21st 1940

I have just been able to piece together the facts of a peculiar occurrence on Friday last week. Apparently the lighthouses are controlled by switches at the town harbour offices, and a sentry on duty there must have been playing with them to see what would happen. The one on the coast road was left alight, and not knowing where it was controlled from, Jerry promptly suspected everyone in the vicinity. Those near Demi des Pas Hotel were shepherded in there, and those going along the coast road were gathered in a group and forbidden to move or talk. After about 30 minutes they were told to clear off home without any explanation of what it was all about – apparently by then they had found someone who knew where the switch was. I guess that sentry won't play with switches again in a hurry.

One of the soldiers (probably the culprit above) is presently in gaol on a diet of bread, water and salt, alternating every three days to bread, water and no salt.

As a fitting conclusion week 16, I have been along to sign on the dotted line for X the unknown quantity (store stocks). They tried to sugar the pill by having charming young ladies to do the clerical work, but it didn't make the job any more pleasant. I will try to keep the store open – there isn't a lot in it now, but the fun will start as soon as we get into communication with the mainland again. That is when my presence will be really needed. I have done my best, making out a complete list of what stocks ought to be in each item, so whoever does it can't go far wrong. Where trouble might arise is in the time factor – arranging shipping and so forth so we are restocked at least as quickly as our competitors. Knowing most of our suppliers personally, I could use the hoped for trip to London to good advantage. All this apprehension is upsetting mother pretty badly and my greatest fear is , if I have to go, it will finish her off, for with things as they are, she can ill afford to lose me. As far as living is concerned, I can leave her enough to last for quite a while, but that isn't everything.

It is now so dark at 8.00 a.m. (half an hour before dawn) that from today everyone starts work at 9.00 a.m. until 6.00 p.m. instead of 8.00 a.m. till 5.00 p.m. we have been working since the evacuation. Even 9.00 a.m. is really 7.00 a.m. so it isn't surprising if I am a bit slow in the mornings.

Jerry celebrated Trafalgar Day by issuing an order for all Jews to register, though most of them ran away during the Great Panic. The only one I know still here actually went and came back (temporarily he thought) to settle things up. They are doing really well in the registering racket – during the past week all British male subjects between 18 and 35, all Frenchmen, Dutch and Belgians have had to fill in forms. And the Italians have been invited to sign up for a return to their native land. I doubt whether many dagoes will accept the kind offer, as most of them are technically deserters from the Abyssinian affair.

The latest German order also forbids the sale of motor tyres – not that it makes much difference to those of us who haven't got the chance to wear any out. They are collecting in 1937 cars now. I haven't seen the Governor's car for a long time – methinks the few minutes I had alone with it weren't wasted after all, or else Lieutenant Volker had the crash he has been asking for.

Thanks to the many millions Jerry had from us, there isn't a cigarette available in town today, and few shops have any tobacco. Every week fewer and fewer cigarettes are made in an endeavour to make stocks last as long as possible. Looks like the day isn't far distant when we shall have to pack up smoking altogether – and we won't have any chewing gum or sweets to ease it out.

On last night's Channel Islands broadcast I was particularly interested because, amongst those sending home messages was Dick De Gruchy's kiddy, Doreen. It was certainly nice to know they were all safe, but I would have given a whole lot to have heard my own family.

With this Jew registration business, I am seriously considering having my nose cut back a bit – I am sure if I walked through town with a bowler hat, I should be yanked in and made to prove I had no Jewish blood back to the 3rd generation.

We just had another official warning of trouble with a capital T for anyone who applauds (or otherwise) at the flicks. Also warned are those poor souls who, having to part with their cars, have been having a last joy ride before they handed them in. Another notice all over town requests people who are hiding British soldiers to produce them, promising no punishment to the hiders and that the soldiers will be treated as prisoners of war. Remembering the Guernsey affair, of which we were officially advised as a warning, I doubt it. I rather fancy they suspect (quite rightly) some of the chaps here on leave when the Occupation took place did not report at the time.

Our poor old town is nearly smothered under with notices – the Germans are very wholesale and put one copy of each notice about every 20 yards and as there have been dozens of notices issued, imagine the result. They stick them on shop doors, windows and anywhere else the fancy takes them.

Our latest arrivals include 400 frontier guards and rumour has it about 150 dive bombers are to be stationed here. Certainly a lot more hotel accommodation has been taken.

We had to hand back our ARP identity cards for signature by the Feld Kommandant and our armlets (presumably for decoration with a swastika). If the rumour about dive bombers be true, we will sure need ARP here. I have a secret hope the need for ARP will help those of us who belong to dodge any consequences of the recent registration. When, in the early days, it was rumoured we should have to wear be-swastika armlets, I had a great objection and would have resigned if that had been allowed. But if that will help to dodge the feared issue of being transported to France or Germany, I don't mind wearing swastikas up both arms and legs and anywhere else they may care to specify.

I must confess this registration business has properly given me the jitters, and I have seriously considered trying a getaway in the canoe should it develop into taking us away. Such an attempt would be twice as difficult from here as from Guernsey. I suppose there would be about one chance in ten of me getting to England – the other nine chances would land me at the bottom of the Channel. But I would take that odd chance were it not for the fact the worry wouldn't help mother much and the Germans might make things uncomfortable for her when I didn't report with the others. I spent hours pouring over charts working out possibilities before I finally decided to stick it out and hope for the best. I won't expect to paddle right across the Channel – merely to get out in the shipping lane in the hope of being picked up. Even that would mean some 70 miles (30-40 hours paddling). I would have done it in easy stages by night, lying up in the day on one or other of the smaller islands or rocks until I got past Alderney. From then on would have been the risk.

October 26th 1940
So endeth the 17th week. One of the air raid shelters in town has been labelled "Reserved for German Troops", to which some wit has added "You can have it – you'll need it".

October 28th 1940
Last night there were mysterious searchlights operating from two to three miles off the coast – I got hopeful at first, but when I found the Germans just weren't doing anything about it, I concluded it must be a German vessel of some description. Nearly every night we see flickers of light out at sea – I have an idea at least one submarine comes close inshore for shelter most nights, and the light we see comes from the conning tower hatch when it is opened.

A Military Zone has been declared, extending right around the island, in which the curfew hours are 8.00 p.m. till 7.30 a.m. It doesn't hurt us much as, near us, it only includes the beach and sea wall, but in some places it extends up to a mile wide, which makes it rather awkward for those poor souls who live inside.

Of those cars which are being bought, many are being reserved for use in Jersey – a tribute to Fritz's driving method, as he smashes up cars so regularly. I believe there is a field near the airport used as a graveyard for those too badly bent, so they need a supply of replacement cars. The roads everywhere are decorated with large numbers and letters – directions to the various posts. All road signs have been duplicated in German, but I don't think they know what verboten means, as it is quite usual to find their cars being driven the wrong way in one way streets. Langsam fahren means go slow, but you wouldn't think so if you saw the way our friends the enemy interpret it. Honestly it is more dangerous now, and there are more accidents with only a hundred or two vehicles on the road then there used to be with 12,000.

We have run out of margarine, but are allowed 2 ounces more butter in lieu. The barges are bringing a certain amount of stuff – flour, coal etc – but not enough to keep us going, especially as they won't be able to run much when the weather gets a bit heavy.

A few shops in town are bearing the yellow and black insignia 'Jewish Undertaking' in English and German as per the best Nazi traditions. That doesn't matter much, but I am wondering what will be the next step taken against the Jews – I understand after all there are quite a few Jews here, although most shops displaying the notices are owned by Jews who thought discretion the better part of valour.

In order to ensure the equitable (?) distribution of available cigarettes, our nice kind Kommandant has ordered a proper scheme of rationing – 20 a day for troops and 20 a week for male civilians – none for females. We are also allowed 2 ounces of tobacco a week. In the case of the available supplies being insufficient to meet this, the Germans daily ration takes priority over our weekly one. Naturally those women who smoke are doing a good old moan. I still have about 600 cigarettes in my hoard, and one of my store hands doesn't smoke so we share his ration. With the pipe going and eking it out with my little stock, I can carry on fairly comfortably for quite a while.

All this time, I am not forgetting the hell in which the family are living, although for the sake of sanity I will try not to think too much about it, and to keep a sense of proportion. Here our major suffering is boredom.

That is 17 weeks gone – I wonder how many more 17 weeks before this silly business is over. The week has included the wreck of at least one large bomber in St. Ouens Bay, the sinking of a barge in the pier and the stranding of a big cargo boat carrying cars also in the pier – probably as the result of avoiding the oil barge which sank. So Fritz isn't having things all his own way.

Just heard the full tale of the above - the plane was a troop carrier and a crew of 7 went with it. Did I hear someone say "Good Job"? Apparently the oil barge which sank in the pier was so well moored that when the tide rose, the side of her caught under a ledge of the wall until she eventually filled with water and sank (Friday morning). When the tide went out, she was pumped empty and refloated. On Friday evening, at high water, they brought in a big cargo boat, which, thanks to clever seamanship, ran amok and hit the barge, sinking it for a second time.

For a long time the Germans have been worrying our States to buy one of the bigger cargo boats and run it under the Jersey flag to carry essential commodities only. The main trouble appears to be getting a crew. At present all boats and barges are run by the Reich Kriegsmarine, as they haven't got any real fleet to play with, and carry a local pilot. I think they fear interference from the Navy, hence the plan for running one under the Jersey flag with a Jersey crew.

I believe the great idea is cars which are going from here are mostly being sold in Spain, where there is a great shortage due to the civil war. The value of the cars is being deducted from the value of the ship - judging by the number of cars already taken, that ship must be just about paid for. I take it any credit left in our favour will be used to buy food and essentials from France. Whilst there may be some truth in the reports of famine in some parts of France, we seem to be able to get what we most need from there – a good deal of meat, flour and 350 tons of coal have already been imported. Generally speaking Jerry's famous credit system looks fine on paper – until settling day comes. For instance, the ship which is offered to us, the S/S Normand, never belonged to Germany so they are bound to make a profit on its sale. In exchange they are taking our cars which are sold, or rather exchanged for a far greater value of goods more essential to them. In effect they are getting 300% worth of stuff they need in exchange for 100% worth of ship which cost nothing and would have to be run and manned anyway. The difference will have to be adjusted eventually by the various governments involved. We shall be left minus more than £100,000 of cars, the owners of which will have to be paid, against the asset of a steamer of doubtful age and value. Obviously it wouldn't have done Jerry any good to seize the money in circulation here. To him, that is just so much paper, as his marks are to us, and by so doing they would merely prevent all transactions here and so kill the goose that, by his present cute methods, he is inducing to lay golden eggs. The more I see of it, the greater admiration (?) I have for their astute and cunning business methods. If they had taken ready cash here – say £1m, it would have been of no value to them until the war was over. Even then, if as they believe England was beaten, English money would be valueless. Whereas by their barter and credit methods, they are getting hold of the real tangible wealth of the Islands and will get more. Thank heavens the banks had the foresight to ship away all securities held here. By reason of the lack of death duties here they were all 'Bearer' and so would have been negotiable anywhere and of real value in his war effort.

NOVEMBER 1940

5th November 1940

I nearly got gaol yesterday. I left a light burning in my office, but, thanks be, some good friend borrowed a ladder and broke the window to get at the lamp before any German patrols passed along.

Another plane came down yesterday – at Rozel this time, and only two casualties. Another one less to disturb sleep at night.

They seem to be working on a system of self extermination, judging by the number of accidents happening. Another motor cyclist had paid written across his account yesterday near the store. When driving, they always think they've got right of way, and take no notice of traffic men. That may be alright sometimes, but when as in this case, there are two drivers with the same idea going different ways, things are liable to happen. We don't hear about all road accidents that happen but I know of at least two loaded buses which had serious smashes and it is a daily event to see cars being towed showing signs of being turned over. We don't know what the casualties are, but they can't be light. Touching wood, although one or two civilians have received slight injuries in collisions with Germans, they have confined killings amongst themselves.

Yet another troop carrier has come to grief. It is rumoured our latest Military Kommandant, Prince Zu Waldeck, was in the first one that crashed. He is supposed to have made himself unpopular, and this accident is said to have been one of the 'fortunate' ones engineered from time to time. But I wouldn't lay any money on that.

In order to satisfy the whim of some big bug, all pigeons here are being put out of action – loud moans from the pigeon fanciers.

Rumour has it that, during this our 18th week, there have been four aircraft come to grief in addition to the three mentioned above and definitely confirmed. If so, it makes quite a nice week of it.

Looking at things now, I realise it was being definitely optimistic in expecting this to be over during the summer of 1941. If, as I fear, this does go to 1942, we will have a most uncomfortable passage during the winter of 1941. Many people here, getting their information from the stars I imagine, have been holding out the belief it would be all over (and England won) by the end of October. Now this has passed, they have extended the time limit to Christmas. These same people, with their wishful thinking, have all been told by someone, who spoke to someone, who knew someone, who had seen a leaflet dropped by the RAF telling the Germans the 48 hours, 72 hours, 7 days, 28 days or 90 days allowed by International Law had elapsed, and would they please go away. (The time limit varied with the time of the telling, but in each case the Germans had been given so many days to clear out.) That is the ever recurring rumour above all others. Thanks be I haven't got the receptive ability to believe all these things. If anything, I have been too sceptical, for some of the things I refused to believe have turned out to be true. Still, if one believes none of these tales, one is right most of the time. The very circumstances of having so little news make a fine breeding ground for rumour.

11th November 1940

This week brings us news the troops are to be allowed to buy spirits in the pubs but not civilians. It is the general opinion this unfair differentiation in cigarettes and spirits is primarily intended to cause trouble. Personally I would have preferred to see all spirits at the bottom of the sea. I must admit there has been very little drunkenness amongst the troops whilst they have been able to get only wines and cider, but spirits will almost certainly cause trouble.

12th November 1940

Another piece of good (?) news. Ever since we were given permission by the good Captain Gussek to listen to English broadcasts, rumours constantly circulated it was to be stopped and receivers confiscated. Constant repetition had made us ignore the rumour, but today brings the official order all sets have to be handed in before the 20th. Reason – espionage in Guernsey. I suppose Guernsey has been told espionage in Jersey. They are surely going out of their way to annoy us and make us obstreperous. It will be very miserable indeed to have no news at all except the German reports of devastating bombing attacks published each night in our paper, but I suppose we must consider ourselves fortunate to have had the wireless for so long. I wasn't looking forward to the winter before, but it will be pretty awful now. I suppose some crumbs of news will trickle through, but it will be so distorted by the time one hears it and so hidden under false rumours, it will amount to nothing.

12th – 13th November 1940

The Germans don't seem to realise their action will make a golden opportunity for false rumours to circulate and be believed. Our local rag has excelled itself by drawing the attention of our friends to the fact we in Jersey are ostensibly being punished for what Guernsey is supposed to have done – not for any misconduct on our part. I admire their courage, but it certainly won't have any effect except as a protest. I also admire the way in which they print the German reports verbatim – the English is very funny, but they don't correct it. Certainly, in view of the very difficult circumstances under which they are working, they deserve praise.

November 14th 1940

Last night we had the most terrific cyclone I have ever known, and nearly every house in the Island has suffered. Our place is alright, but I lost my wireless pole and 100 feet of fencing. This epistle looks like being put aside for a day or two, as I can see it will be coats off for us – chimney pots, tiles and slates till further orders. The damage is so great I am afraid it will make a terrific hole in my stocks. It was as bad as an air raid – I believe the gusts were over 100mph and the average was 85mph.

22nd November 1940

The first chance I have had of carrying on with this. We have had one hell of a time, working all the daylight hours and about very other day another gale, though not quite as bad as last week's cyclone, but in conjunction with rain, hail and thunder, it has made things unpleasant and difficult. By dint of much scheming and worrying, I had previously managed to clear our working expenses for this year, so this extra rush is putting money in my pocket. It is rather upsetting our stocks, but I just can't help that.

Not much has happened other than the wind and its effects. We still have our sets, after having registered them. Rumour has it the recent trip to Paris of the Civil Kommandant was to try to get the order held over – nothing official has been said, as they won't contradict the original order, but the date specified has passed and we are still able to listen – maybe it is intended to hold the execution of the order over our heads to keep us good.

The measures against the Jews are working up – the latest registration is of their investments and interests.

During the past few months, I have broken the all time low record for business by selling exactly nothing on four separate days. Now, however, I can also claim an all time high record, for we have put out a phenomenal amount of stuff this week – I haven't had time for meals or anything except work. The extra work is helping time to pass – here we are at the end of the 20th week, much to my surprise.

Some time ago, an order came out for cyclists to ride in single file, but that had joined the limbo of forgotten things. Now the German patrols are enforcing the law with a punishment to fit the crime – a week's confiscation of the cycle. Naturally quite a number have paid the penalty.

Also amongst the news of the last week is an RAF bomber which was brought down by AA fire off Guernsey. Four of the crew passed through Jersey on their way to the prisoners' camps, but the encouraging remarks of the quay workers to the RAF chaps were stopped. A number of Guernsey people have also passed through here, believed to be for court martial in France – offences unknown but much and colourfully imagined. Another German bomber in trouble let go a load of incendiaries at St. Ouens but luckily only one barn caught fire and was quickly put out. 54 were found after, and I have seen the remnants of one, which is unmistakably German.

Having apparently satisfied themselves with the cars of 1937/40, they have issued a warning to owners of these models who may as yet have avoided the issue. Also they demand that all motorbikes of whatever age be taken down for valuation and possible purchase this week. I am lucky, as ARP lets me out. I could have cheered when I learnt from the office that exemption for our bikes was being arranged.

26th November 1940

A day of great tribulation for the motor cycling fraternity. I have just ridden an evacuee's bike down to the centre (glad to get a chance of a ride again) and you should have heard the moaning and wailing and gnashing of teeth. They are only taking the really good stuff.

I have learnt Guernsey people have already lost their radios, as a result of two British officers landing there for purposes of espionage. Six other people, as well as the two officers, were arrested for harbouring them and have been taken to France.

Trading here is rather difficult thanks to the cleverness of some folk who apparently think silver coinage has an intrinsic value up to its normal value and so have been changing all their notes to silver. It shows a wonderful faith in Britain – I don't think. There is about £50,000 worth missing, and it is a double nuisance because these days everything has to be paid for in cash, so there is a greater need for small change than usual.

Also some moaning from housewives as the fat ration (2 ounces) is dispensed with and we are expected henceforth to manage on 4 ounces of butter for all purposes. It is becoming increasingly difficult to buy anything at all except rationed goods. I can see this Christmas won't be the overeating time it usually is.

At last official comment is forthcoming on the subject of radio sets – together with a vague threat should we take undue advantage of the kindness of our 'owners' in allowing us to retain our sets. It is believed this concession is due to the intercession of the Feld Kommandant during his recent visit to Paris. If so, many thanks.

DECEMBER 1940

2nd December 1940

Masses more orders over the weekend, including one all dogs have to be muzzled and on a leash. Poor old Mick won't like that a bit, and if it weren't that the order is for three months only, I would seriously consider having him destroyed. Apparently many Germans have brought dogs over picked up during their travels in France, and have reason to be afraid of rabies.

The chalk line which we are expected to follow is becoming more and more difficult - we are hedged in on all sides by restrictions and orders. One of our best known solicitors is paying the penalty of too free speech to one of his clients, who made herself most unpopular by transmitting the solicitor's remarks about the Kommandant direct to that gentleman himself. The poor devil has to serve two months in gaol, but as he is in very bad health, he is doing it a bit at a time. I don't know whether we are supposed to be daft or what, but proceedings of the above sort are not given any publicity, so presumably it is intended to be secret.

Another little detail calculated to add to the popularity of the Germans is an adventure of theirs at St. Martins, when two of them held up a chap and his girl, and whilst one kept the fellow covered with a revolver, the other – well, I leave it to imagination. Of course, such things have happened with men of the British Army and one must admit it isn't smiled upon by the German high ups. I believe they found the culprits, thanks to scratches inflicted by the girl, but we don't know what has or will happen to them.

I am getting a bit fed up with hearing on the wireless about communication with the Channel Islands. I have no doubt England and Geneva are sincere about it, but I know for a fact the enquiries which we were invited to send on October 10th have not yet left the Island. We have a peculiar crowd here now, including some in civvies wearing green armlets. I haven't found out whether they belong to the forces or are just refugees; also some Feld Gendarmerie wearing moon shaped metal plates hung around their necks on chains. When I saw the first one of these latter, he looked so sorry for himself I thought the metal plate detailed his crime, and he was under one of Jerry's peculiar punishments to fit the crime. It wasn't till I got close enough to read what was on the plate that I realised what he was.

Last Wednesday about 5.30 p.m. we heard heavy gunfire and a little later saw the lifeboat go out. Rumour insisted a RAF plane had been shot down in the sea, but I withheld judgement until I found out the following definite facts. One of the local pilots was detailed by the Germans to bring back a boat from Gorey to town, and on getting within sight of town, an overzealous German gun crew opened fire on him. Fortunately every shot missed, but they were so certain of their aim the lifeboat was set to pick up survivors.

I hear people moaning, whatever they want to do, it is becoming more and more difficult. It is even becoming difficult to find ways of committing suicide should one find it too much of a strain to live, what with no poisons left, and gas rationed, besides not being allowed near the sea without a special permit, not to mention having no firearms.

December 7th 1940

We had the letters which we tried to get through to America returned this morning marked 'no service'. Although it is four months since we sent them, they hadn't even been stamped with the local postmark.

December 9th 1940

We had an example last night of what happens when the RAF gets annoyed. Jersey wasn't included in the itinerary, but for about four hours airports on the adjacent coast were hammered. The explosions were terrific, with only seconds between them, and it made the whole Island shake. I was quite amused at the futile efforts of the local searchlights to pick up our blokes. We knew it was the RAF around long before the searchlights woke up to it. I always send them my blessing and thanks whenever I hear them.

December 14th 1940

There isn't a great deal happening except land mines are being laid all over the place in the Military Zone and a most persistent rumour all Germans are clearing out in January on condition these Islands maintain strict neutrality – which doesn't make sense to me.

December 16th 1940

Some poor old duck of about 65 was heard in town referring to our guests as 'swine' and is now in gaol until she apologises – from the way she talks, that will be never. Actually, she is in the hospital, as they found when they got her in gaol one of her legs would have to be amputated. Also in gaol for a month are two men for holding a copy of the last leaflet dropped more than two months ago – I wonder what I would get if they found out I had been making copies and distributing them.

The latest piece of 'busybodiness' is everyone over the age of 14 has to carry an identity card complete with photograph – don't ask me why, unless it is to keep someone amused.

As a prelude to a happy Christmas, we have had our Income Tax demands at 4/- and have also received the wonderful news next year earned income will be subject to 50% on this. In other words, if you're got money you pay at 4/-, and if you haven't you pay at 6/-. I expected heavy taxation, but I didn't expect the working man to bear the heaviest brunt of it.

December 24th 1940

This is the first Christmas Eve we haven't had a slap up feed of tea and buns. Never mind, the pubs are open until 2.30 a.m. tonight and on New Year's Eve, with a curfew of 3.00 a.m. I rather fancy it won't be very healthy in town at closing time, but I shan't be there so I am not interested.

Much rumour about a barge loaded with soldiers being sunk this week – supposed to have been rammed by a boat piloted by my friend who posted letters for me from France, and he is supposed to be in gaol under suspicion.

December 28th 1940

There goes Christmas – not really such a bad one as might have been expected, thanks to a pretty general draw on food reserves. I must admit, contrary to my expectations, the troops were quiet and well behaved – what rowdiness there was, they kept amongst themselves. Many of the pubs didn't open; all drinks were on the Germans, who were full of goodwill.

I am rather over busy – very worried over business details - it isn't so good when there is no one to turn to for advice and help. Anyway, I can't do more than my best, and I have certainly done that.

The espionage business in Guernsey which resulted in the arrest of several people and the confiscation of all radio sets has at last been brought to light officially. The Germans are making great propaganda over their generous attitude and, as the result of court martial in France, the two officers who landed are being treated as prisoners of war, and the people who sheltered them are allowed to return to their homes. All radio sets were returned in time for Christmas and the only one being punished is Mr. Sherwill, the big noise in Guernsey, for his connivance. He has lost his job, as the Germans say they can't trust him.

Which ends our first six months of this inglorious affair – may there not be too many more six months. I reckon I can stand one more half year, but more than that will send me nuts. It gives me great pleasure to come to the end of 1940. May 1941 bring us all those things which 1940 should have done.

1941

JANUARY 1941

January 2nd 1941

The employment problem is becoming more and more difficult. Some 300 to 400 girls are employed under the aegis of the States, knitting, sewing and generally making as far as possible the essential clothing which is not now available in the shops. Many thousands of men are being employed by the States on mostly unproductive work. A considerable amount of road widening is being done, and those trees which blew down in the gale are providing labour to saw into blocks. Experiments are being made at digging peat both at St. Ouens and Grouville, but the number to be employed is being constantly increased as more and more firms have to close. I can see ahead for Pirouets until the end of 1941, but the prospect further than that definitely does not please. Financially we are in a strong position, and become more so as we sell stocks and realise the money.

Mother looks hopefully at the postman every day, as we often hear of others receiving news, but the most exciting mail received has been my Income Tax demand. I have no doubt I shall be pleased if and when I do hear from family, but meanwhile I am not allowing myself to become unduly disturbed by absence of news. For one thing, news takes so long to come through it doesn't mean much when eventually you do get it.

January 6th 1941

There is more specific information about the photographed identity cards. The forms which we have to fill in are as long as your arm, and once again include enquiry as to whether one has served in any of HM Forces – including the OCT and Home Guard. The latter was only formed about three weeks before the Occupation. Those who belonged to the Home Guard are wondering whether, if this is to be taken as service during this war, they will be taken as prisoners of war. I am indeed pleased to be able to put a definite no to that question.

The house which the Kommandant had taken for his own use was burnt out last night. I suppose the British Secret Service will be blamed, as they are for all untoward happenings. It made a lovely blaze.

There is also news of an alteration in curfew time – 10.00 p.m. in town and 9.00 p.m. in the country. Although we had expected something of this sort to happen early in the winter, we thought, having left it unaltered for so long, we were to be left with the 11.00 p.m. curfew. So consequently we are doing a good moan. Folks in town are not so bad, but we will have to leave town soon after 8.00 p.m. to be in by 9.00 p.m. We have been lucky to have had so much freedom, and Mum and I at least have made the most of it while we had it. As is usual with most of the regulations, there appears to be neither rhyme nor reason for it, except as a reminder we are under German Martial Law. We have also had definite orders to destroy all pigeons – not being interested, that isn't my pigeon – joke.

One thing I notice during this cold weather is most of the 'other ranks' either don't possess or never wear greatcoats except on guard duty, for which purpose I suspect a small stock of greatcoats is kept. Neither do any of them possess the knitted comforts which are considered indispensable for the British Army.

I hear the French people are quite jealous of the treatment we receive from the Germans. We were described on the Paris radio the other day as Hitler's pets. The French quite naturally don't appreciate the many tons of coal, meat and other foodstuffs which have been brought here from France when so many places there need the stuff as badly as we do. In many other ways it appears we received better treatment. The curfew in France has been the same as it now is here right from the beginning.

I have hopes now, which I hadn't got a little while back, we might be free before the end of 1941, and am quite certain it won't be later than the middle of 1942. A month or two back, it appeared as if it might go on for years – in fact until such time as the civil population on one side or other cracked up under the strain.

One hears, truly or otherwise, of many Germans not expecting to win. I haven't heard them as I try to avoid contact, and anyway would hesitate before discussing such a matter with them – they are quite capable of drawing one on to say too much. It is a fact they have a very wholesome respect for the RAF. One of them, spotting an RAF plane high overhead on Thursday, drove his motorbike and sidecar straight into the air raid shelter at St. Aubins (the old railway tunnel) and stayed there. I do know conditions of travel in France and Western Germany are pretty terrible, which impress the German mind a whole lot. I am certain the old arrogance and complete confidence in a German victory doesn't exist in the same way now. When first they came here, they expected to be in England in a few weeks, but this inactivity isn't doing any good. We don't seem to have as many troops here – probably about 1,000, and I am wondering whether the daylight raids over France means they are attacking troops concentrated ready for invasion. This end of France was catching it this morning – we got this information not through the BBC, but direct from the RAF. I still see why we have been left in peace in Jersey. The airport was machine gunned about a fortnight ago, but I don't know what the casualties or damage were – only that the buildings were pitted with bullets. I am hopefully keeping the motorbike in running trim so if the fun does start, I can enjoy it.

13th January 1941

Our friends have allowed us to do what we took the liberty to do a long time ago – keep all our clubs open unless told to do otherwise. For some unknown reason they want a triplicate copy of rules, roll of members and declaration the club will only be used for the purpose stated in the rules.

We had a long rigmarole in the paper the other night about all the benefits they had conferred on Jersey, and how they were making it self-supporting. It would take a magician to make an island of 40 square miles support a population of 40,000 plus an occupying army of up to 3,000 men. There aren't enough bear skins to go around and the restrictions on fishing don't help the food situation much. It is intended to grow some wheat this year, but I can't see enough tons of flour being produced from what we can grow, even if we turned over the whole available ground to it and we need other things besides bread – unless Adolf in his Godlike way, can reproduce the miracle of two loaves and five small fishes.

We have found a way of defeating the boredom of early curfew. One or two neighbours and I gather together for a game of nap most evenings. Living close together, we can make sure the coast is clear before we slip out home, and so we put our fingers to our noses at their 9.00 p.m. curfew. It won't be so good if one was caught – four days gaol now, which would be a new experience.

A lot of Red Cross messages are being delivered, apparently in alphabetical order. Some have been as long as five months coming and the quickest I have heard of is ten weeks. They don't mean a thing, as so much can happen since they were sent. Mum is being very hopeful, and I should imagine one of us at least should get something any month now.

Jewish shops are now being run under Aryan administration – I bet that isn't for the benefit of the owners.

January 18th 1941

All the Red Cross messages of this batch have been delivered, but we have not been amongst the lucky ones. I expect now the service is really working, we will get news more promptly, and we may have better luck next time. Meanwhile Mother is bitterly disappointed.

January 20th 1941

We are being entertained this 30th week by sundry loud bangs – rumour says it is drifting mines being exploded close inshore. The majority of the troops here now are very young – average 16 to 19 years old. It is a peculiar thing usually there seems to be little or no drilling and practising done. Now as during last August and September, one sees them crawling on bellies with machine guns on their backs and generally looking like the worms they are. Ergo, another invasion attempt is foreshadowed. May they all be dead before they land on the shores of our England – it is bad enough poor little Jersey should be so defiled. Fortunately England realises the possibilities and from all accounts are ready and able to give our friends the sort of reception they deserve – bless em all. There also seems to be some movement of heavily camouflaged shipping – no doubt in the same connection. It is mighty bad medicine, but a dose which must be swallowed; for there is no doubt a really expensive attempt at invasion would do much to shorten the misery.

I have just got my latest identity ticket, but although a space is provided, up to date no mention has been made of the photographs which were to adorn them. Methinks it is because of a shortage of photographic materials.

All fishing has been stopped. For 24 hours this even included low water fishing, so it looks as though the theory of the big bangs being mines is reasonable.

More moans - the ration of butter is down to 2 ounces which, with no other fats, is not so good. In compensation they have doubled the sugar ration for children, but not being a juvenile, it doesn't help our household much. This reduction is only supposed to be temporary – I certainly hope so.

There have been persistent rumours during the past week about another Channel Islands broadcast – this time giving the names of CI air raid casualties. I disbelieved the latter part from the first, but no one seemed to know the station or time, or even the day. The last of the rumoured times has now passed, and I have yet to hear of anyone who knows anything about it. These false alarms and excursions give one the creeps.

This 30th week of seemingly never ending misery is made more bearable by a reversion to the 11.00 p.m. curfew as a reward for us being good. The 9 o'clock racket was just lousy, as although I did not observe it strictly, one had to observe such circumspection as to make it hardly worthwhile.

I don't know if I mentioned earlier we are rationed for electricity and coal – the former based on previous consumption and the latter at half a hundredweight a week. Also there is some talk of rationing bread.

I just had proof of the inquisitive nature of our guests. A pal was told over the phone by a friend he had a few eggs available if he would go and get them. But before this could be done, a German was at the poultry keeps to collect eggs, which is proof positive of the phone tapping which I suspected, and the reason why we just don't see eggs.

January 27th 1941

Life is very quiet – there is the usual change around of garrison and most of the arriving crowd seem to be aircraftsmen, so maybe it is intended to use this place for raids on a larger scale than they have done for a few months. I also heard yesterday, from a usually reliable source, it is believed to be their intention to use this as an invasion base and to fill our harbour with barges. If this be so, what ho for the RAF – welcome little bombs.

Freemasonry was never popular with the Reich and this week they have been venting their spite on the local branch, taking away expensive regalia and destroying what had no intrinsic value.

FEBRUARY 1941

February 3rd 1941

I have managed to get hold of some 6 lbs of illicit pork, so this week we are making pigs of ourselves. There is quite a bit of 'black market' business going on, especially in pork. Pigs are not allowed to be officially killed until they reach 150 lbs, but with shortage of feeding stuff, they just won't make the weight and so obligingly die. Of the Jersey pork which does comply with the law by being killed in the official way, the civilian population never see a bit, it all goes to the Germans, so we all grab what we can get. I got mine from a bloke who owes us money, sort of blackmail, and am hoping to get more in a week.

A local man was killed whilst attempting to escape from the Military Guard when he was caught out of after hours in the Military Zone. He had already been caught twice before, the first time being warned and the second time getting five days gaol. For the sake of those who doubted it, we know now the rifles which they carry so carelessly are loaded. I can quite see the official German point of view in this. They obviously can't have people playing the fool with military regulations, and the bloke wouldn't have got hurt if he hadn't tried to break away. For a change publicity was given to this event, presumably as a warning.

As there is so little to buy in the way of eats, the price of vegetables, amongst other things, has been steadily rising until during the past week such prices as 3/6d a lb for haricot beans and 5d each for leeks have been paid. So henceforth the prices will be controlled.

Bread rationing starts on February 17th: 6 lbs 2 ½ ounces for male manual workers, 5 lbs 6¼ ounces for female manual workers, 4 lbs 10 ounces for others, male and female, and 3 lbs 1¼ ounces for children under 10. That gives us 9¼ lbs of bread a week and I can see myself rapidly losing the 7 lbs weight which I have put on since we had perforce to return to the simpler life. Tobacco ration is down to one ounce, with the prospect of none at all in the future.

From facts which have come to light, I am not so sure my sympathies about the killed man are all with the Germans. I gather from people living near when he was actually shot he wasn't in the Military Zone, although he may have been before. The body was completely riddled with bullets (this came from the undertaker) and was left where it fell overnight even though it is possible he wasn't killed outright. No civilian doctor was called in, and the undertaker was the only civilian to see the body.

There is a serious shortage of meat and experiments are being carried out with supplying soup in milk bottles in lieu of the meat ration – each ration of soup to contain a normal 1½ ounces meat. Altogether prospects in the food line are not so good, especially as it is only reasonable to expect, while the invasion is happening, we will have to rely entirely on our own very meagre resources. Food is our first thought and topic of conversation. With the sole exception of vegetables, rationed goods are all it is possible to buy. Even things as aren't covered by coupons, such as jam, are being unofficially rationed to those with children only (quite rightly) as available stocks are so small. We are still eating last year's new potatoes – they are getting a mucky, but are all one can get.

February 10th 1941

Jam rationing has become official – 1 lb a fortnight to children only. A very serious shortage of fuel oil for generating electricity has become apparent – it is understood there is only sufficient for three weeks ordinary requirements. Therefore it has been made Law, except in an emergency, no lights must be used between 11.00 p.m. and 7.00 a.m. and all electric fires, irons, cookers etc. are banned. Also revised is the meat ration, which may now be taken partly in the form of readymade soup and partly in meat cuttings, or alternatively in meat cuttings only. About once every six weeks we are to be given our meat in one lump for roasting. In addition to not being able to have a ration of cooking fat one is not even able to get any on the meagre ration of meat, as all fat is cut off before the butchers get it. This has been so for some time and at first it was said this was to build up a reserve for when we got short of butter. Well, we are short of butter, nearly none, and I rather fancy the real reason that fact hasn't been released is it has been taken away to make soap.

I expected February to bring trouble in the grub line and I have not been disappointed. I expect things to get even worse looking far into the future, between the time the Germans leave us and our own food ships start to arrive – though that hard patch will be worth putting up with.

I believe the French are annoyed about even the small amount of stuff being brought, and an armed guard is necessary over the loading of every ship. I often wonder what would be our position if France decided to throw in their lot with Germany – I suppose we should once again change our nationality.

Another batch of letters has arrived and is being delivered in alphabetical order. I am so optimistic this time I have already drafted out a reply – I want the greatest value possible out of my 25 words.

The Germans are getting interested in local education in accordance with usual Nazi practice; German officers are overseeing the work done at the local boys' college.

The place is lousy with all grades of German services. There must be 3,000 here now, all clamouring to change their dud money into goods of some intrinsic value, but there is precious left in shops for them or anyone else to buy.

13th February 1941

Now footwear is only available in odd sizes and fancy prices, a ban has been placed on Germans buying them. It is so kind of them not to want to take all our stocks! I reckon we have supplied shoes to the best part of the German Army, Navy and Air Force and all their families.

We are still rubbing along at the store, barely clearing expenses each week. One can't look ahead much, and everything depends on how long this Occupation lasts. The store will be empty, to all intents and purposes, by the end of the year, and then what? Meanwhile, the hardest work is to find something to fill in the time.

14th February 1941

After a lapse of some weeks, a 2 ounce ration of fat is to be issued next week – presumably to grease our first week of rationed bread.

I am finding this diary quite useful as a reference, as at the request of the local wholesale newsagent, I am preparing a series of notes for an article for the English press later on. I don't suppose anything will come of it, but meanwhile it keeps me amused and is no harm to anyone.

My tame spies have been active and have brought the news Granville is closed to our ships – reason, apparently invasion preparations. They have a large steamer there and are practising horses at going aboard and disembarking. Despite, or because of, the hammering the Navy and RAF have given the place, Cherbourg is definitely pro British and completely blasé about bombs and shells. The harbour area is in a bad way, but the town is hardly damaged.

From facts to rumours. The best recent one is everyone is to be moved off the Island. Version (a) insists it is to be heavily fortified, and version (b) it is to be put under the American Red Cross and become neutral. I can just see the Germans presenting our people with a nice air base when the time is rife for the move towards Berlin. Some star or crystal gazer has said the war will end on May 5th at 5 o'clock (I didn't ask whether morning or afternoon). You would be surprised at the number of people who have implicit faith in this.

I have been faced with the problem of supplying nonexistent firebricks and slabs for bakers' ovens – an essential commodity at a time like this. By dint of much brain picking, I have evolved a scheme for the local brickworks to make some to my specification and so, having found an answer to my problem, I am feeling pleased with myself.

During the course of my brain picking, I learnt the Electricity Company which had been making salt can no longer do so as electricity is so precious. So now it is proposed to dry some from salt water in the destructor. I told the bloke in charge it would be dirt not salt unless they altered their arrangements. And lo, it was so, for I have seen him again and he agrees with me now. There are so many little things which we have hitherto taken for granted, but which we now have to find out for ourselves.

February 21st 1941

All the Jesuits (training to become Catholic priests) were taken from here this morning – probably because of the food shortage – not that it is any better in France, but as they are French, the Germans think they ought to be there.

Some, if not all, of the Air Force have gone, owing to the difficulties of bringing petrol here to operate. One might have expected capable people like the Germans to have thought of this before they went to the trouble of the considerable extensions made at the Airport.

Owing to the oil shortage, German engineers are arranging for a pipeline to be laid from the Gasworks to the Power Station. This is being done post haste, and when necessary alterations have been made to the machinery, the electric generators will be driven by gas. We have a fair supply of coal for making gas at the moment and apparently no difficulty is anticipated in getting future supplies.

Inconvenient though this oil shortage is, I am mighty glad to have such proof of Germany's need for economy.

It is rumoured a boat with Red Cross letters was sunk off Portugal. If this be true it would be just our luck to have our letters aboard it. You may think my diary comprises nothing but rumours, but I haven't reported most of those around – only the most probable and a selection of the most fantastic.

24th February 1941

24th February brings the news our butter ration is to be doubled to 4 ounces – for one week only. It was true about the Air Force going – they took 400 personnel away and brought 300 new ones.

I have learnt a little of the reasons for bread rationing. Before the Occupation, with a population of 55/60,000, our weekly consumption of flour was 70 tons. The consumption has been rising steadily as less of other food becomes available, until we were eating 140 tons a week between 40,000 of us still in the Island. Bread and potatoes are our main fare, the other items being only to camouflage the menu. They reckon to bring the weekly consumption back to 70 tons, so as an average, our allowance is only a little over half what we have been eating. This doesn't include the Germans, who bring their own rye flour for their bread.

I am pleased to see the troops' cigarette and tobacco ration has been halved. Many shops have been unable to supply the one ounce of tobacco this week, but I have been lucky.

I can see I shall soon be on my flat feet again as the tyres on my poor old bike are getting very moth eaten. I get two or three punctures every week and new tyres are right out of the question. The only thing I can do is to buy a second hand bike with decent tyres, but that wants some getting hold of. The trouble is no one has much need of money, and it takes a lot of it to tempt anyone into parting with such a valuable possession as a bike with decent tyres.

Bus services are being again reduced and it is only a question of a few weeks before they stop completely – unless a miracle happens and our friends bring us some petrol.

Mum and I are feeling a bit sore because everyone else seems to be getting news but we are still left out in the cold.

The Germans have been here nearly eight months and the first fruits of their visit are becoming apparent. Amongst those attending the hospital are one child of 11 and two of 13, and there are many married women amongst the crowd. I don't think I am exaggerating if I say 30% to 40% of all females between the ages of 15 and 30, married or single, are going out with Germans. No doubt when this is all over, tales will be told of assaults, as a cover for the obvious results, but they are not to be believed, for the girls are positively throwing themselves at the Germans. The special 'pash' is pilots, who go nightly to kill their friends and relations – and husbands – but the demand for pilots exceeds the supply, and the less important private need not go short of female company. I will admit the readiness of these women to co-operate has prevented the few decent girls from being molested, but I have a great deal more respect for the average prostitute than I have for this dirty rotten crowd. If I had my way, the whole lot of them would be branded with a swastika when this is all over. It is repugnant to me men should be fighting, amongst other things for the freedom of these Islands, whilst their wives are volunteering their bodies to their enemies. Had I a friend whose wife carried on so, I should not hesitate to tell him when this is over, even though he would almost certainly not believe me. The worst aspect is the children who are not to blame but who will be the principal sufferers. I do not attach any blame on the Germans for this state of affairs – as strangers in a foreign country, they naturally will take what is so willingly offered.

27th February 1941

I have bought a push bike – had to pay five guineas for a second hand one, and got it cheap, being friends with the auctioneer. I guess I should have had to pay a lot more if I had waited much longer, especially when the buses stop running. A decent second hand bike fetches anything up to £30 today.

There are a surprising number of second hand shops springing up and more surprising still are the prices they ask (and get) for stuff which in normal times would be put in the dust bin. For instance, a second hand vacuum flask which new cost 10d or a shilling will fetch 7/6d. People will pay just any price for stuff like that which can't be bought new, and which we have got so used to having we can't do without. Auction sales too bring more proof of this when people will pay 35/- each for pullets and 8/- for a dozen eggs. There are many people, especially those working for the Germans, who are better off than they have ever been, with less rent to pay and less to spend their money on.

One of our chief amusements is card playing – one has to do something but just sit and think which isn't a healthy occupation with things as they are.

The shops now don't open on Mondays and Thursdays, so are only open 18 hours a week. Each week brings additions to those closed down for the duration. It is pretty hard on the smaller shopkeeper who has worked hard to make his business and now finds it completely collapsed.

My latest labour making device is to buy up all the hundredweight kegs of white paint I can find and put it up into 7" tins. White paint is one of those things which people will pay almost any price to get. There is plenty of white lead, but no oil or turps, or I might be able to make quite a big thing of it. When I bought up all the old firebricks for crushing and incorporating in the new ones, I managed to salvage quite a few usable ones, which are fetching as much as new ones used to.

Further proof of Jerry's weakness is his latest order all old motor, cycle tyres and tubes must be produced for purchase – he can't be so wealthy or well organised as we read nightly he is. Last night too, the paper contained a notice revoking the order for two meatless days – a fat lot of difference that makes when our allowance is one ounce meat and ½ ounce bone per day.

People here are getting annoyed at the way our officials, according to reports, are feeding themselves, and posters and chalked signs are appearing overnight on the subject. Although I do agree at a time like this there should be genuine equal sacrifice, I don't like the idea of washing our domestic linen before German eyes. Obviously, dissatisfaction expressed about our form of government gives them fine propaganda, as well as the opportunity of dispensing entirely with local government. The moaners might then find the present snags are the lesser of the two evils. The trouble is people are not getting enough to eat and are dreaming of nothing so much as the day when they can again have eggs and bacon for breakfast.

The following, for instance, is what I am expected to live on each week - bread 4 lbs 10 ounces, sugar 4 ounces, meat 8 ounces, bone 4 ounces, ½ tin of tomatoes, cooking fat and salt two ounces sometimes (it doesn't average out more than ½ ounce per week), butter 2 ounces, milk 3½ pints; potatoes are unlimited and what other vegetables one can get. Fortunately Mum had some foresight and stocked up and people who have too much bread (only those with very young children) help those who haven't enough and have something to swap. Even so, I am always hungry. The summer will bring smaller appetites and more plentiful supplies. We will be able to get fruit, more variety of vegetables, and maybe even more butter and an occasional egg. So roll on the summer.

MARCH 1941

March 10th 1941

And we have had 36 weeks too long of Occupation. The latest and daftest rumour is a plebiscite is to be taken as to whether we are satisfied with German

Occupation. If such a thing did happen, I suppose most people would be too scared to say no, but to say the least, I do not think it likely such a question will be asked. One could not truthfully say at the moment we have been treated as badly as most of us expected. I, for one, expected much more interference than we have had, and in the panic of the first day or so destroyed many papers and things which, in the light of subsequent events, proved totally unnecessary. At that time our nerves were a bit ham strung and we wanted to keep on the safe side. It amuses me to remember, when the war started and I promised to run the store, I thought it was money for old rope. Whereas it has turned out to be a big strain on my worrying department with precious little recompense – the sort of job I would not willingly have taken on. Now I am not at all sure that I will be content to remain here when it is all over. Pirouets will always bring me a living, but Jersey will never again be the prosperous place it has been. Anyway, I have ample time before it becomes necessary for me to finally decide whether or not I want to stay. If I decided to go elsewhere it would mean dropping all I have worked for and starting right from the bottom again. Maybe it is natural I should feel a bit disgruntled towards the place just now and shall feel different about it all when prospects are brighter.

The flow of Red Cross letters has stopped for a bit so I have to be patient again. Whilst other people are not getting news of their loved ones, I don't feel so bad about it, but it hurts to feel left out in the cold.

The high prices of push bikes works both ways – I had £3 for my poor old bit of iron, which was in a deplorable condition and couldn't possibly be made roadworthy with the repair material available in the Island. Not so bad – I wouldn't have got 2/6d for it a year ago

Heigh ho, they are after all cars now, irrespective of age – at least, we have once again to furnish full details in anticipation thereof. I don't know whether my old wreck will have to go - the trouble is, it is in better mechanical order than most cars of its age.

Our States have decided to control a whole lot more items of building and decorating material. As usual they intend to control things which are already unobtainable. I am afraid this interference will rather upset out profitable little retail trade, but I suppose we have been lucky to carry on so long without it.

I wondered why there were armed guards everywhere this morning, and now learn some unidentified ships appeared off Guernsey at 3.00 a.m. and, coming so soon after the Norwegian episode, it gave Jerry a real fit of jitters. We always get a good laugh out of seeing them that way, and from the precautions they take, they do not think an invasion of the Islands is as ridiculous as we do.

For instance, one poor chap whose house overlooks St. Catherine's breakwater (probably the most likely place for the unlikely to happen) has a German guard parked in his drawing room 24 hours a day keeping watch. Fritz surely thinks he is here to stay for he has built (or rather made us build) huts all over the place, on all the headlands etc. and has also put up a big wireless mast at the north of the Island. They have installed a radio direction finding apparatus at St. Martins and enlarged the Airport considerably. I haven't seen it, as it is forbidden territory, but I am told the hedges for a long way around have been flattened so planes can be taxied well away from the landing ground and parked under trees or between farm buildings for cover. I imagine a good deal of overhauling is done here, as there are more planes there than we see in the air, and many of those which go up for short flights sound unhealthy as though it was a trial flight between adjustments. Many a time our hopes have been raised by the sound of a faltering engine, but up to date I haven't had the pleasure of seeing one come to grief. It is amazing as they often come very low over town with their spluttering engines and there ought in theory to be lots of crashes.

There is talk of arranging messages relating to births, marriages and deaths will shortly be taken at this end, but as I can't very well be included in the first two categories and am not interested in being the subject of the last, the announcement leaves me cold.

The curfew in the Military Zone has been relaxed to 9.00 p.m. till 7.00 a.m. which is a little better for those unfortunates who live in the area.

Our States have been taking measures to stop the black market in pork – no doubt it will cut down the pig mortality rate a bit, but the farmers will turn to cattle instead. This black market racket pays too well and pigs have been fetching up to 3/- a lb live weight. We have vague hopes of buying half a pig – if it comes off, we will share what we can't eat or salt down amongst those friends who have helped us in the past. There is no difficulty in selling the stuff at any price.

12th March 1941

As a result of the German panic on Monday, numerous rumours are floating about. One says that five destroyers landed men in Guernsey and took away 100 German prisoners. Another insists an RAF plane landed at our Airport and the Airport buildings were ransacked before the plane took off – I don't know what the Germans were supposed to have been doing whilst this was happening. And a new edition of the ever recurring one the Germans have been warned to leave here – this time the date is the 13th. If this latter should by some queer chance be true, I haven't noticed our guests making very much preparation to accede to the request. I believe some of these 'ultimatum' rumours start when one of the Germans tells his particular woman he is leaving Jersey on a certain day, and this is assumed to mean the whole German forces. Some are leaving and fresh ones arrive all the time for this still seems to be regarded as a rest camp. I never imagined in any Army there would be so little drilling and training done as is the case here. It is very much a rest centre and the troops are wandering about town each morning waiting for shops to open so as they can carry on with the organised looting which is one of the benefits we derive from Reich protection.

I don't know how the girls will be managing now as silk stockings are unobtainable, as is elastic - I suppose they can manage without stockings, but it will be rather a nuisance to have no elastic. As far as that goes, the male population is liable to suffer the same inconvenience, as braces are among the unobtainable items. The answer to both problems seems to be a bit of string and a lot of hope. At the moment there is just nothing in the clothing line one can buy, and I am afraid by the time this is all over, I shall be looking even shabbier than usual. It is a small point and easily remedied. If this goes on for too long, owners of fig trees will be making good money.

Thanks to the recent heavy rains, at least five aircraft have been damaged in landing at the Airport in the last few days. As a result of which a big extra batch of men are working long hours and under armed guard, as the field has to be got in trim for this weekend. They are making the Airport so big that soon it will cover one end of the island. To what purpose this work is directed, I don't know, but I suspect as the weather improves we shall once again be the base of air operations on a big scale.

March 15th 1941

The end of the 37th week brings also the end of my cigarette hoard – henceforth I have to exist on my bare ration.

We are being allowed to take our 12 ounces of meat all in one piece this week, and are also being allowed 4 ounces of butter instead of the usual two – quite a red letter week, in fact, I am quite amused whenever two or more are gathered together, the subject under discussion is always – food.

Judging by the distant explosions this last day or two, the Navy or RAF are having target practise on our friends' encampments nearby. It gives one rather a headache when it goes on continually for days on end, but it is indeed music to our ears. It is just like midsummer down here, instead of March, but instead of appreciating the change from the everlasting rain, we all feel it is bringing to England more blitz and more hell. Please God this can't go on for long. It hurts to see their infernal pilots strutting around as if they were the lords of creation, very proud of themselves – and to see their planes leaving from here with a load of misery for some poor devils – to see all this and yet not be able to do anything at all about it. Sometimes I feel, for the sake of my self-respect, I must destroy what small part of their war machine I can, though it would be suicide and bring misery to many other people. It seems almost pro Nazi to stay here and just quietly see the preparations made for carrying slaughter across the ditch without ever attempting to prevent it. I am only glad I am not brought into contact with them, although as individuals, they don't seem to be such a bad crowd as they are painted.

Those who signed on to serve on the S/S 'Normand' under the Jersey flag, and with the guarantee of carrying only foodstuffs and essential commodities, now find themselves carrying Jerry's war material, contrary to all promises. How much more must the crews of ships and men working at the Airport feel about it than I do, for they are working directly for a German victory, whereas I at least am only a passive observer? It doesn't seem possible the world will ever be straight again – certainly not the nice pleasant old world we used to moan so much about.

Amongst recent orders, the use of public telephones is banned and we are allowed once again to applaud at the pictures, but only popular heroes and comedians. Thus are our minds directed along the proper path.

I am experimenting now with making paper hanging paste from potatoes. They have starch and glucose so should have enough stickiness to stick wall paper. It is worth trying if only to keep us amused. I believe quite good flour can be made from potatoes, in much the same way as we are trying to make paste but there is a lot of work attached to it.

Another plane crashed into the sea on Friday night off Corbiere. Although I hear of these things, I don't usually report them here until I have confirmed or otherwise, the items with our Saturday night nap school. They comprise a master plumber (and the son of a head of a States Department), a headmaster, a bank cashier, a grocer, and a States official looking after imports from France; so that, amongst the very varied experiences, we usually manage to get the truth or thereabouts of all rumours, whatever the subject.

We are getting French tobacco issued now, and thanks to the difference between French and English weights we had 1¾ ounces this week instead of 1 ounce. Unfortunately, supplies won't last more than a week or two, but I consider even the small amount bought to be a waste of the precious credit we have in France and which should only be used for buying essentials. A smoke is doubly appreciated these days but it certainly doesn't constitute an essential under present conditions.

Another of the land mines has exploded at St. Martins, injuring a woman and two children.

I see the blue envelopes being delivered again this morning – maybe we shall be lucky with this batch.

March 18th 1941

March 18th brings news of a new order of the clearing of inflammable material from attics and roof spaces, an order which England had many moons ago.

During the night a large number of notices have been chalked up over town 'Workers need more food – search houses of rich hoarders'. I am wondering whether this is intended to appeal to the sympathy of the Kommandant and to enlist his help in getting a house to house search started. Whoever is responsible for the notices can rest assured if the Germans do make a search, the workers won't get much of the proceeds. The Germans themselves had their rations cut down very considerably lately, and any proceeds would be used to their own advantage.

Some weeks ago a party of young Frenchmen, with more courage than skill, managed to get away from France with the object of joining the Free French Forces. They apparently lost their way and landed in Guernsey under the impression it was the Isle of Wight. The sequel occurred yesterday when one member of the party, aged 21, was shot at St. Ouens for espionage. Others have received sentences of up to 15 years. The tale goes they took the young Frenchman out in the same lorry as his coffin, and he died bravely singing the Marseillaise and without the traditional bandage over his eyes.

The latest proof of Jerry's intention not to leave here yet awhile comes from the import of 900 tons cement and 600 tons sand (coals to Newcastle) for his own use. It is believed to be for use in building a road down to the proposed barrack site at Noirmont. I wouldn't mind if they would spare me 100 tons or so. I am forgetting what cement looks like.

I have just bought up more second hand stuff from demolitions. It will all help to keep the wolf from the door.

Once again we are disappointed – the latest batch of letters is finished and there are none for us.

It has become the fashion to express the local topical moans in verse and some quite fair efforts have resulted. Everyone seemed to want a copy, and after knocking out quite a few I decided to sell them at 2d each in aid of our Spitfire Fund. I have sold quite a few and it tickled my sense of humour to collect money towards a Spitfire (at some future date) yesterday within sight and hearing of a German soldier – wouldn't he have been pleased if he had known.

We have had the RAF around here these last few nights, as well as the Luftwaffe, and have heard the bursting of bombs at L'Orient – 110 miles away, so it couldn't have been small stuff, although no doubt the wind helped the sound to carry.

They have brought in the biggest ship that ever came into our harbour – a 4,000 ton Danish vessel, loaded with guns and general stuff of all sorts. There are enough anti tank guns here now to hold up an entire army.

March 24th 1941

Once again we are unlucky, as the enquiry which I addressed to Bill has been amongst those not accepted, and we have had it returned to us.

I am also feeling more than a little annoyed about our States, who managed to secure 200 tons of cement from the Germans, and are intending to retail it to the building trade. Naturally I have started a row. How the heck are we supposed to pay rates and taxes and keep our men employed if the first building material to be imported in nine months is handled by the States themselves? So altogether I may be forgiven for feeling a bit liverish this morning.

I learn from the coxswain of the life boat it is definite at least one plane carrying Red Cross mail has been lost around here, which may explain why we have heard nothing.

One of the snags of Occupation is the number of little trifling details which one can't get. My snag just now is unbreakable watch glass having broken four of the other sort in three weeks.

The local Jew shops are being sold up by order of the Aryans – nice people with nice manners.

March 27th 1941

March 27th brings news from Bill written in November which relieves mother's mind considerably. I have also heard from my mechanic pal who evacuated.

Guernsey is in disgrace again as someone has cut the telephone cable. As punishment they have to supply 60 men each night to patrol the affected region and are subject to a curfew of 8.30 p.m. Darn fools – the day may come when we shall be able to do something really useful, but if they go on with all this pinpricking, the Germans will be wholly suspicious and expect it.

The latest orders forbid the use of electricity except for light and wireless, coal for anything but cookery, and gas for light and cooking only. No more perms or electric gadgets, no more gas, electric or coal fires. The attempt to operate the electric generators on gas has proved a flop. Reason unknown, but variously rumoured to be insufficient pressure of gas, and the factory making the adapting machinery has been bombed and put out of action.

No tobacco ration is being issued this week, and the stew in milk bottles is being discontinued, much to everyone's delight. It has been most unpopular and looked as though it had been eaten before.

31st March 1941

The raid on the enemy raiders at Brest last night was not only audible here, 100 miles away, but the glare of the fires was reflected in the clouds. The sight of which pleased me mightily.

In conjunction with other merchants, I raised Cain about the cement to such good effect we are to have the handling of it, each in proportion to our pre war imports.

For the last few weeks I have been trying to fit my second store hand into other work, as I have so little for him to do here. Of course success crowns my efforts at the same time as the above happens and I could use him. The bags this French cement is packed in are rotten, a good half being broken, and it isn't possible to get casual labour now for any hard work. Pleading small rations men prefer to work easy on relief schemes then to earn good money on hard and dirty work. So, off comes my coat for the job.

Following the example of Guernsey, Jersey has issued a new postage stamp, not a very beautiful one, but will have some historic value.

APRIL 1941

1st April 1941

Our street has been quite animated today as the shop next door has released its stock of summer shoes (unrationed) and about 1,000 women are clamouring for some 200 pairs of shoes. It is only leather boots, shoes and slippers which are rationed, so there is a proper grabbing competition when anything else becomes available.

We have some German Field Artillery here now for a change and they are amusing themselves (and us) mounting guns at Noirmont. They must either have lots of war material to spare or else be firmly convinced our people will invade these Islands.

Another lot of letters are in course of being copied and sorted, so once again my hopes rise like a gas filled balloon.

The S/S 'Diamande', which the RAF bombed, has arrived here under her own steam and is quite serviceable – apparently it wasn't a direct hit and the damage is superficial.

Due no doubt to the unbalanced diet (spuds and more spuds) a lot of people, including me, are suffering from peculiar bumps which come up under the skin quite suddenly in the most awkward places. They are rather a nuisance and are the first sign I have had of any trouble at all. Except for this, I am well as ever. The trouble is due, I suppose, to the ever recurring potatoes and swedes and the potatoes are still last year's early crop, which by this time are not so palatable. I believe in Paris they haven't seen a spud since Christmas and here we are moaning about a surfeit of the things. Altogether things don't seem so good in Paris where, when anything in the vegetable line becomes available, people queue up all night outside the markets. And we moan!

7th April 1941

I can note today as a red letter day, for it has brought me the first news of family, dated December 20th. It has been 15 weeks coming but I feel so much better for having it.

The latest proclamation is a most awe inspiring document, full of threats of the death penalty and reprisals on the whole population if acts of sabotage and general unfriendliness towards the Germans continue. We have been informed by the Kommandant the acts referred to happened in Guernsey only, and up to date we have been very good boys – but we had better carry on being good, or else.

Straight on top of sending my reply I was quite well, I proceeded to spend a day in bed with a particularly vicious cold. Even the short ten word message I received seems to have brought the family so much closer to me. May it not be too long before I get further and more up to date news.

It looks as though my efforts in making firebricks have been wasted, as in order to conserve coal, more than half the bakers' ovens are to be closed down, and nearly all those remaining in use are the modern steam type which won't want the special big bricks I have been making.

It amuses me, although it doesn't amuse the victims, to see the huge queues whenever food stuffs appear on sale – anything from limpets to rhubarb attracts crowds. I call it the great game of 'grab'.

We don't seem to have any aircraft at all stationed here now, although we are still disturbed at nights by them passing over on their way to the West Country and the Midlands.

12th April 1941

42 weeks of our time are up – we are worse off than criminals, who at least know how long a sentence they have to serve.

No tobacco has been issued for three weeks, and the little store I had accumulated is looking very sick as quite a number of friends have been helping me to smoke it. I am sure it isn't doing us any harm to smoke less and it is good preparation for the not far distant future when we shall to pack it up altogether.

One of the shortages which is really making itself felt is soap and many people confirm they are entirely without. Had they any sense they might have included soap amongst their hoarding, for it was not to be expected Germany could afford to be generous with it. I believe a small factory is making soap at Granville, and it is hoped soon to have enough to issue a ration here.

The tea ration is down to 2 ounces but thanks to my having claimed and got an office tea ration (what a racket) we have a few lbs ahead – which pleases me mightily, for I should loath to go without my cup of tea.

The week's daft rumour is the Islands are to be garrisoned by Italians. If that happened I am afraid the troops would get a hell of a life – and so should we. There is also a rumour, with some foundation, some 10/15,000 German personnel are to be brought here. This is borne out to some extent by an order furniture and equipment must not be removed from evacuated houses. This surely won't add to the amenities of the Island, and will mean a proportion of one Nazi to every three British. It will be more necessary than ever to keep a strict guard on one's tongue.

April 14th 1941

Today is Easter Monday, and I am working but on improving the occasion by adding a contribution to my growing diary. We are allowed an extended curfew till 1.00 a.m. for the holidays, with a 12.30 p.m. pub opening. In view of the fact regulations do not permit any lights after 11.00 p.m. (in theory) and no lights in places of public entertainment after 10.00 p.m., it doesn't do the civil population much good. These relaxations of the curfew are intended primarily for the Germans and their 'friends'. Except on duty the forces are subject to the same curfew hours as us. When the curfew is at 11.00 p.m. and a jollification is to be held, it gives the girls an excuse to sleep at the German hotels. I heard some gorgeous screams coming from an upstairs room at the Ritz last night, and said to myself "serve her right" – if she goes upstairs in a German hotel, she deserves something to scream for. I fancy most of the girls don't know what is happening to them as it seems to be part of the German technique to get them drunk first.

April 15th 1941

Whoopee – I am to have an evening out with my motorbike next Monday after a lot of wangling. All the DRs have to take their bikes, one each evening, for a check over and I am first on the list. Fancy getting excited about being allowed to ride a few miles on one's own horse and petrol, here's looking forward to a most enjoyable evening.

April 17th 1941

Can you imagine me getting four smokes out of every cigarette? The last bit is finished in a cigarette holder to get down to the last 1/16th. I am only able to allow myself a pipe about every other day and that won't be for long. Many people are smoking dried watercress, coltsfoot and other weeds but I don't fancy these ersatz concoctions.

We are getting a 2 ounce ration of block cocoa and a 2 ounce ration of potato flour this week. It will surely be a treat to have the cocoa.

As a result of the fuss I kicked up a week or two back, I have a little more cement coming into the store – which is quite good news from a business point of view, though the price is drastically controlled to prevent us from doing more than clear our working expenses on it.

Quite a few people here seem to be losing faith in England's ability to win this little war – I suppose it is an excusable result of nerves, for you can take it from me that this does get on your nerves, after nearly ten months. The complaint is far from general, but there are enough sufferers to make me bad tempered – I hate to hear anyone who can even doubt the eventual outcome and the only question I want answered is "when?" I could wait so much more patiently if I only knew how long. I am resigned to another year of this, whilst all the time hoping I am being pessimistic.

Jerry has brought some new searchlights, real ones this time, so he has a little hope of seeing the RAF next time they pass this way. But they haven't yet learned how to operate them and we get a good laugh at the haphazard way they dart around the sky, crossing each other and generally working entirely without co-operation.

April 21st 1941

Adolf's birthday has been celebrated by a showing of 'Victory in the West', the film which has been used to try to terrify the Balkan countries into submission. I should have liked to see it, as a historic film, but I doubt my ability to sit still through it, and therefore won't go. It is only showing for two nights, the first of which was for the troops only. The Forum is all decorated with huge swastikas for the occasion.

April 22nd 1941

I had my 'evening' out with my motorbike, an evening which extended from 11.00 a.m. yesterday till 11.00 a.m. today. I surely haven't wasted this, my first opportunity of a bit of enjoyment – I had my happiest day since the air raid. Naturally, there wasn't much work done as I had to treat myself to time off in order to get the maximum amount of value from the occasion. I had a nose at the airport 'improvements' (from as close as one is able to get) and at the radio direction finding station on the north coast – in fact, there wasn't much of the Island left unvisited when I went to bed last night. It surely was great while it lasted, and I know I wouldn't be such an infernal misery if I had the motorbike on the road every day.

Jerry is after all cars, lorries, tractors and motorbikes of 1936/40 vintage, but that doesn't include any of my vehicles. The motorbike is the only one which comes in the age group but is covered by ARP. I wouldn't be surprised if they go back a year or two further to get spare tyres and batteries.

April 23rd 1941

Yesterday we got another message from Bill dated December 10th that all was well with them, and wishing us a happy Christmas – I don't know which Christmas he meant.

Now spring hath come, our visitors have reverted to their 1940 tactics of giving their troops a day trip here and a day trip in Guernsey. As four or five batches pass through the Islands some weeks, the best part of the Germany Army will have visited us before this is over.

Things here are very quiet, apart from a mine drifting onto the rocks in Grouville Bay and exploding itself a few days ago. We got all excited thinking the RAF was starting.

One of the facts published in our local rag to illustrate what a bad way England is in, is that tobacconists in London have to close one day a week. As propaganda to people who have to manage on 20 cigarettes a week it is funny –

as are their remarks on rationing in England when addressed to us, who, to say the least, are not overfed.

They are using the windows of some unused shops to propagandize us – photographs of Hitler and his wonderful works and so forth. If it wasn't for the extra expense to the tax payer, these windows would be getting busted methinks.

April 29th 1941
Meat ration is down to 8 ounces, with 4 ounces for children and 10 ounces for Reich Germans – the latter are credited with a much bigger appetite in all things than we are.

MAY 1941

May 1st 1941
May 1st brings the news henceforth all textile and shoe shops will only open on Tuesdays, Fridays and Saturdays, not having much left to sell, and butchers' shops are only to open on Fridays and Saturdays, so the town will be deader than ever. The only time there is any animation (apart from the Germans, whom we don't count) is when any shop has anything extra to the bare rations, be it watercress or baking powder; there will be a wrangling mob on the great game of grab. If a farmer's van loaded with rhubarb, for instance, is seen going through town, the crowd follows it until it reaches the shop or stall, and the stuff disappears before it gets a chance to get into the shop. It is amazing how quickly the news of anything in the food line travels.

We are being issued this 44th week with a one ounce ration of tobacco – stuff at which, in normal times, we would have turned up our noses, but as we have had none at all for some 6 weeks, we are very grateful to get it.

I am glad Britain is putting clocks ahead another hour. It will relieve us of the mental gymnastics necessary when listening to BBC programmes – our only contact with that world. Often, lying in bed, I have heard the bloke announce the seven o'clock news, and think I have lots of time to spare, until I wake sufficiently to realise it is really eight o'clock.

It would seem that perambulation after hours in the Military Zone is not encouraged, and it is also likely there is not much challenging done if one is caught.

It is apparently a case of shoot first and ask questions after – or how do you account for the fact two German were shot; one is dead, the other in a bad way.

May 6th 1941

The meat ration for this 45th week is 4 ounces, with 5 ounces for manual workers and 2 ounces for children, and from what I gather from the butchers, it seems there is likely not to be enough available to supply even this reduced ration. Certainly unless some comes in the ration next week will be exactly nil. This cut comes at a very bad time, when even the vegetables which have been our principal diet are getting scarce. About the only things which are available without fighting are potatoes (still last year's earlies) and swedes. A little fish appeared in the market on Saturday, and two women are in hospital as a result of the scrimmage which occurred to get hold of some. A small 2d tablet of soap is being issued this week – the first for many months and we are warned to use it carefully as it will be a long time before more is issued. Quite a lot of people are in a bad way for soap and some I know have to borrow their neighbours' soapy water on washdays. Probably as a sop for the reduced ration of meat, we are getting an extra two ounce ration of rancid cooking butter this week.

The town is being spring cleaned of the many and various posters of proclamations and threats. There were so many issuing orders, describing the fate of those hardy souls who had defied the Reich and threatening dire penalties to anyone who invoked the wrath of the authorities that the place was getting to look most untidy. The display of these notices was chaotic, for besides defeating their object by being so profuse, they marred the prominence of the many German sign boards erected for the benefit of newcomers. Another and more comprehensive system of sign posting the whole island is being carried out – the third different system used in the 10 months of Occupation. The whole thing becomes more complicated as, instead of erecting boards, they have been painting the letters and figures on the walls of houses, and it is quite usual to see cross roads decorated with the three systems.

Now the tea shortage is becoming acute, the supplies of ersatz coffee (made from barley) are being withheld against the day when no more tea is available. It has been found quite a tasty ersatz (better than barley) can be made from parsnips roasted – it would be a struggle at the moment to find parsnips, but we shall be able to get a palatable drink later on in the year.

The black market is flourishing, money being no object. 100 bags of sugar, which could only have cost about 10/- are being sold for £20 or more, whilst tea changes hands at 15/- to a £ per pound. A tobacco ration card for 6 months fetches from £2 to £5 – a lot to pay (as an extra) for 20 cigarettes a week and a very occasional ounce of tobacco. As may be expected, one result of all this is the amount of thieving being done – the quantities are too large to be anything but a well organised vamp. Last week, for instance, a case of 160 lbs of tobacco was missing from the pier – and every man and vehicle coming off the pier is regularly scrutinised by the sentries on duty. Quite a few chaps have got members of the crews of the ships to buy them cigarettes in France, and have been searched when trying to get them away from the pier. Considerable quantities of foodstuffs are being stolen quite regularly and farms are being pillaged of vegetables, mostly during curfew hours. There was a case a little while ago of a pig being stolen (alive) during the lunch hour – and they got away with it.

May 10th 1941

Thanks to the shortage of leather, wooden soles for boots, with just a leather edging, are being made now. I imagine they won't be very comfortable, but they will fill a need.

The suggested immigration of some 10/15,000 Germans mentioned here previously seems to have fallen through – probably because of the increased feeding difficulties.

May 12th 1941

We are getting a special treat this week – a 4 ounce ration of semolina; it doesn't thrill me much, but any sort of food is acceptable. There is also an extra 2 ounces of butter, but the kids are minus their jam ration for a bit. The 4 ounce meat ration is being maintained only by killing off some of our valuable Jersey cattle.

This 46th week is distinguishing itself with more business worries. Whilst taking in another small lot of cement (like the first lot, mostly loose), I had a phone call from the officer in charge of the Noirmont 'improvement' scheme asking for our stocks of distemper and paint, with the object of commandeering. I got an hour or so grace to make the required list and used the time to good advantage in finding places to 'dump' as much as possible of our stocks. More than 30 hundredweight is not now in the store, so if the commandeering comes off, it won't be quite as bad as it might have been. Meanwhile, we just wait and see. The request for stocks was a general one, but other people weren't as lucky as I, as the officer concerned went in person.

May 15th 1941

It is now an offence to paint or decorate exteriors without official permission – this order, no doubt, is in connection with the paint commandeering just mentioned.

They are being generous to us this week, as we are getting another ration of potato flour and a tin of beans. Many people are making potato flour, which is a lot of work, but anything in the food line is worth any amount of trouble these days. I have made a gadget for grinding the spuds, and we have made a useful quantity. A year ago, every rock was smothered with limpets, but so many have been taken that now, if you want any, you have to go down the beach a mile or more. Any sort of fish on sale causes a free fight – not that Jerry allows much to reach the public, as all fishing has to be done from certain places between stated times, and Fritz is always on the top line to grab it as it comes from the boats.

Chatting to a friend from the Treasury this morning, I learnt the cost of Occupation alone is between £5/6,000 per week. Which added to the cost of unemployment makes my guess of £1m a year not unreasonable.

The one ounce tobacco ration seems to be regular again. Although my non smoking store hand is not now with us, we are still lucky enough to share his ration – I only hope he doesn't get to hear of the good prices being offered for ration cards.

Although considerable extensions have been made at the airport, it is not being used at all, and it is quite unusual to see an aeroplane – in fact there are very few of the Air Force stationed here. We have more than enough of the Army to make up for it, but I imagine they aren't the crack troops. I saw one the other day with a glass eye – on sentry duty. Many others wear thick glasses or look to be very weakly specimens – I have got to see a German private who has what we would consider a soldierly bearing. Their antics on sentry duty are funny to watch – apart from the changing business, accompanied by much goose-stepping, they are most slovenly and lean against anything handy with their rifle slung on their shoulders by the sling, and chat to their pals or any girls who happen along.

Another two Germans have gone to the bitter land, having stepped on one of their own land mines at St. Martins. Apparently the warning notices are posted above the beach, and the land mines may be just anywhere below that point, so it is not safe to go anywhere on beaches so labelled. Fortunately our corner of the island is not so cursed – maybe they realise our rocks are sufficient guarantee against any invader.

The Germans don't seem to appreciate practical jokes, such as turning the direction arrows of their road signs the wrong way, and have promised reprisals if it continues. Methinks it be possible the idea will spread now they have reminded people they can have a pennyworth of fun at the expense of the troops.

Referring back to ancient history, when the S/S 'Normand' was first commissioned to run under the Jersey flag, it was publicly guaranteed she would carry only essential commodities. Some little while ago, the captain was ordered to carry ammunition and, in accordance with that guarantee, he refused. In consequence he is at this moment serving two months hard labour; all honour to the man.

Dissatisfaction with our States is becoming more widespread and publicised. I have not much reason to be pleased with them myself, but many people here are so short sighted as not to realise such a movement now is giving Germany good propaganda, as well as opportunity to replace our form of government by a type of Quisling regime, which would not be an improvement. Unfortunately, one isn't in a position just now to publicly argue out the rights and wrongs and I can see trouble ahead if the dissatisfaction comes to the ears of the Kommandant. Already many of the more ignorant threaten to appear to the Kommandant about every petty grievance, and the Germans are far sighted enough to insist on each occasion on generous treatment, thus making the working man feel that he would be at least as well off under German rule as under British. There is no denying German methods are most insidious. Local people working in the hotels and so forth are most generously treated, and I have heard such people say they have never been as well off in their lives, and hope it will go on for years. German generosity is done with tax payers' money, yet these people are ready and willing to credit the occupying forces with all the virtues of justice and generosity. Of course, they are generous and just – it costs them nothing and if, as they hope, they win this war, it will be half the battle in introducing their 'new order' if the working classes are biased in their favour. Personally, I suspect every concession made to us, but a far too big proportion accept it all as another proof of magnanimity. I will admit, as a whole, we have been treated a lot better than British propaganda would have had us believe, but Germans are not such fools as to cause too much irritation amongst people whose support they hope to want later on. They know that, after the war (under the assumption they win) it won't be possible to keep every town and village under military occupation, and so are preparing the way for the 'new order' to run itself – under the wing of Germany. I can begin to understand the hold which Nazism has secured on the mass of the German people. It is based on very clever psychology, and by offering immediate advantages, it causes the masses to see no further than the end of their noses.

May 26th 1941

Another prominent bloke is doing a fortnight's hard labour – for taking photographs out of doors and another civilian has paid the penalty of getting in the way of a Jerry car. I don't know what the score of road deaths is for the past 11 months, but I reckon it is as high as the previous 11 years.

The week's special treat is a ration of tinned tunny fish – a whole lot has been brought from France so we look like getting the treat repeated. The grub position has improved somewhat in the last week or two. We are starting to get spider crabs now to help things along.

May 30th 1941

I have just had a word with a friend who is in the Red Cross office and find they will now accept messages about every 3 weeks, provided one hasn't received an enquiry in the meantime. Full publicity is not being given to this facility as people flood them with all sorts of ridiculous and unimportant messages. Anyway, he has promised to get one through for me so here goes to concoct another 25 words.

The curfew in the Military Zone has been brought into line with the rest of the Island, 11.00 p.m., which no doubt pleased those unfortunates who had to be indoors by 9.00 p.m. or latterly 10.00 p.m. or take a chance of being shot. It also places the beach within bounds for us of an evening.

We have 2/- local notes in circulation now, which helps the shortage of change a bit.

I thought the fun had started last night until I remembered reading in the paper about practise. It was the guns at Noirmont in action, as well as machine guns and rifles. This is the first night practise we have been treated to, although they often practise on the beaches in the day.

JUNE 1941

June 2nd 1941

The poor old Jews are catching it again. By the latest proclamation, they aren't allowed business or investment interests of any sort; neither are they to be employed in any job which might bring them in contact with the public. Further, on the orders of the Germans, they can be sacked for no other reason than they are Jews. If there is any doubt about their origin, they are given the benefit of it – and are called Jews. I don't think the order affects Jersey much, but they surely hope all Jews will just curl up and die. Those without money are, it seems, not to be given employment, and those with money are only to be allowed just sufficient, decided by the Germans, for bare needs.

It rather looks as though my scheme of hiding stocks to prevent commandeering is going to work. We had to hand in written details of our stocks a few days ago, and some other merchants received orders to give the Germans what they want, whereas I have heard no more. Apparently the figures which I put in are so small as to leave us right out. I know some others have regarded this as a good opportunity to get rid of their old stocks at the States' expense on the assumption the States will meet the bill; but I would prefer to bury my stocks – one never knows what might happen if Jerry once gets into the habit of coming in the place. They are a saucy crowd, as instanced by the following. They have been in the habit of borrowing hand carts and so forth from Doris' father, and the other day, one of them opens the door and walks straight upstairs – and Doris is still in bed. It was alright, she preserved her honour, but I reckon it must have given her heart failure to hear jack boots coming up the stairs.

June 6th 1941

We nearly got yanked in last night for curfew breaking, it being just after 11.00 p.m. and we still a few hundred yards from home when two patrols, fully armed, passed us on push bikes. They half stopped, but we crossed the road as though we lived in one of the houses there, and they went on, to the accompaniment of sighs of relief from Mum and a neighbour who was with us.

Most of the crowd here now seem to be infantry or artillery plus the usual crowd of frontier guards, gendarmerie and clerks. Both day and night have been made unpleasant by their practise with every weapon from revolvers, rifles and machine guns, to mortars and 7" guns. We still occasionally get the day trippers, 4,000 of whom arrived for 2 hours last Friday. By now there is precious little left in shops for them to buy. De Gruchys, Voisins and some of the other bigger shops are still open, though with rapidly emptying shelves. Smaller shops have either closed or gone in for the 2nd hand and exchange business. There isn't a street in the town which hasn't at least one place offering to exchange a piano for a sideboard, or sugar for eggs. The phrase 'for what' is used to get the best offers and has become a proper catch word. Wandering around and comparing the bargains is a favourite and entertaining past time, and the things one can get in exchange for cigarettes, cycle tyres or foodstuffs are legion. A dozen eggs, officially worth 4/3d, will carry one further than a pound note, and a hundredweight of sugar, if one can find anyone to accept cash for it, is worth up to £25. But usually cash won't tempt them – it must be in exchange for food or other essentials.

Presumably in order to protect us against those wicked English, we now have the privilege of having our roads pulled up by tanks – only a few small ones, but decidedly detrimental to tarred roads in hot weather.

June 8th 1941

The exchange racket has resulted in so many robberies the latest orders ban the barter or sale for more than the authorised price of all foodstuffs; which merely means that it will become part of the underground black market.

As from this week, the local drivers of staff cars will be replaced. I am not displeased for their driving methods have become at least as bad as the Germans, and now they aren't getting all the perks, maybe they won't be quite so pro-German.

I have just spent a morning at Victoria College House to see the Feld Kommandateur with Father Pirouet. A phone message came through for him to present himself at Room 19, which turned out to be the Paymasters Office, and as he is so deaf, I went along with him. When we got there, no one knew anything about it – the usual way with officialdom, be it German or Chinese. I've got an idea the message was for another Pirouet altogether, but we couldn't get any sense out of it. Some of the army clerks speak English fairly well, but it isn't very easy to make oneself understood. I must say those with whom we came into contact were polite and tried to be helpful. In trying to elucidate the mystery one of them asked me if Father Pirouet was a Jew. I didn't repeat that one for his benefit, or there might have been a row, as he is not one of the most tactful of individuals.

I have been busy preparing the little Morris and my friend's Standard for the Purchasing Commission. I originally intended to call the latter a 1934 model and then decided it wasn't worth risking jail to save someone else's car. I have arranged they won't get the best of the tyres, which are the most precious part of the car to them.

A little fuel oil arrived for the electric power house just in time to save us from going lightless.

This 50th week's only bonus ration is an extra ounce of salt – not thrilling, but useful, as until the last week or two, we only had a ration and most people cooked with sea water.

June 13th and a Friday

June 13th starts with disposal of the Morris. I had rather hoped it might be rejected as too small or too much mileage, but no such luck.

We had a pleasant surprise this week – a 2 ounce ration of brawn without losing a meat coupon and also jam is to be issued at 1 lb per head, taking people in alphabetical order, so that we have a month or two to wait for our turn.

June 19th 1941

Coming to the close of our first year of Occupation, I think it would be an idea if I tried to paint a more complete picture than the foregoing disjointed scraps provide. The keynote is boredom, and the primary snag is the almost complete rupture of communication with England. Yet in overcoming the many little difficulties presented by the lack of so many little things which we have grown accustomed to, we lead quite busy lives. Life is far nearer to normal than one would imagine it to be, although there is a not inconsiderable shortage of many items of food and of those many things which go to make life pleasant. The town presents a desolate scene of empty shop windows and stopped clocks. Even those shops which have not closed only open for 14 hours a week. A certain amount of trading is being done with France and a permanent buyer is kept there to handle purchases of essential commodities. For special traders, the trade organisation is expected to nominate a buyer who will be sent there with money in his hand to buy the required items – not a very satisfactory arrangement, but then these are not very satisfactory times. During the course of enquiring into the matter regarding the import of drain pipes and building material generally, I have learnt a little about it. The necessary funds for purchase are provided either as credit against the potatoes which were shipped away last year and the car and lorries which have been shipped away since, or from the Reich Credit Marks spent here by the forces. Last year the troops were flush with 'victory' money which had to be spent in the occupied territories, and our shops were full of the wherewithal for them to purchase. So we were really well off in exchange currency. At that time there wasn't such a lot purchasable in France, and in order to dispose of the apparently useless paper, our buyer bought some things of doubtful utility with the credit which we now need. I don't blame the States for that, as looking back to the then known circumstances, I should have advocated such a plan, goods being better than dud money. Now our needs are greater and our available income of credit and marks less and becoming progressively smaller, so every purchase must be considered in the light of the Island's essential needs. Transport across France to Granville is a bit difficult from all accounts; though shipping between Granville and the Islands is left untouched by the RAF and Navy. Despite these factors we still have food to eat and clothes to wear, although most people are looking a lot thinner and somewhat shabbier. The general health of the people is better than might be expected, though naturally some of the older people's lives have been shortened, and the younger generation will probably feel the effects in later life. But the same effect might quite probably result from the shortened rations combined with the discomforts of air raids if we were under like conditions to Britain. We still have supplies of gas and electricity – both are strictly rationed and can only be used for vital necessities. Buses are still running a much shortened service, thanks to the import of occasional small lots of petrol. One can go to the pictures, if one doesn't mind being pumped full of propaganda, though I understand the showing of the German news films is not now general. We still even have a smoke – just. Providing we are indoors before 11.00 p.m. and we cycle in single file holding both handlebars firmly and generally walk a straight line between the many pettifogging regulations, our personal liberty is not greatly interfered with. Taking it full and bye, I think we have good reason to congratulate ourselves we have rubbed along so well. But the prospects for our second year of internment are not so good. We started on July 1st 1940 with good stocks and all the necessities of life which, in proportion to the size of the place, must have been an eye opener to the Germans. For this year we have to be much more dependent on our natural resources. Provision for this, as far as possible, has been made by the planting of a big proportion of the land in wheat, corn etc. in place of the hitherto inevitable potato; by the excavation of peat for fuel and by strict economy in all things. Employment is a major problem, but all spare labour, male and female, is used, mostly under aegis of the States, in combating the problem of food, clothing and fuel for a population too large for the land it lives in. Such a state of affairs is all very well for what we hope to be a short term policy, but it is not an economic possibility for it to continue indefinitely. But we face this second year with high hopes, each week bringing us so much nearer to the release for which alone we live. We have lived a year of being glad that each day has passed, a year of wishing our lives away. If, during this full period, there have been many days when we have lost heart, we can hardly be blamed. For the few, it has meant only a comparatively slight deviation from the previous hum drum existence, but for many it has been the temporary replacement of living by mere existence. May it soon end, that we may again pick up the threads of life which we laid down, through no fault of ours, in June 1940, that blackest of all months?

From all accounts there seems to be panic movement of troops and barges from France to Guernsey – due, maybe, to the intensified RAF activity. Of course, our 'guaranteed essential commodity' vessels are on the job.

The weekend has been notable for the audible RAF activity and for the inclusion of Jersey in the panic troop movements. Rumour has it we have 8,000 here – certainly more than we appreciate.

Soap is being issued this week, on special application, at the rate of one tablet about the size of a matchbox per family per fortnight.

We have been working hard this last day or so, the place next door having been commandeered as a food store for the Germans at short notice, and they don't give one much time to clear. We have come to the help of the owner, and given him a little corner in the store – as a reward, we will have the pleasure of a sentry on the door step day and night, leaning against the door frame, as is their habit, with a rifle slung over the shoulder by the strap.

June 24th 1941

I have just sent another 25 words via a Red Cross letter which I can do every three weeks. I wish I could receive news as regularly, though I have no doubt the family are doing their best.

Latest orders include keeping to the right of the road – one which I am surprised didn't come before, but which we are finding a little awkward to get used to. Gas will henceforth only be allowed to be used from 7.00 a.m. to 8.30 a.m., 11.30 a.m. to 1.30 p.m. and 5.30 p.m. to 7.30 p.m. In between these hours only sufficient pressure will be available to just fill the pipes. It will be a little awkward, but the hay box which I made when gas was first rationed will be of even greater value than it has been. A considerable quantity of the coal, which we had imported, has been re-shipped to Guernsey, who were just about bust for gas. But it cuts us down very near the bone, as I am told that we have only enough for 7/8 weeks gas supply ourselves.

During the course of my enquiries, I find the difficulties of importing stuff are so great that I am experimenting in making drain pipes. There are exactly none left, and I can foresee that the lack of them at a time like this might quite easily be the curse of an epidemic which, once started, would be almost impossible to stop.

JULY 1941

July 1st 1941

The V for Victory racket is being worked here – some hardy souls have even marked the walls and notice boards outside German premises. We have another mass of traffic regulations, but boiled down, they all mean little.

Reprisals for the V campaign, failing the finding of the culprit within 48 hours, are to take the form of civilian patrols to prevent a recurrence, the confiscation of wireless sets, and a fine – but all this only applies in the affected district. It is generally agreed it can hardly be the work of 'Britishers' – the wording "Victory is British" is hardly the way an Englishman would express himself, and the workmanship in all cases was so good it must have taken some time to do.

It doesn't seem reasonable to suppose it was done before the curfew time of 11.00 p.m. after which it was rather dark for decent sign writing. Ergo it must have been done in the early morning, when a civilian would have been taking a big risk walking around with a paint pot and brush let alone painting over a German signboard under the nose of a sentry. Had it just been done in chalk, it might conceivably have been a civilian, but painted, and well painted, it seems to point to being either the work of a disgruntled soldier or, more probably, an organised attempt to justify reprisals.

A whole string of orders relating to fishing have been issued, whereby amongst other rules, 20% of all fish caught belongs to the Germans. Hitherto they have been commandeering considerably more than 20% and the public have seen very little of what has been caught. These last few days I have been push biking out to Gorey each evening on the off chance of getting some from the fishermen, but that won't be any use now. I am lucky to have had any at all, and what with a little extra 'black market' meat and the products of the garden now coming along, we have been feeding much better than for some time past.

Cor, there goes an ME110 – the first plane we have seen for many days.

The latest step in Nazi infiltration is an offer to teach the school children German after school hours – I fancy very few children will be allowed to volunteer for that. Sufficient unto the Island is the female population who, for the furtherance of their seduction of the troops, have learnt to speak German.

July 7th 1941

Orders dated July 5th demand firstly all mains wireless sets belonging to evacuees should be brought in and secondly, a complete duplicated inventory of the effects of such persons should be handed to the Befehlshaber (Military Commandant) in order they may select what they want. This order is a bit late, as many hundreds of mattresses etc. belonging to evacuated persons and in storage, are already being collected for the use of a ship load of troops who arrived today. It would appear they are not getting a very restful time in France, thanks to the attentions of the RAF. Even Granville, which has hitherto been left untouched as a channel for supplies for the Islands, has had a couple of eggs laid on it. Merton Hotel has been fitted out as a hospital, and a number of ambulances are on the job, so our friends expect (and will get) bother.

The gas ration is cut by a further ⅓rd, which isn't so good, but better than none.

I have been busy these days making inventories of the governor's place and of my pal's house near home. I have bought the latter's radiogram and refrigerator, and will sell them back to him afterwards. I know I am taking a bit of a chance about the radiogram, which should have been delivered to the collecting centre, as they already have particulars of all wireless sets from last November's contemplated confiscation.

Since the V 'outrage' civilian patrols have been on duty at each German notice board every night in the affected area, and now confiscation of wireless sets is proceeding. But I fancy this is a good sign, and another example of the jittery feeling of the forces in the game they are playing in still further fortifying the Island. They sent for 1,000 men on Monday to work at the airport, but when they arrived no one knew what it was for and they were all sent back. The airport isn't being used at all just now, despite the terrific amount of work done on it enlarging and so forth, but one of these days they will use it – and then we shall be treated to that long awaited raid. Guernsey has had two lots recently, and we are quite jealous.

July 14th 1941

Just sent off another 25 words, but I wish I could hear from those in Britain for a change.

Following swiftly on the registration of evacuees furniture comes the order to hand in all their single mattresses immediately.

July 18th 1941

The Germans, unable to stop the V campaign, have decided to adopt the V, complete with laurel wreath, and this morning German hotels, cars and all sorts were decorated with Vs, which makes us laugh. We are wondering what the

BBC Overseas news is talking so loudly about the 20th for. As usual there is a packet of rumours going about that the invasion of France is to take place, the Channel Islands are to be re-occupied by the British, and someone heard the announcer say the RAF will raid the islands – as though they would send a postcard they are coming. My own idea of the most likely to happen is a mass sweep, but being as the announcement was made to all occupied territories, and it wouldn't be possible to make the sweep as extensive as that, even that it is improbable.

Many German civilians have arrived here, and have been reshipped to Alderney which it is apparently intended to populate. I think I mentioned Alderney was completely evacuated, even to the cattle, and since then has been occupied only by a party of a few Guernsey men who went there to more or less keep things going. Many of the empty houses here have been taken, and are now occupied by troops, who apparently feel safer well mingled with the population.

July 22nd 1941

Our old friend rumour has been most active recently on the matter of the reticence of troops stationed here to being sent to Russia, and it seems generally accepted that at least one lot was encouraged aboard the ships at the point of bayonet. The patrols lately, contrary to usual practise, have been going round in dozens instead of pairs and armed with hand grenades as well as rifles.

Since the RAF started specialising in disturbing shipping, we see a lot more ships as they now come south of Jersey, hugging the French coast more closely than previously. I am looking forward to coastal Command getting wise to this move.

July 28th 1941

The wireless sets confiscated as a reprisal for the Vs are being returned today; which will, fortunately, relieve me of the job I have done for the past few days of keeping a written summary of the news for Father P, who was in the affected district.

Despite the Germans officially joining in the game of Vs, our attempts to help them are not encouraged – they don't seem to have any sense of humour. One person at Havre des Pas who decorated his house has been very seriously reprimanded, and another case in which two young girls were noticed picking up paper Vs in the road has resulted in at least one of them being sent to France for nine months – full and accurate details of the latter case are not available yet, but the foregoing seems to be generally accepted.

July 29th 1941

The official version of the above V sign racket is the V is considered subversive to German authority.

Additional to the above, there are two men waiting shipment to Germany for internment, one for chalking V on the road after curfew, and another for having possession of 100 sticks of gelignite, stolen from a quarry. I don't know what the latter chap intended, but he must have had some scheme in his mind to use the stuff, which is sufficient to blow up a small town.

July 31st 1941

Masses more traffic orders and also more proof of the German expectancy of trouble from the RAF. This being orders relating to the precautions against incendiary leaves in grain crops, as well as a repetition of threats of death to anyone harbouring the crews of 'enemy' aircraft. The curfew in the Military Zone is again back to 10.00 p.m. and adjustments have been made in the bread ration to cut out the odd ounces – so henceforth we get 9 lbs. a week instead of 9 ¼ lbs. The issue of the minute ration of soap is cancelled, but we are getting a packet of soap powder per head next week – I think for one week only.

AUGUST 1941

August 1st 1941

A big ammunition dump is being made about a mile from town in the yard of our principal competitor – I sincerely hope there are no accidents. Terrific quantities of all kinds of war materials have been brought into the island, as many as 16 ships unloading in the harbour at one time.

At the store, we are getting progressively slacker as stocks run out, until now we only average to clear one to two days expenses on each week's business. And still we can't see much daylight ahead.

August 2nd 1941

The good Col. Britain amuses me, with his orders to the V army, and the latest one to buy as much food, clothes and anything else we can lay hands on shows, whilst he has some knowledge of what is going on in the occupied zones, his knowledge is neither up to date nor complete. It is reasonable to suppose, with certain minor differences, the circumstances in these Islands are parallel with those of France, Belgium, Holland etc. and in all these places, as well as here, the German troops, flush with victory 'money', have for more than a year been changing their phoney money into something of tangible worth. The troops realise the paper credit mark is merely a ticket telling them how much lout they are entitled to, and despite Hitler's wonderful system of trade by credit and barter in place of gold, his soldiers like to change their dud paper into gold articles or other goods of intrinsic value. Therefore in 13 months of occupation the place is just about drained dry. You couldn't buy a new saucepan or cup and saucer or blanket for love nor money, and the German purchases have even included suites of furniture, and practically all new clothing has gone. Against this, the only acceptable form of International exchange within the occupied zone is the Reich Credit Mark, and as we must buy, we must sell our goods to obtain those marks – we don't like it but what would you do? In telling us to buy whatever we can on the principal goods will always have a value which phoney marks won't, Col. Britain shows knowledge but no understanding. The money in circulation in each country at the time of the Occupation is still in circulation now, being as it was no use to the Germans. The Germans are paid in, and spend, marks, but the general currency here is still the pound sterling, the paper credit mark being only used to a small extent to alleviate the acute shortage of change. There will only be a very small, almost infinitesimal proportion of marks here when the Occupation ends, although no doubt there will be a bigger ratio in France, for instance. On the other hand, in a country like France where the goods sold are replaceable from their own factories, such a policy will result in an internal trade boom which, though only temporary, won't hinder the German war effort. In telling us to buy food and fuel for the winter, Col. Britain wants to try teaching his grandmother to suck eggs. During the whole of this lousy period, everyone here has bought whatever they could lay hands on, almost irrespective of cost. Tinned and other non-perishable foodstuffs have vanished long since, but the Germans made sure of their own pickings first. Even in Jersey where the differences between town and country are less defined, we learnt very early the country is the place to go for ones 'grabbing', and don't need Col. Britain to tell us that. There may be a deeper purpose behind all this than I, with my common or garden mind, can grasp. It seems the idea is to keep us occupied and 'oppressed' peoples alert and feeling we are doing something. It is true the feeling which we have been getting we could do nothing to hinder Germany is mighty bad for ones morale, so maybe the foregoing treatise is merely the ramblings of a naturally fault-finding brain.

AA guns opened up here last night, presumably on an RAF plane, but without effect. The big quantities of guns and material I mentioned yesterday continue to arrive, and from all accounts really big stuff is being mounted all around the coast. Reading in a book of Lord Fisher the other day, I came across the information during the Napoleonic Wars, the coast of France adjacent to these Islands was considered the most vulnerable spot for a landing, and geography hasn't altered since then. Therefore it may be deduced our friends are preparing in case the BEF decide to enter the continent that way. If such did happen, the Islands would be of great strategic importance. Recent ARP regulations mention 'alarms or air raid alarms', so it is certain the full possibilities are not being overlooked, and equally certain Germany realises the growing strength of Britain, and realises too the invasion racket is not so one sided as it was last year.

August 5th 1941

For the last 10 days we have been living under some apprehension. A German officer had a fountain pen and 'important papers' stolen from his clothes whilst he was bathing – no money was touched, so it would appear likely to be the work of some kids. Both he and the local police have mentioned the possibility of the confiscation of wireless sets in our district if the culprit isn't found, but up to date and touching wood, nothing has yet happened.

We are the latest victims of the pinching racket, having lost a not inconsiderable amount of soap and other cleaning accessories to some individual with enough cunning to put his arm through our larder window. As the things are not replaceable, we quite naturally are not so pleased.

August 6th 1941

A couple of Germans cut up rough last Saturday night with an old lady, breaking in by firing revolvers at the lock of the door. They knocked the poor old soul out and pinched some money, and when two local policemen were sent along, damaged one of them as well. No publicity has been given to the affair – the Germans only advertise things which show to their credit, not incidents like this. We believe it to be an old soldier's dodge to get gaoled and dodge being sent up to the Russian show.

Another German variety show is being staged at the Forum. I mention this not as of special interest, but just to show some occasional effort is made to entertain the troops (and us). This crowd apparently consider themselves first rate, for whereas previous shows have been entrance free, a charge is now being made. Not having seen any of their shows or band performances, I am not in a position to judge.

This 58th week brings a reduction of the tobacco ration and the reduction of the cigarette ration to 10 per week. The black market price of the cigarettes smuggled in from France at the moment is 3/- per 20, but the added demand created by this further reduction of ration will considerably increase the price. And I moaned about paying 1/4d last time I was in England for real cigarettes – not that I pay the 3/- rate – I prefer to spend liberally for food when I can lay my hands on it, not for cigarettes.

A considerable number of horses have been brought here, and a lot of the German transport is being done by them in order to conserve petrol – a very good sign. The economy racket has extended so far that, instead of towing the anti tank guns to the drill grounds, they are now man handled. I reckon the horse vehicles they are using are a remnant of the 1870 war – the same sort of things which, according to Hollywood, were used by the first American settlers. In direct contradiction to this economy, there are a number of huge caterpillar transports which seem to do a round tour of the town every day for no more apparent reason than exercise the crew. The adventures of these colossal semi-tanks cause trepidation in the hearts of those people who have houses and shops on corners of streets, and when they are drawn in close to the kerbs, sparks and chunks of granite go flying in all directions.

August 11th 1941

Saturday night's paper is a most interesting one. The recent pigeon round up is explained by shooting a Frenchman for sending messages to England that way. The second item of interest is an advertisement for 200 men to work at the airport. Hitherto, the Germans have ordered our States, who in turn have ordered contractors to do the work. Now the contractors have found that, according to International Law, they cannot be forced to do work of this kind, and have accordingly downed tools, even though it means losing the equipment on the job. I am afraid the men will not back their employers, and will flock direct to the Germans to get jobs – not only do they get paid better wages and danger money, but they get extra rations, which counts these days more than money. Thirdly is the latest order relating to the property of evacuees – this is now requisitioned for the use of the Army of occupation, and the keys of evacuated properties have to be handed over immediately. I have no doubt the Germans will have some nice pickings from some of the bigger houses – stuff which won't be seen in Jersey again. Although we don't like to see our protectors helping themselves in this way, if I had left Jersey I should have said goodbye to everything I left behind, and those people who went can hardly expect to come back and find things exactly as they left them. It makes me feel as if the Island is under the finger tip of the blood sucking cancerous growth which is spread over Europe, and is being sucked dry.

August 16th 1941

I have bought a new (or as new as possible) push bike – a rather super one which I was lucky to get for £12. I know I am being extravagant, but push biking is a long way from being a pleasure to me, and I thought it worthwhile to reduce the misery of it as far as possible. I shall get a few shekels back for the other bike. The week's misery is – no tobacco again. Some actually arrived in the Island last week, but is not yet released because they haven't yet had the invoice and so don't know what to charge for it.

August 18th 1941

It seems to be true there was a fracas amongst the Germans billeted at Five Oaks on Friday night, including some shooting. Casualties unknown, but the tally grows every time someone tells me, the latest being 14 men and 3 officers killed and others wounded – which seems to be a little exaggerated.

A good sign is the almost complete lack of planes about here – we don't see more than one a week on average. Up until the time of the Greek business, troop carrying Junkers were over all the time, being used to bring petrol and oil and to take away the loot, as well as for their legitimate purposes. Since then, we haven't seen a single one.

Neither do we see much of the RAF, whose attentions are in the main directed where they ought to be – Germany itself. Another recent feature are the route marches to which the troops here are being subjected – hitherto, they haven't marched for half a mile a day, but now they are doing forced marches – maybe in training for Russia.

August 21st 1941

We are officially informed we are to have one ounce of tobacco as well as 10 cigarettes this week – which makes pleasant hearing. I often smile at the jokes on the radio about cigarette queues – if you were trying to make 10 cigarettes last 7 days, you would find it a little more difficult. Single cigarettes on Fridays, the day before the ration is issued, are worth 6d.

The good work (from the German point of view) of rounding up evacuees' furniture and stuff is proceeding apace. It is the best stuff first. I gather there is no intention or pretence of compensation for this, either from the Military authorities or the States. Our latest attempt at finding soft jobs for some lucky blokes is fuel rationing – henceforth this is to be done with ration cards, and I gather it will be based on so much per head of family – not a very fair means. The scheme covers coal (if any), coke (if any), wood and peat.

Butter ration is cut to two ounces, and as this is our only source of fat (no margarine or dripping or lard) it is not so good. I think it is this lack of fat which is the most serious omission from our diet.

August 25th 1941

There is news, unofficial but confirmed from many connecting details, of a young soldier at present at large after shooting an officer. He appears to have got hold of civilian clothes and to be getting sustenance from the countryside. We all hope he won't be caught, but there is not much one can do to help.

It may be a 'follow on' of the German attempt to employ labour direct, but a German builder appears to be setting up here and is advertising for all grades of labour at very good wages. I only hope this won't bring us into the foreground as suppliers although financially we might benefit considerably, as such a demand would put us in a better position to import from France, with corresponding advantage. I hope our competitor, who is much larger than us, takes it on, as then we could just horn in for a share of the imports without the unpleasantness of handling German business - or am I being selfish?

The phenomenal amount of rain has ruined our harvest of wheat, oats and so forth, and although there is considerable gnashing of teeth about it, I for one am not sorry, being convinced if the harvest had been a good one, the major portion would have been taken over by our friends. A poor harvest such as we have will probably be left to us, though no doubt it won't be anywhere nearly enough for our requirements.

I have concocted another 25 words to send to family. That job is the bane of my existence – there is plenty to say, but it wouldn't pass muster, and being confined to 25 words, I find it hard to express myself at all.

The petrol shortage is so acute French engineers are here engaged on altering our buses to burn charcoal, and meanwhile 100 gallons of reserve held for ARP services has been handed over to keep the very restricted service going. Gas coal too is just about on its last legs – failing further supplies, we shall be entirely without gas in about 3 weeks from now; which will remove the moans about the quality of gas rations.

August 30th 1941

August 30th ends this 61st week with a further reminder the winter food shortage which we have been dreading is getting nearer. Bread ration is being cut by 1 lb per head, so Mum and I will now get 7 lbs. a week. In lieu of this we are to have ¾ lb of wheat flour a head, which seems to me to be just plain daft – we are severely rationed for all types of cooking fuel, and there is prospect of no gas or coal for domestic use in the near future unless supplies arrive soon. And yet we are being given wheat flour which must be cooked. Surely it would have been more economic on fuel for the flour to be cooked in the dozen or so bake houses and issued as bread, than for the 10,000 households to each be cooking their small ration. But the ways of officialdom are weird and wonderful, and beyond human understanding. A bright spot is indicated by the use of a huge tanker barge which has been bringing fuel oil for the electric generating plant and for the quarries machinery (for German use). Although this barge could carry at least 1,500 tons, she has only brought 290 tons altogether in the last four trips. This goes to prove our officials are not alone in their uneconomic ways of life, and also shows oil is far from plentiful in occupied France. Prior to the first of these 4 trips, we were within 4 days of being without electricity, but are in a comparatively safe position now.

The mention earlier this week of a deserter has been confirmed by his capture in the loft of a house – the confirmation is not official, but is reliable, having come from the fellow whose house he was hiding in.

Later -

I learn my foregoing remarks about the bread ration were unjustified – one can, if one wishes, have the ¾ lb flour in lieu of 1 lb bread, but it is optional; which isn't quite so bad, but still seems to be a daft scheme.

I think the ingenuity displayed in overcoming the many difficulties and in making the most of our meagre resources deserved to have a paragraph to itself. In transport, for the delivery of goods and the transport of the younger members of the family, the cycle trailer is quite the thing, with the cycle sidecar a poor second. Much ingenuity has been shown in the matter, and most of the efforts are sturdy and good looking. In the early days one saw people shopping with those little garden-baskets-on-wheels and I even saw one case of a hand truck made from a lawn mower minus the works, but that sort of thing just isn't being done now.

Then too, old methods of extracting flour from potatoes have been revived, but today's generation has produced many weird and wonderful inventions for the necessary grinding of the potatoes in lieu of the old method of hand grating.

Thus, with the aid of a hundredweight of spuds and much labour one is able to produce 7 lbs to 10 lbs of flour. The more handy amongst us have produced devices for saw dust burners, which work well and save quite a lot of fuel – whilst one can get the necessary sawdust. In this connection, the use of hay boxes for cooking has become almost universal. We make quite palatable ersatz coffee from parsnips, and tea made from blackberry leaves isn't too bad. In more specialised lines, the use of lino and wood for the soling of boots and shoes, the making of old-type besom brooms, and buckets from zinc with wooden bottoms, and the use of potato flour for paper hanging are all the products of various peoples' fertility of mind. My own contributions to this world of make shift are the firebricks and slabs referred to earlier and the manufacture of drain pipes on which I am now engaged. My first pipe is at present in the mould, and my fingers are itching to take it out, but I must abide my soul in patience till Monday. This making of something out of nothing, even when it is such a prosaic article as a drainpipe, brings a little thrill – one realises one is doing something for the common benefit. I can foresee we shall make very little money out of this venture, and shall more probably lose on it, but I still feel it to be worth doing. I regard it as a duty to do my little bit towards keeping the draining system in working order and thus preventing an epidemic which, if it once started, could not be stopped amongst a people under-nourished and ill provided with medical necessities. Even in such things as the servicing of cycles ingenuity rears its head – we have wooden brake blocks fitted now, instead of rubber ones, and the many and wonderful methods of patching up tyres which, in more normal times, would be thrown away, are too numerous to mention. There have been one or two instances of rubber hosing being used, but there are snags attached to it, especially now that the rubber vulcanising can no longer be done through lack of material. Lack of H T wireless batteries has produced clumsy and expensive, though efficient, apparatus made from old Ford car coils powered by car batteries.

I could indeed go on for hours instancing the many little ways in which necessity has proved once more to be the mother of invention, and paying homage to the many fertile brains which have so minimised the inevitable inconveniences resulting on a complete cut off from the sources of supply on which we so heavily relied. Unfortunately for us, we have had the benefit of modern science for so long as to have come to regard luxuries as necessities, but the foregoing will, I hope, be some indication that we are not laying down under things, and are indeed, creating a 'new order' of our own – a new order of compromise and makeshift, and of greater appreciation of the many little comforts which, before this bad dream started, we accepted as a matter of course.

SEPTEMBER 1941

September 2nd 1941

I had a laugh last night when cycling home with neighbours riding three abreast when we were hailed by two patrolling tin-plated Nazi Military Police with "Hey, mister, stop". Cycling two abreast is regarded as a heinous crime, and results in a fine of 2/1d on the spot, so naturally I expected riding three abreast was going to cost a lot more. But when stopped, the nice Nazi policeman, with the aid of some little English and a lot of gestures, indicated to one of the party his light was out. We demonstrated with more gestures and a lot of laughter that it had bumped out, whereupon the policeman shook hands and off we went, much happier than we had been a few seconds before. It goes to show that, although these Feldgendarmerie are generally loathed even amongst the Germans, they are not all so bad.

September 6th 1941

A little coal has arrived, just in time to save us from going gasless – we were within 48 hours of it. Also a little cement has arrived for civilian use, which would please me more if it was delivered in its bags as sent, and not lose as received. The week has included quite a lot of RAF attention all around here – Cherbourg, Granville and Brest – audible to us, but we are still being left alone. I can't make out why the big convoys which come here are left unmolested. For some weeks past about 50 ships and barges have arrived each week, but I suppose the RAF realise the impossibility of avoiding those which are bringing in food, so leave all alone. I cannot believe this lack of action is because they don't know about it.

Just had another bit of 'black market' meat, the second recently and more promised for the future. We have not been amongst the most unlucky ones in the food competition, and thanks be, have managed to get hold of quite a few small extras to the rations on which we are supposed to exist. Were I in England I wouldn't countenance the racket, and indeed, I didn't like it here at first, but I have come to find the local meat goes to the Germans and the imported meat to us civilians. Ergo, black market meat is so much less for the Germans, as well as being so much more for us.

Talking to someone who works in a laundry which used to do the German work, I am told it is quite common for uniforms to be taken to be washed blood stained and bullet holed, presumed to have been taken from German bodies for cleaning and reissue. Our friends seem to have more soldiers than uniforms and are certainly not considerate for the finer feelings either of their men or the laundress.

After many failures and disappointments, and only after much experiment and perseverance, I have managed to produce a presentable and usable drain pipe, of which I am naturally rather proud. Now we have to set to and get it on a production basis, if only a small one.

September 12th 1941

Once again last night the district around here was pounded by the RAF, the raiders passing this way. Despite the fact the planes were obviously British, no searchlights or ack ack went up, we presume because our local 'protectors' were afraid of the consequences or else afraid to assist the raiders by giving away the position of the Islands. The falling bombs made music in our ears.

Had another bit of black market luck this week, thanks be. I have got in with the right bloke this time, methinks.

September 16th 1941

I have been keeping myself busily engaged with making pipes and other little experiments. The first pipe mould was a quite elaborate and therefore expensive affair, but I am trying out ideas of my own for making a much more simple, though I hope equally efficient, job. I am experimenting making chimney pots.

In the days ahead when this becomes a family heirloom (maybe) I hope that posterity will forgive these lapses and will understand that life here does not solely compose of standing on street corners looking admiringly at the German soldiery as they slouch past singing their charming ditties about all they will do to England if and when. We work far harder than before, despite lack of trade, in trying to create the essentials of trade and in overcoming the many snags resultant on our complete cut off.

September 18th 1941

By direct orders from the Germans, extra rations of fat and meat are to be given to very heavy workers, but I fancy very few will get the bonus ration except those who engage to work for Theodor Elsche, the Nazi building contractor, and it will be another inducement for the men. It would appear labour is being a bit shy about taking on the job he offers, and his Jersey foreman is also advertising (under his own name) for labour of all kinds, hoping to catch those shy of working directly for the Germans.

On the strength of my pipe making efforts, and with the aid of friends in the appropriate department, I have managed to get my bread ration increased to the workmen's 6 lbs instead of 4½ lbs. a week previously. What a wangle.

Early this morning a loud bang was heard whilst planes were overhead and unconfirmed rumour has it that an egg was laid on the new fortifications at Noirmont.

September 19th 1941

Last night, for the first time since I don't know when, we were treated to the sound of bombers going over to raid South Wales, and flying so low we could see them despite the darkness. They left here heaped up with our curses, although only about six went.

Letters come and letters go but we wait on forever. Everyone else seems to be hearing except us, but with great patience and perseverance, I am sending family another 25 words in the hope that in the end someone will receive and reply to one of our many attempts.

No 'baccy' ration again this week, and it is believed there will be no more – so be it.

Further details of the fuel rationing show that we are expected to stay warm on ½ cwt of coal and 1 cwt of logs or peat per family per month. Strikes me we will be suffering from cold feet in a literal sense this winter.

September 23rd 1941

Not much happening except the reported arrival of some 2,000 civilians – the purposes of this influx are variously and ingeniously conjectured in the current rumours to be connected with Nazi intention to have only German business houses. Today's rumours also concern our local Nazi builder – he is starting to build a tunnel to France, he is making a tunnel at St. Ouens from the beach to the Airport, and another at Gorey, and he is building another aerodrome at Gorey. Actually, he appears to be wholly concerned with fortifications, building pill boxes and gun emplacements. Another juicy rumour worth recording for its unbelieveability is that, as a reprisal for the internment of Germans in Iran, all English born people in the Island are to be taken to concentration camps immediately. A modification of this one says all males are to be taken and all the females left to supply the needs of the Germany Army - this latter was told to me in all seriousness by a fellow who works for the Germans. I fancy some at least of these fairy stories emanate from the Germans in an effort to keep us on the jitters. Unfortunately by the time they have been handed on a few times, the tales become too ridiculous to be believed by anyone but a raving idiot.

September 27th 1941

One of the questions being asked here is why we are quite so quiescent under German authority. This same question will probably be asked when this Occupation is all over, and to understand the reasons it is necessary to take into consideration the fact that whereas, in Paris for instance, the male civilian population outnumber the occupying forces very considerably, here in Jersey the armed troops outnumber the unarmed potential revolutionaries by at least two to one. The very size of the Island and the impossibility of getting away from it render any action of force right out of the question – unless one wants a quick and certain method of suicide and to drag many others in it. Many of us would willingly take a reasonable risk to help the common cause, but as things stand there isn't any risk attached to it - sudden death is just certain. I and others sincerely hope the opportunity will come, and meanwhile we abide our time quietly so that if it should come we will be ready and able to take full advantage. At the moment a passive resistance is all that is possible, and the greatest damage we are able to do is in such minor things as misdirecting their vehicles. Sabotage in a small way might be possible by those working for the Germans, but for the most part these men are all too eager to keep in with the Germans to get extra cigarettes etc. In fact, for the sake of what they can get, a small minority of men here are just as bad as the girls in their creeping methods.

A second firm of German builders has started up here, and are applying for unlimited number of mechanics and labourers. Thanks be, it seems materials will be imported without the assistance of we local merchants. It also appears certain practically all German work will be taken out of the hands of the few bigger firms who have been doing it, leaving no civilian work at all except the small jobbing repairs which can be done with the very limited materials available. This influx of Nazi builders will thus result in the enrolment of nearly the whole of the local building industry to work on the German schemes. A considerable number of Czechs and Austrians are employed here, and a few hundred French passed this way during the week en route to work in Guernsey. The recent heavy shipping between France and the Islands seems to have been mainly devoted to bringing cement and building material for the various schemes.

OCTOBER 1941

October 4th 1941

October 4th ends a quiet week. My drain pipes have received the approval and blessing of the sanitary authorities, and I have gained some considerable kudos thereby. My only assistant is off sick, having gone all gooey principally through under nourishment. Still no tobacco is being issued, but I have been doubly lucky, having been given English stuff in a sweepstake. There is news another issue of jam is to be made at 1 lb per head, again in alphabetical order. The tobacco has come as a wonderful blessing to me, for during the period I have been without, I have sucked an empty pipe so much my jaws have ached too much to eat the unappetising meals to which we hurry home as though we hadn't seen food for weeks. An unusual and unpleasant feature for Jersey is the verdict at one or two recent inquests into sudden deaths – 'due to under nourishment'. This is affecting those who were not strong before more than those of us who can stand it better, but I am afraid the 'under nourishment' verdict will be used more during the winter.

I have just had another ration of black market meat – I don't intend to figure as the corpse at one of these inquests if I can help it.

There is an almost complete dearth of English currency and we have to use the Reich Credit marks extensively. Reasons for this are variously conjectured, but I discussed the matter with bank and treasury people and find the reason is partly hoarding on the part of local country folk, and partly through members of the German forces taking cash away with them. The Reich Credit Marks with which the troops are paid are valueless in Germany itself and it is useless for the soldier to send or take home this special Occupation money. He prefers to hold English notes. I am given to understand by a local business man, a Frenchman with many connections in France, the troops are swopping our £1 notes there and getting 250 Francs instead of the official 192 – another proof the French expect our victory.

October 13th 1941

We had a thrill yesterday afternoon to see a couple of silvery planes playing high up – too far to pick out the markings with the naked eye, but we were certain of what they were by the sound of the engines. A few minutes later, as they passed westwards towards the Airport, Jerry showed he too was sure of the nationality of the planes, and wasted a whole lot of ammunition. Everyone here this morning is bucked to death they have seen an RAF plane – the first for many weary moons, and a welcome reminder our existence is not forgotten. It is the first time I have seen the RAF since, on the day before our friends arrived, those Blenheims passed over when I was at one of the fires started by the air raid and made us all duck for cover until we recognised them.

Despite many vain attempts, I have never lost sight of the possibility of getting my motorbike back on the road on the strength of ARP, and now our friends will only allow 12 phones to cover the whole island in event of trouble, our importance has grown. Therefore, we D.Rs have together taken up the matter of having one of us on the road the whole time, which would give us one week on the road out of four. It would only cost ½ a gallon of petrol a week, and would undoubtedly make for greater efficiency in ARP – though that aspect is not the real reason behind our application – we are being completely selfish, and want to have our bikes on the road.

I feel contaminated – for the first time I had to shake hands with a German. I know that sounds almost cowardly, but what can one do when one comes into direct contact with a German officer who puts himself out to be polite and who insists on shaking hands at parting. Or maybe I am being more fastidious than most people here.

October 14th 1941

Sunday's RAF activity seems to have been accompanied by a couple of small eggs on AA guns and it seems generally agreed there were at least six planes involved. Last night again, at about six o'clock, we heard flak and went out in time to see six planes and a lot of flak smoke bursts. The RAF got here a little late yesterday, as throughout the day ships had been arriving bringing some thousands more troops. At the time of the RAF nosiness, only one largish ship was left out in the bay, and she quickly settled into harbour. We were bitterly disappointed not to see that ship attacked, for we should have had a grand view of the proceedings, but German planes had been active during the day escorting the convoy, so no doubt some of them were upstairs too, making any sort of attack difficult.

October 17th 1941

Apparently the present influx of war material is only a prelude to the arrival of a real horde of Huns. Victoria College has been taken over at short notice, presumably for their accommodation. In addition to the not inconsiderable amount of billeting possible in our hotels, a large number of houses have been taken over, the occupants being given 3 to 7 days to clear. In the case of the owners of the houses being the occupiers, in order to keep inside of International

Law, they are not expelled but have troops billeted on them – which comes to much the same thing, for who wants to live in the same house as Germans. Also numerous suitable stores have been commandeered for the storage of foodstuffs for the approaching hordes.

A German officer has told a friend of mine it is intended to station 200 fighter planes here – if this be the reason for all this preparatory work, look out for sparks. The RAF will surely break up our dreary monotony. The building work going on here certainly points in that direction and includes a deep cave being built within easy reach of the Airport, presumably as an ammunition dump, as well as coastal defence works. Another possibility is all the preparations here are being made for the reception of German wounded from the Russian front, though this is a heck of a long way to bring them. We notice almost all the troops leaving here now are equipped with greatcoats, so are presumably en route to Russia. Despite the number leaving here daily, the place is just lousy with all grade of Army and Air Force, with still more due to arrive.

October 18th 1941

For the first time for many weeks, we are to have a 2 ounce ration of dripping next week – our only fat extra to the weekly 2 ounces of butter. I am working harder now than I ever have before, cycling to sales whenever building material appears on the list, in addition to our ever growing output of concrete pipes, ridge tiles, and latest addition, chimney pots.

The clothes ration coming into operation at the end of this month includes second hand clothing and footwear (just about all that is obtainable) and even such items as sewing cotton, shoe laces and boot polish.

I mentioned back in July the place next door to our store was being commandeered, and we had to do a panic evacuation of the contents into our store. We heard nothing further for a long time, and the owner of the place had been quietly taking his stuff back. These last few days German officers come around regularly to inspect the place, and it seems almost certain it will be taken as a food store – actually it was contact through this which brought me the displeasing handshake mentioned as the owner lives in the country and I hold the keys and more or less look after things.

October 24th 1941

The RAF passed this way twice during the course of last night, their passage being marked by much flak. Some parachute flares were dropped, but I gather nothing else.

As from tomorrow the curfew is to be from 10.00 p.m. till 6.30 a.m. Some while ago we lost our old Kommandant, Col. Schumacher – it was understood his family had been killed in an RAF raid in Germany and he had a nervous breakdown in consequence. He has been replaced by a Col. Knackfuss, who seems to be tightening things up a lot, as instanced by this shortening of curfew. I fancy it won't last, for it applies to the troops as well as to civilians.

Tomorrow we are to have a one ounce ration of tobacco in addition to our weekly 10 cigarettes. Which is doubly pleasing, as for a few days we shall not be fumigated by the vile smells emanating from the pipes of those hardy souls who concoct ersatz mixtures from the leaves and flowers of every plant, be it weed or vegetable, and who often even gild the lily by introducing eau de cologne.

October 25th 1941

From a welter of reports of damage and casualties all over the Island in Thursday night's incidents, the only one which, I gather is authentic is an RAF plane probably damaged on the raid over Brest, dropped part of its fuselage and its whole load of incendiaries at Victoria Village, damaging a couple of houses and wrecking some greenhouses. The sole casualty appears to be an old man who, weak in mind before, has gone completely nuts over it. As is usual in these incidents, no publicity has been given, so whilst I believe the above facts to be a true version, there may be other damage and casualties in other places, as reported in the various yarns. I thought at the time the explosions were very heavy for flak, though the stuff sent up from here is very heavy. I sincerely hope, despite his damage, that plane got safely home.

I tried to send the family a message yesterday, but it could not be accepted, there being some 4,000 just arrived. May there be one or more for us.

October 27th 1941

Again last night we had a few seconds excitement at about 11.20 p.m. when we were at a neighbour's house playing cards. (Note how well we keep the curfew). We heard a plane flying very low, followed immediately by the most intense flak. We all rushed outside to see the sort of firework display which always used to draw "ah" from the crowd. Strings of many coloured lights were criss-crossing the sky in all directions, and instead of the lines of lights going straight, they zigzagged, so the whole sky was an intricate pattern of red, green and white lights, each light going out as it exploded; and behind it all, powerful searchlights searching every opening in the low flying cloud. It all lasted less than a minute, but for that short time the sky must have been a most unpleasant place to be in. We don't know what happened to the plane, but presume it managed to hide in the clouds and get away safely. There is no doubt this place has become a veritable hornet's nest of ack ack, and the searchlights here now are very different to the poor affairs of a few months ago. Jerry seems to appreciate the possibilities of invasion in the reverse direction, in which case the possession of these Islands would be a big factor. His recent instructions to ARP personnel mention 'when' (not if) fighting develops in the Island, in which case we are supposed to stay indoors – they hope.

More painted Vs have appeared on the Ritz, Royal Court and West Park Pavilion, resulting in the confiscation of all wireless sets in the surrounding areas, totalling most of the town and suburbs, and an order for the provision of civilian guards at the above spots as a preventative of a recurrence. In view of their having pinched the V sign, I think they would be wiser to ignore the unofficial ones – we are all delighted at the way they get rattled about it.

It has been suggested, and it seems reasonable, that last night's fireworks were directed against a German plane which was a little tardy in giving the recognition signal. It fits in with the brevity and abrupt termination of the show that, being so rudely reminded, Fritz remembered to indicate his nationality in time to save his skin.

October 29th 1941

Another message arrived yesterday – a month after the last, and yet sent a month earlier.

Again last night AA guns were in operation, though this time they gave the flaming onions a rest and concentrated with heavy stuff, I presume because the height was greater. The explosions were so heavy at times I shall not be surprised to hear some of them were caused by eggs – in any case, I can foresee the RAF getting tired of being potted at without hitting back, and am expecting sparks any night now though.

NOVEMBER 1941

November 3rd 1941

Most of us, me included, find the courage with which we decided we could not do other than face this lot out, is steadily evaporating. We haven't abandoned all hope exactly, but we are rather fed up with things in general. My own particular grouse at the moment is the requisitioning of a builder's yard, the owner of which evacuated, by yet another of the firms of German builders, and we have to get many tons of stuff cleared at very short notice so that I am working really hard. Blast the Germans.

A recent Court case has brought to light some interesting facts of the black market, 2 cwt of sugar having changed hands for £130 and 40 lbs of tea for £60, the enterprising salesman being a big business man and a competitor of mine.

November 6th 1941
We have cleared the building yard, and I am feeling pleased we managed to get away 3 concrete mixers and a crane by keeping them hidden until we could smuggle them out one at a time in between the frequent visits of the new tenant. He had already put the 'stay there' touch with an expressive movement of the hand on the wood-working machinery, and would certainly have done so on the concrete mixers if he had seen them. When I started on the job, I didn't realise what I was tackling, and I am mighty glad it is finished except for the clearing of some stone and bricks which I sold direct off site. Our poor little store is overflowing. Still, there is some money to be made out of it, in addition to the pleasure of not leaving it all for Jerry. The new arrival is apparently a large bloke from the Saar district, and has brought some £2,000 worth of Mercedes car with him and half a dozen foremen equipped with motorbikes. He can't talk English, but his hands express his wishes perfectly. Whilst perfectly polite, he seems to expect immediate obedience to all his commands – I suppose he regards us all as so much scum. Being as his wishes to clear the place as quickly as possible coincided with mine, we didn't quarrel.

November 10th 1941
The shipping rush still continues, and one day last week, there were over 50 ships in our little harbour, ranging from tugs and patrol motor boats to barges and steamers of 4,000 tons. They still bring huge quantities of all manner of material, ranging from office furniture to ammunition. Milk ration is cut down to ¼ pint and potatoes are becoming increasingly difficult to procure, although foreseeing this, I have taken necessary precautions.

November 12th 1941
People not normally resident here before July 1st 1940 – that is, English people who got caught here at the time of the Occupation – have to register, and there are many rumours as to what this is for.

It has been common knowledge for some weeks that one Denis Vibert managed to get away from the Island and arrived in England safely. Unfortunately, tongues wagged far too freely about it, and now the German Feldgendarmarie are demanding information about him. Of course, such information will not be given, and we are expecting some sort of retribution will be taken from the civil population – maybe in the form of a still further shortened curfew. We will worry about that when it happens, and meanwhile are all glad to think the authorities in England have some definite knowledge of events here, and of the fortification being carried out.

November 15th 1941

The local Girls College has now been taken over by the Military, and all householders have to give details of the number of rooms and number of occupants in their houses, in order billeting arrangements may be made. Thanks be our bungalow is only a bandbox of a house, for it would be just about the last straw to have Germans living on the premises. There are some 9,000 troops here now, and from all accounts it is intended to bring more than double that number before Christmas. It won't be a happy Island. When I come to think of the unimportant little things we used to moan about, it seems the present difficult period has been sent to teach us to appreciate when we are well off, and not to moan. Another snag is the cessation of the one ounce tea ration, so I suppose henceforth there will be more frequent issues of the ersatz coffee and ersatz cocoa which I understand is here but not yet released.

We are all a little disgusted the RAF have allowed the heavy spate of shipping to flow around here unmolested, more especially since we had the heartening evidence of their presence around here a week or so back. Guernsey received some attention last week end, but as usual Jersey was forgotten – even though I am sure we have at least as much worth bombing here as in Guernsey. It makes us jealous, and you would be surprised at the way many of our elderly ladies are looking forward to our boys coming along and disturbing the peace, even though we all realise, however careful the aim, it is inevitable some of us will get hurt in the process; but none of us here (except their paramours) like the idea of this being a safe hideout for the Hun.

I mentioned gas rationing some months ago and that it was only to be used during certain hours. This rule having been honoured more in the breach than the observance (in common with most regulations). It is now definitely shut off except from 7.30 a.m. till 2.00 p.m. and from 5.00 p.m. till 9.00 p.m. This comes a bit hard on those who rely on gas for lighting, and is dangerous both from the point of view of leaving taps turned on and from the possibility of air locks and explosions in the mains. It isn't much use telling the poor souls who now have to go to bed at 9.00 p.m. to use some other form of lighting, as even the few who get a paraffin ration have to manage on one pint a month, whilst the few candles which are about go at about 1/8d each.

November 18th 1941
The skipper of Jersey's S/S 'Normand' has been awarded two years gaol in France, believed to be something to do with the smuggling racket and a couple of Dockers have to do a couple of months. All these rewards are handed over in secret, and received no publicity.

November 22nd 1941
There seems to be a game of General Post going on, and all night troops and ammunition have been shipped way. Maybe it has summat to do with our Libyan push.

A friend just back from Guernsey tells me things there are much the same as here, only more so – some 12,000 troops and much fortification. Alderney, which once had a population of 1,000, now has 1,500 troops and many guns, whilst even little Sark has a garrison of 150 and is being prepared for the worst. Despite the Dame of Sark's edict banning motor vehicles on the Island, vans and motor bikes are being used there for the first time in history. General conditions in Guernsey seem to be much as here, except few children have been left there, having been evacuated school by school. Food seems much the same, but the fat ration is more generous – 4 ounces butter and 2 ounces cooking butter against our 2 ounces altogether – but against that they get skimmed milk only.

Our own tally of troops has risen to 11,000, which figure includes some hundreds of Hitler Youth, not actually soldiers, who do not salute but use the Nazi sign.

The recent visit of a 'high up', reputed to be General Von Muller, has resulted in a persistent report he found fault with the immense number of troops idle here, and issued orders the number was to be cut down immediately, which could coincide with the rumoured scuttling of the billeting order. Certainly there seems to be a thinning of Army uniforms about already, but I notice a lot of Air Force uniforms wrapped around beings wandering around aimlessly as new arrivals always do, as well as new signs around town with unintelligible wording except for the 'Luftwaffe' part. So maybe we are to be handed over to the Air Force – I don't know which I like least. The Air Force pilots consider themselves IT, but the ground staff, like Army privates, seems to be a harmless sort of animal. Many of the Army officers speak English too well for my liking – I had one in the store this morning, and found it unnecessary to talk with more than usual clearness, whilst he understood English idioms as well as I did. I imagine he must have lived in England for some considerable time. Unlike some others with whom I have come into contact, he was the sort of bloke I could quite easily hate in person as well as in the abstract as we all do. He added fire to my early dislike by wandering down the store and looking around to see what we had in stock, after I had told him we were out of stock of the paint he wanted – we always are out of stock of anything out of sight. I imagine it to be a trap, for this afternoon, a private came along and asked for the same thing – probably hoping to be attended to by someone else, and catch us out. I have known that sort of thing to happen on previous occasions when we have said 'nix', and I have felt a bit nervous once or twice when a glance in the right direction by the German would have proved me a liar.

It looks as though the long rumoured spud rationing is to come into force, as we now have to give details of the potatoes we have – they hope. We are also re-threatened with dire penalties for using electricity between 11.00 p.m. and 7.00 a.m. except in case of extreme urgency.

DECEMBER 1941

December 6th 1941

The meat ration is being doubled to 8 ounces and the butter ration to 4 ounces. I am afraid the former doesn't thrill me much, as I have been doing quite well in the black market of late, and have even bought some 200/250 lbs of pig for Christmas – no, not all for me, or I should be pork myself, but it gives me a chance of making sure all our friends have a decent Christmas dinner. If I got found out, I would stand a good chance of having Christmas dinner in gaol.

Our bread is the subject of some moans, being made from this year's local harvest, threshed in our own mills. It is so good it includes the shucks and straw, is nearly chocolate colour, and of a texture like damp sawdust. Our efforts at being self supporting in this line certainly have not met with much success. I haven't mentioned the taste, you will notice, because I can't find anything good to say about it, except whilst the bread is like it is, we don't mind so much being rationed.

The coming and going of troops continues, with apparently more going than coming, for the number here is certainly less than half what it was. Several houses in our neighbourhood have been taken over by them, which makes curfew breaking a more hazardous business. I notice troops this winter are all fitted up with greatcoats and woollen gloves, although some of the coats look as though they have been pinched from the Belgian Army. They don't look quite as miserable as they did last winter.

December 15th 1941

Extra rations for Christmas are double sugar ration (making 6 ounces) and 2 ounces of tea for adults, 3 bars chocolate and 2 ounces cocoa for children. And joy of all joy, 50 cigarettes and 2 ounces tobacco for adult males – the first tobacco for many weeks. The tea is also very welcome, for neither tea nor ersatz coffee has been issued for some weeks past.

Shipped to France is a 75 year old local farmer, notorious for his temper, who got into an argument with an officer billeted on him and struck him. On being hit back, he grabbed a whip, so accounts run, and gave the German something to think about. This case was settled without publicity, and it would appear without any sort of trial.

We don't see or hear anything of the recent raids over Brest, neither do we hear German planes en route for their infrequent raids on the West Country – it looks as though both sides have changed their routes.

December 20th 1941

Further concessions announced for Christmas are an extension of curfew till 1.00 a.m. on Christmas Eve and Christmas Day and on New Year's Eve, and an extension of gas and electricity hours on each of the holidays till midnight. In order we may not get too jubilant, or else with singular lack of tact, the order granting these various favours is printed side by side with a reiteration of the threat of the death penalty for anyone keeping pigeons.

December 27th 1941

With the aid of the pig which so aptly died, we have not fared too badly in the grub line – Mum even managed to conjure up a Christmas pudding of sorts, and altogether we did better than might be expected for a second Christmas under occupation. Such things as sweets and fruit were markedly absent, although a few walnuts were available, and school children were each given a few sweets.

On Christmas Day, we had the doubtful pleasure of being fellow guests with a German Corporal. I can't say I was very pleased about it, but must admit that, leaving aside my prejudice against his uniform, he didn't seem to be a bad sort of fellow. With the aid of much mimicry, imagination and concentration, we managed to make each other understand. He is a peculiarly good tempered chap, and we were able to discuss the bigger aspects of the war quite peaceably. He is very definitely pro Hitler, and instanced the considerable improvements in conditions generally since 1933. He blames England for starting a war over Poland, which he seems to consider to be populated by people very little better than savages, and certainly not worth fighting over, and he seems to genuinely look forward to a time when England and Germany shall be friends. I, of course, acted the Ministry of Information against his Goebbels tactics, but we neither succeeded in convincing the other. Discussions of this nature might lead to unpleasant complications if carried out with anyone of less equable temper than he, but despite the possibilities we finished up more friendly than we had started. I on my part thought the discussion to have been worthwhile to hear at first hand of the other point of view, and to have the opportunity of giving the British one, and, maybe, to have sown some seeds of doubt in his mind – though probably he thought exactly the same thing.

1942

JANUARY 1942

January 2nd 1942

The good news of the week includes the crashing of a M.E. at St. Ouens killing one and disabling the other member of the crew, and an increase in the tobacco ration. Lending libraries have received orders to withdraw from circulation all books which contain disparaging reference to Nazi Germany – some job, as every recent book will have to be read.

There is not much change here during the last 6 months. More shops, houses and buildings of various kinds have been commandeered, and shops left for civilian use and still open, have almost no stocks left of new stuff though with an increasing quantity of second hand. In addition to some 3,000/4,000 troops, we have crowds of Arabs, French, Spanish, Moroccan, Dutch, Belgian - in fact every nationality in Europe – brought here as labourers. Poor devils are clad in rags, but are so unprepossessing a sight one hesitates about helping them even if we had the wherewithal to do so – added to which we are especially wary in dealing with strangers. People generally seem to have stopped losing weight – probably having got more used to the changed diet. Which is as well, as some of the more portly lost up to 70 lbs in a very short while. I must say, that with some exceptions, no-one seems to be in much worse health than before.

When America entered the war, American citizens here were required to register at the German Civil Kommandant's office, and it seems they are being shipped away today to Germany as prisoners of war. I can't quite see why that should be so when English men of military age are allowed to remain – after all, Germany is at war with both countries. I do know some weeks ago our States were required to furnish a list of definite English people – with what object I do not know. I also know, although I was born in England, my Jersey name causes me to be left out of that list, thanks be.

I have lost a great deal of faith in human nature. These 18 long months have proved patriotism, when divorced from flag waving and band playing, and brought into competition with profit making, doesn't mean a thing. I find a too big proportion will do anything to make money, and, in a smaller way, many others creep around the Germans for cigarettes.

I have a feeling Jersey won't be a comfortable place for a lot of people when this is over and the Union Jack is again flying here. Thanks be, 1941 has brought such an improvement the pessimists cannot see how Germany can win. I enter 1942 in the high hope we may be free before it ends.

January 5th 1942

As an instance of Nazi justice, let me quote the case of an elderly woman who was knocked down while on the pavement by a German lorry. As soon as she came out of hospital, she was summoned to the Kommandatur and fined £1 – for obstructing the German forces. This sort of thing is not unusual. I only mention it as an example.

We have again been hearing the RAF at work over Brest, and on Friday last the AA guns on the north and west of the Island opened up seawards, so there has been some speculation as to whether a German convoy was being interfered with.

An old rumour has recurred after a long absenteeism all Germans have received orders to be ready to leave at an hour's notice, and we are to be left alone within 6 weeks.

January 6th 1942

The RAF were over early this morning, and delivered another batch of leaflets, receiving in return a short but heavy burst of flak.

January 8th 1942

Last night again the RAF were around and much ammunition wasted in 3 snappy lots of flak. The Germans surely know how to make a lot of shells burst all over the sky, but their handling of the searchlights strikes me as being decidedly amateurish and unlikely to pick up any raider. They swing the beams across the sky at such a speed that even if they lighted on a plane, they would miss it again immediately. A good deal of shrapnel is scattered around this morning, and I hear many windows in close proximity to the guns have been broken by blast. As usual, I got quite excited while it lasted, all for nothing.

January 10th 1942

Our fuel ration for January is 200 cwt of wood and ½ cwt of lousy coke – thanks be I made some provision in the wood line. The ration is for the month, not per week.

An acquaintance of mine is just out from spending a couple of days in gaol, interspersed with frequent searching cross examinations. The crime is a bonfire which he had lit in his garden earlier in the day was alleged to have blazed up again on last Wednesday evening, the day on which the RAF last visited us, so he was accused of signalling to the enemy. When he was released he was warned henceforth he was a suspected person. Another case, which occurred a week or so back, concerns some German soldiers who broke through the windows of a public house after curfew time. The proprietor naturally came to see what it was all about and got slashed with a bayonet. His wife laid hold of something heavy and laid one of the soldiers right out. The foregoing is bad enough, though I suppose such a thing could happen in any Army when drink gets the upper hand. The cream is the woman got fined 100 marks for hitting the soldier. Nice visitors we've got this year.

January 14th 1942

We are having a little snow and ice, and whilst negotiating same on my poor old push bike, I managed to lay a German Corporal, trying to do likewise, on his back. He swore at me in German (I imagine) so I gave him a 10 second burst in the good old cockney style of England, which made me very pleased with yesterday.

Our friends want more lorries of the 1930/40 type and motorbikes from 1935 onwards, so for the umpteenth time details have to be given.

Large notices have been displayed by our States, calling the attention of working men to the fact, under the Hague Convention, no civilian can be forced to do work of a military nature. Whilst they are a bit late, it is a good move.

We are doing well in the ration line, receiving a tablet of toilet soap and a packet of soap powder this week, and 4 ounces of chocolate and 2 ounces of fat next week. The shortage of soap has resulted in high prices for the small amount smuggled in from France – 4/6d per tablet. Other black market prices worth recording are 1/9d each for candles, whilst over Christmas chocolate was fetching 21/- per quarter and pork 17/6d per lb.

January 19th 1942

We are feeling rather jealous of Guernsey for once again receiving the attention of the RAF – in daylight too. More Vs have appeared at St. Ouens and Millbrook on military signposts, but this time wireless sets in the neighbourhood are not being confiscated. Civilian pickets have to do duty from 10.00 p.m. till 8.00 a.m. The wireless sets commandeered last October for V punishment have not been returned to their owners, and it is believed the sets have been taken for military use.

The spud ration is 7 lbs per week, which sounds enough but isn't when it is a case of spuds for every meal.

January 24th 1942

Not much is happening just now. There seems to be a thinning out of troops, but a decided increase in the number of French prisoners and labourers of other nationality – according to one of the French prisoners, there are 1,500 of them here. Most of the unloading of ships carrying war equipment is now done by them, as well as the preparation of gun positions, ammunition dumps and block houses which grow like mushrooms in every conceivable spot. We have this morning again been treated to the magnificent spectacle of Nazi military might in the form of a massed parade and march past, complete with bands.

I am feeling very tired, having borrowed a cycle trailer and brought home a whole pig from a farm some 9 or 10 miles from home and, of course, it poured with rain the whole time. I was just about in a state of collapse when eventually I did get back, but it was worth the effort to be assured of a meal for some time to come. There is some tightening up on the black market racket and there appears to be a chance the risks will soon be too great. I had intended salting down some of the Christmas pig, but the demand was so great that I could not. This little man has been bought for just that. I am not broadcasting the news this time.

January 28th 1942

There has been a great hoax going on. For some days I have been hearing reports of gramophone records having been dropped by the RAF containing all sorts of news, including warnings to expect raids and assurance of very early relief. Naturally, I had to track down such reports, and eventually found out the small aluminium discs which were spread around the country were advertisement records for De Riseke cigarettes. These were in the Island before our friends came, and my theory is the Germans decided to pull our legs and started all the rumours, after spreading the discs around. It would probably have been scotched earlier but the records have to be played with fibre needles, and of the few who still have gramophones, only a very few have the needles, so people who found the discs were confirming the rumours without having heard the record.

January 30th 1942

Owing to my only assistant having spent the last fortnight in hospital, this diary has been rather neglected these days – running the store and carrying on with my various manufacturers is a bit of a handful for one alone. Ever since the RAF's last visit to Guernsey there has been comparatively little shipping about in these waters. It looks as though our friends have taken the hint. Numerous huts and defence works are appearing like mushrooms, being erected by the released French prisoners and our other cosmopolitan visitors under the direction of the 'Organisation Todt', the khaki clad equivalent to a cross between our sappers and pioneer corps. Only other news is a German order no trees or shrubs are to be cut down without special permission, which, being interpreted, means no tree within 300 yards of any gun position or ammunition dump can be cut down – we are not allowed to burn what is necessary to the Germans for camouflage.

FEBRUARY 1942

February 2nd 1942
Again on Saturday night the RAF were guided to and from Brest and St. Nazaire by heavy flak from here, sent up as a barrage, being moonlight and therefore the lights being useable. We had the pleasure of hearing and feeling what the RAF can do when it gets annoyed, although we were over 100 miles away.

February 3rd 1942
Last night's Evening Post contained a reprint of an obviously German inspired account from the Guernsey paper of the recent raid, which is rather funny, for in being evasive, it does confirm a direct hit was scored on a ship in the harbour and there were some casualties amongst the Germans as well as among the French, Dutch, Belgian and Guernsey men working on the piers.

Not so official, but confirmed by the presence of an armed guard over Merton Hotel, the Germans' own hospital, is the picking up at sea of 4 crew of an RAF bomber after Saturday night's affair. One is said to be in our own hospital in a pretty bad way, the rest at Merton pending removal to prison camps. Embroidery to the foregoing is the airmen were rescued by a Dutch cargo boat which, leaving here empty after discharging coal, decided to make a run for it to England, and, after picking up the RAF blokes, was stopped and brought back by a German patrol boat. This latter part may or may not be true..

Further authoritative news of Guernsey's raid, coming in a letter from a States official there, confirms the sinking of a 6,000 ton ship in the harbour. Casualties included 23 foreign labourers and one Guernsey man killed. The casualties amongst the Germans are estimated between 70 and 150. The RAF didn't do too badly – it is nice to have some confirmation they can aim straight, in anticipation of when we shall be awarded our share of fun.

February 4th 1942

It looks as though Americans are classed with Jews, for after taking away the few American males of military age, our friends now require full details of all investments held here by American citizens, companies or the American Government, much the same as happened to the Jews. I have an idea the USA is not so popular with Germany just now.

February 9th 1942

Latest order is photographs will have to be appended to Identity Cards as per instructions to be issued shortly.

I had a most interesting chat, or rather listen, to a Dutchman whom I met at the house of a neighbour. He was able to give a firsthand description of Brest and its RAF favoured battleships and of the horrors of the breakthrough in Holland and Belgium that weekend long ago, and of the horrors of the super-blitz which Rotterdam got during that weekend. He is one of the many who are only waiting the day when they can have an opportunity of repaying the Germans for their treachery and brutality.

February 11th 1942

One of the dozen or so German building firms here has rather spoilt today by worrying me to make pipes for them, offering me unlimited supplies of cement, sand and labour and a good profit if I would undertake it. But I want to do what very few people here will be able to do when this is over and hold my head up.

Today's tale is bodies have been washed ashore on the north coast from the two vessels which were left sinking by the Navy a few days ago. One was supposed to be the body of the ill famed Miss L referred to earlier, who was on her way to or from France. I hesitate to believe it, but would only shed crocodile tears if the latter part were true.

February 14th 1942

February 14th brings the end of week 85 and the importation and ensconcing in Hotel Victor Hugo for the benefit of the troops, a number of ladies of easy virtue. There were also tales of a lorry loaded with troops which went over the cliffs at Bonne Nuit with satisfactory results.

February 16th 1942

Again last night the RAF were greeted on their way to and from St. Nazaire with very heavy flak. One of the aircraft dropped a parachute flare, and we hopefully anticipated at long last the patience of the boys was exhausted, and they were going to answer the flak in a way that our friends would understand. Again we were disappointed.

February 19th 1942

On Monday evening another snappy but very short burst of heavy flak was sent up after a flare which sounded to be a Jerry. Judging by the abrupt cessation of firing and the fact no mention has since been made on the news of RAF activity at that time, it would appear our light fingered friends let drive without waiting for the recognition signal. Time past I used to stay outdoors to watch the fun and see if flares were dropped, but the flak now is so intense, and shrapnel falls like rain, so it is more sensible to stay under cover. I will give credit to the powers that be that up to date all these little disturbances occur before midnight and so don't disturb our sleep.

February 20th 1942

Unless I had a few weeks at my disposal to go around and peep at all the widespread and intensive work which is going on all over the Island, and another few weeks to write it up, I could not hope to give any fair idea of the extent and scope of the German building activity. Whichever way one goes, be it inland or on the coast, there is evidence of work in progress, the object of the majority of which it is difficult to decipher. In general it appears it is all part of the job which the Todt Organisation (O.T.) has undertaken in providing defensive equipment along the whole western coastline. It appears these Islands are receiving their full share of attention. Some thousands of men, local, German and nearly every nationality in Europe, are engaged in the work, and a quantity of heavy machinery including excavators and trains are on the job.

I had an overdose of these O.T. Jerries this last week. The chap who was so keen on me making pipes (he kept trying to persuade me) turned out to be not an imported German builder, but a member of a black uniform clad crowd in civvy clothes. He isn't a bad sort and speaks English quite well, having spent two years in London with an aunt. I have also seen quite a lot of an O.T. bloke whom I have christened Goebbels from a certain resemblance, especially in expression, and who has bought quite a quantity of stuff and paid cash on the nail each time with their oh-so-cheap Reich Credit Marks. You can bet your life he hasn't had anything for nothing, but I can't quite place the bloke. He always seems to be sizing one up and strikes me as being just the sort of louse who, if he suspected one was keeping something back or trying to twist him, would call in the Feld

Gendarmarie and get one 'shopped'. He talks a little English, but I have a shrewd suspicion he understands more than he would have one believe. After several visits he appears to be getting more kindly disposed towards us, and yesterday even went so far as to give us each two cigarettes – a noteworthy occasion. Having these fellows in and out of the store keeps me on tenterhooks lest they should decide to take the place. I have a feeling it is only the very narrow street and awkward entrance which has kept me free of such a pestilence.

February 21st 1942

The RAF passed this way yesterday morning in the course of a daylight sweep and as usual were greeted with heavy flak. They chose the wrong day, for on Thursday and again today, there were some big vessels in the bay which would most certainly have been spotted and considered worth attending to.

February 25th 1942

For the past month or so the troops have been doing more intensive training than usual. It is uncommon not to see at least one batch of singing soldiery on route march or going to or from their various drill places every time one goes out. No doubt this is in preparation for the much advertised spring offensive. I also hear of non combatant soldiers (butchers, bakers etc) being taken back into their units, and of the older of the Hitler Youth here being transferred into the Army proper.

I have lately been feeling bitter towards myself for staying here and doing the job nearest at hand, especially when I hear people (and sometimes catch myself) criticising what people in England are or are not doing. A fat lot of right we have got to criticise, we who having the choice, preferred to put our own petty interests first, and to rely utterly on the efforts of Britain to get us out of the mess. I can see now, what I failed to see at the time, it was the duty of every able bodied man to get away from here to a place where one could have been of some service instead of a hindrance. I do believe a few of us have partly justified our stopping by minor sabotage and by keeping as much as possible away from the Germans. The British Government were partly responsible for the attitude of mind from which we suffered because, of those who did go, 90% went in panic to get away from the Germans. Certainly their main reason for going was not to be of service, although they have since had to shake down into various duties, and will be eager to impress on us laggards when they come back how they helped to win the war and to save us. I have no doubt now, as I had none at the time of those nightmare days of indecision, that we Channel Islanders on both sides of the channel have, and will often do so, regretted our choice whichever way it was made. Please God we won't any of us ever be faced again by the choice of two such bitter alternatives.

The face of the town is changing as, following on several 'bottles through windows' incidents (believed to be the work of our guests), most shops which have no shutters to cover their windows at night are having them boarded over. Extra precautions have to be taken in the case of butchers, bakers and tobacconists shops, all of which have recently been the subject of extensive robberies. What a change from a couple of years ago when a few loaves or 4 ounce rations of meat would have been beneath the dignity of any self respecting thief.

MARCH 1942

March 3rd 1942
We have received another rude official reminder the consequences of refusing to supply goods or do work as ordered, or to do it in such a way as to jam the purpose thereof, will be fines, imprisonment or, in extreme cases, death. This follows the refusal of one of our biggest contractors to do certain work, as a result of which the firm has been taken over. We are also treated to a long list of regulations governing 'enemy' property, which is not to be disposed of, and must all be registered forthwith. I don't fully understand the notice, written in lawyer's English, but it seems the store is considered enemy property and will have to be registered. I cannot yet see the object of this. It may only be intended to legally justify some of the commandeering already effected or perhaps with an eye on future possibilities of requisitioning of firms and properties.

March 5th 1942
Several foreign labourers have died as the result of eating some poisonous weed. Poor devils, their only food ration is two ladles of soup a day – not even any spuds. I have recently seen some of them scratching in the earth looking for the odd few green potatoes left in last year and eating them unpeeled and raw. No need for Col. Britain to ask them to go slow – they just haven't enough energy, through starvation, to do otherwise.

I am sorry, too, for the raw recruits now undergoing military training – they are so young and so raw they don't know what to do with their hands and feet. Judging by the intensity of their training, it is intended they shall be ready for the boasted spring offensive. They seem to absorb youngsters from Hitler Youth into the Army as soon as they reach about 16.

A whole lot of shipping is going on around here – there seems to be a convoy of six to ten ships arriving every day. But it is only on very rare occasions we see an isolated unit of the Luftwaffe. Now that the 'Scharnhorst' and 'Gneisenau' have gone from Brest we don't have the pleasure of entertaining the RAF.

I have been given sight of the most recent French leaflet – No. 36 of the "Journal de L'Air" dated 1941 but not received here until early January. It gives a map of the world and a summary of the positions at that time on each battle front.

March 7th 1942

We received a regular spate of Red Cross messages yesterday – one for each of us from Bill, and one from a 'Pompey' friend. All of them are replies to our enquiries, the first time we have received direct replies.

Jews have now to be indoors between 8.00 p.m. and 6.00 a.m. Hitherto they have enjoyed the same curfew as we have, but it is apparently considered necessary to remind them their existence is not forgotten.

March 13th 1942

We see few queues these days, the reason being there is just nothing available to queue for. The sole exception is on rare occasions when shoe shops are able to accept repair jobs. All 'extras' in the food line are rationed. It is not easy to portray the position on the food front without going into unreadable detail each week, but in general we have our regular ration of bread, milk, potatoes, meat, sugar and butter usually plus a ration of one of the more or less luxuries – jam, ersatz coffee or cocoa, saccharine, soap, sardines or some type of cereal, each of which recur only at long intervals. The only unrationed foods are swedes and more rarely turnips. Occasionally our buyer in France excels himself by getting hold of such things as olives or salted mackerel which, being priced far above their food value, are unwanted and therefore left unrationed.

Training has intensified during the past week, and one hears of large numbers of troops going away, presumably en route for Russia. We hear the noise of rifle and machine gun fire in the playing fields near home all day, every day, which gets on one's nerves, and constantly meet companies of field gray soldiery marching to or from drill grounds. Drill in the parade ground fashion of the British Army seems just not done.

March 18th 1942

I waited to report on RAF activity last Sunday in the hope of getting more detail, but without success. There were a series of heavy explosions during the forenoon, and the only explanation forthcoming is given by eye witnesses on the north coast, who report at the time a convoy of one large and five small ships were just visible through glasses. The convoy stopped after the loud bangs and when it proceeded there appeared to be one large and four small ships. No planes were seen or heard, though the distance was pretty great, and no subsequent mention has been made by the BBC, so it may have been just accidental explosions. During the afternoon two planes, believed to be coastal command Beauports, stuck their noses beneath the clouds for a look see, and received the attention of enough flak guns to persuade them it was time to go home for tea.

We can only buy footwear (if available) after we have persuaded the authorities we are entirely without wearable shoes or boots of any description. Clothes rations here are just a farce. Almost the only imports from France are of footwear, and precious little, whilst a comparatively small quantity of socks, underwear etc. is made locally. Except for that, ones ration card is so much waste paper.

March 21st 1942

I am doing quite well in Red Cross messages, having received the third in six weeks. I am duly grateful.

I am rather unpopular amongst certain of our neighbours. There are in our immediate vicinity four females, with their husbands and families of two to four children, who regularly go out with Germans – some even have their amours home whilst their husbands are there. Don't tell me it isn't possible - it happens. I have got into the habit of flashing a torch on these bright females when they are being walked home by their Germans, and have suffered the corresponding displeasure of the females and their escorts. In fact some of the females, on behalf of their Germans, are threatening all sorts of unpleasantness for me. I have at least registered my disapproval of this fraternising with one's enemies, although I should prefer the methods which the Dutchman mentioned earlier on tells me are used in Holland – they get hold of the females, take them to a quiet spot and shave their heads – whereby they are known to those people who were previously unaware of their carryings on.

March 24th 1942

From time to time, in their efforts to ensure civilians should not see the results of bombing raids if and when, our friends have issued various orders relating to the calling out of ARP. Sometimes our orders have been to get out on hearing the first siren, sometimes we are supposed to wait for the second. Now it is a punishable offence for anyone, ARP or not, to go out during any alarm. Which makes it a farce – we have to wait until we are sent for, but being as there won't be any wardens out to report incidents, none will know when ARP services are required. I can see a good reason behind it all. Apparently our friends agree with my theory at no great distant future there is a distinct possibility of a landing attempt being made in our immediate vicinity, accompanied maybe by a parachute landing. In which event the ARP service might easily be a real nuisance to the Germans by cutting phone wires and generally upsetting arrangements. I shall be bitterly disappointed if no attempt at a landing is made during the next two months. Failing the attempt, it appears to me (as an armchair critic) there are two alternative possibilities. Firstly the long heralded spring offensive will finish the Russians, in which event Britain would have to be in a much stronger position before an attempt could be made. It could take some years to attain the necessary supremacy over the whole German forces. The second alternative is Russia might beat the Germans alone unaided by a British landing. Added to these salient facts, is the presence in England of a token force of USA troops. The first deadly earnest attempts to save shipping space and sundry small things, such as the recent Commando raid near Le Havre thrilled us to the marrow and were apparently designed to test German defences and British attacking arrangements. Putting these things together and adding them up, I believe the sum total to be an early British landing, bringing with it (we hope) an early release for us from our state of suspended animation.. The German powers-that-be seem to agree to the possibility of the foregoing, as evidenced by the immense amount of work being put in by Organisation Todt, with about 4,000 labourers of all nationalities, by German building firms employing local and their own imported labour, and by many of local building firms working for the Germans, ostensibly on work of non-military character. The general design of things seems to indicate an attempt will be made to withstand a long siege if necessary.

Prophesies are dangerous things, and I have often scoffed at hardy optimist friends who for nearly two years have foretold the collapse of Germany three months ahead. But I have great faith in this belief of mine, which has grown stronger in recent weeks – hence my courage in putting it into writing, where it will always be able, should I prove wrong, to laugh me to scorn as I have often done to other people.

March 26th 1942

We each received messages from Bill yesterday, both replies and both sent in mid January. We are doing well.

Last night we had aural evidence of the presence in the vicinity of the RAF – no planes or flak was heard, but plenty of heavy explosions, so the show must have been quite a distance away. For the second night running the Luftwaffe passed this way en route for Southern England – they carried my curses on their expedition with them.

Further evidence of Jerry's preparedness against invasion is the arrival of ten medium tanks and the appearance at all strategic points barbed wire barriers ready to be thrown across the road. It makes me excited to think of the possibility and to know, far from being out of the question; the Germans believe it to be quite possible.

March 27th 1942

Last night more proof of Jerry's breeze vertical was forthcoming in a series of mock battles around our district keeping us awake most of the night with machine gun and rifle fire – unfortunately all with blanks.

I made a bet of £1 last night the Union Jack will be flying here by June 30th, so I hope the British Army doesn't let me down.

March 28th 1942

Again last night our sleep was badly disturbed by the heaviest AA barrage we have yet heard, heralding the RAF on their way to and from some target near here. Flaming onions, poms poms and heavy stuff contributed to making the night hideous, culminating with a heavy burst at a plane which was flying homewards at 3.00 a.m. low – so low we imagine it to have been damaged previously, but it appears to have got safely away from the Island, taking with it our prayers for a safe landing.

March 30th 1942

The St. Nazaire affair, reported above as extra noise and less sleep, has resulted in even greater precautions being taken to prevent a similar occurrence here.

No more English money is being issued, the few remaining £1 notes being called in on German orders to balance the small Jersey notes about to be issued.

Our only reminder we were once English will be the copper coinage.

APRIL 1942

April 7th 1942

Another petrol economy drive is going on and results in further cuts in the almost nonexistent bus service, orders doctors have to share a dozen cars between them, and a scheme for converting all lorries on the road to gas producing wagons. Also our friends are requisitioning 50 cycles (for a start) believed to be for the use of officers in lieu of cars. Those whose cycles are not being used for essential purposes are asked to present them for valuation. Methinks there won't be many fool enough to take their bikes in until forced to do so – push bikes are a very valuable commodity.

April 8th 1942

For the first time since the Occupation, with the exception of pre advertised practises, the air raid siren was set going just after noon yesterday, the all clear being sounded about 10 minutes later. There certainly were some planes about, but no guns were fired, so maybe they weren't sure whether they were British or not. People in town took exactly no notice, except to remark they didn't know a practise was taking place, despite official orders everyone was to clear off the streets when the alarm was given. I wondered at first whether it was sounded to see if people would obey orders, but I have heard of no cases of people being run in for it, and it is the opinion of the ARP office it was a genuine alarm. We had to hand back our swastika identity cards and ARP has, for now at least, ceased to exist.

April 15th 1942

Yet another registration is taking place of all motor vehicles. Due no doubt to the recent quashing to all intents and purposes of ARP, my motorbike has for the first time to be registered – hitherto it has been listed on ARP reserve. Fortunately it has a bad fault in the engine due to lousy workmanship when last overhauled. I have cursed many times, but may yet be grateful for it.

Mum has received yet another reply from Bill, dated February 26th, in reply to one sent in November.

All of Guernsey's Police Force has been replaced, having been involved in a big black market racket. Much the same would happen here if the truth ever became public – but then, if nominal justice were done, there would be few of the 70,000 in the Channel Islands out of gaol. Another big case of the racket is being worked up here, and several well known people have been arrested and many others are shaking in their shoes.

The anti-invasion panic goes on, and hundreds of miles of barbed wire have been used to protect all sorts of places, especially flag staffs which our protectors think might tempt any Commandos to run up the Union Jack.

The complete failure of the voluntary system of procuring push bikes has resulted in the commandeering of cycles being used as punishment by the Gendarmerie for such offences as riding two abreast, or failing to carry one's identity cards.

April 18th 1942

We had ample evidence of the weight of recent raids extending from Le Havre to St. Nazaire, bombs audible 100/140 miles away must be not inconsiderable. It culminated yesterday in evidence visible to some parts of the Island when troops drilling on the north and east were machine gunned. The Germans' own air raid warning went into action several times, and last night's paper contained another reminder the sounding of the general sirens means it is probable bombs will fall immediately after, and therefore civilians should take cover. Apparently they expect bother as much as we hope it will come.

April 20th 1942

This Occupation seems to have brought out the worst traits in most people, and all sorts of hitherto law abiding citizens are being arrested for various offences. In many cases it is for black market traffic, which under the present circumstances, is in itself no disgrace, though the profits made are. Another case now concerns the supply of cooked potatoes to the O T labourers. It is forbidden to supply them with food, though they are only given two bowls of soup and less than ½ lb bread a day. They are receiving big wages which tempted them from their homes and will offer a lot for anything to eat. In the case referred to, they have been paying one mark for about 3 lbs of cooked spuds. Another well known grocer is under arrest for replacing half the sugar supplied to him for jam making with saccharine and water – the sugar thus saved netting him 12/- a lb. Also under arrest is a big grower for neglecting the crops of potatoes and tomatoes in his greenhouses – the Germans got him for sabotage, so methinks he will be spending a holiday in France.

We are to have local notes for £1, 10/-, 2/-, 1/- and 6d issued. We won't mind holding those as they will be stabilised and cannot be repudiated. The German money may fluctuate, and the less kept in Island circulation, the less the loss when we come to settle things up.

It being the unworthy Adolf's birthday, ships in the harbour (some two dozen) are dressed with bunting and German lorries decorated with flowers and greenery. May it be his last.

April 21st 1942
News trickling through in letters from Guernsey shows they are worse off than we are, having had neither potatoes nor sugar for several weeks – potato peelings are fetching 9d a lb black market. We are being educated in the various ways of using peelings, probably in anticipation of a week or two without potatoes before the new ones are dug.

April 23rd 1942
I was interested to hear on the news last night we had been the subject of a parliamentary question, and whilst I was glad to hear there was to be no silly softness in sending us food and so relieving the responsibility of our guardians, I was puzzled at the phrase "the few remaining in Jersey and Guernsey". Either the Government is under a misapprehension about numbers of people who evacuated from or else they wish to convey the impression nearly all the population evacuated. In fact, some 18,000 left here, leaving about 40,000 and the proportion in Guernsey is about the same, so the 'few' is in the region of 70,000. There is not any noticeable difference in the crowds one sees in the streets now to what there were before the evacuation – in fact it seems more crowded now on the days when the shops are open than before, although our uniformed friends are a crowd in themselves.

April 25th 1942
The case of sabotage through neglecting crops has resulted in a fine of 1,000 marks (about £100) and some publicity to prevent repetition.

April 27th 1942
Latest evidence of Jerry's flair for regimentation are forms which each householder must fill in giving details of each occupant; one copy to be sent in and the other fixed inside the front door. Object, I assume is to get a quick check in the event of British landing accidentally or otherwise and being sheltered by someone - more evidence of the jittery state of their nerves.

April 29th 1942

As from May 1st, the general curfew is to be 11.00 p.m. again, curfew in the Military Zone is to revert to 10.00 p.m. and that for Jews is advanced to 9.00 p.m. so everyone feels a little more cheerful.

Nowadays when the RAF passes this way, the searchlights are the only indication the Germans are awake. Members of the soldiery are supposed to have said they have received orders not to waste ammunition in the lavish way they have been doing whenever the British planes appear – they must now only open fire if an attack develops.

I have been told the tale of an intended escape which resulted in the arrest of the intending flitter. The fool made no secret of his plans and his landlord with whom he was lodging got windy for fear he might be held partly responsible when his lodger was reported absent. Accordingly he reported the matter to the local police who in turn passed the information to the Germans. The man is now in gaol here, and others who were aware of his intentions are living in fear of being called up and questioned. They want to corroborate the man's story, but don't know whether he will just deny everything, or insist he told people just for a joke and had no real intention of attempting to escape. Up to now he has not revealed the identity of even the existence of the man with whom he was to make the attempt; neither does anyone know where the boat and equipment is. Whilst agreeing the fellow was a damned fool to tell so many people, I don't think much of his landlord for valuing his own skin quite so highly, or of our local police for passing on the news, even though that is the order.

MAY 1942

May 1st 1942

Latest registration is of all livestock from cattle down to chickens – maybe our friends want all the meat and eggs instead of only most of it. Fuller details have been published of the Guernsey Police racket mentioned earlier. 16 sergeants and constables were sentenced to terms varying from 4½ years downwards by a Military Tribunal held in public for pinching stuff from German stores. It reads like a fairy tale, and one could have a lot more sympathy with the Police if they had confined their pinching to German stuff, but they are now to be tried for taking civilian stuff. It is almost unbelievable ⅔rds of Guernsey's Police force could be involved in such wholesale robberies and get away with it for so long, especially as the Inspector is a man, who from all accounts, would hang his own grandmother, and who has the reputation of being one of the smartest policemen ever. He was not involved in the case, though it is believed he, in common with the few remaining police, lost his job. The plea put forward in each case was they were hungry. Apparently they have been hungrier in Guernsey than here, but it appears to be mostly due to even less foresight being shown than here in the early days. They have had no sugar at all for a long time, but they made sweets for a long while after the Occupation. Cakes and rolls were still being sold up to the time when the bread was rationed. Once upon a time we used to hear people remark how much better off they were in Guernsey than us, but now, although we are not exactly overfed, we do get a bare 'enough'.

May 4th 1942

Another unsuccessful attempt at escape was made last night by three youngsters. Details are lacking, but they were using an open dinghy of about 12 to 14 feet with no motor or sails – it was washed ashore on the beach near home this morning. They were spotted and fired on. Either the boat was hit or capsized, for one of the youths was drowned and the others captured. It was a silly attempt and doomed to failure. To get away from Jersey one would have to make a big detour to avoid being spotted from any of the Islands' When it comes to rowing, one would think several times before attempting the nearly 100 miles. Whilst I don't know what arrangements they had made, I doubt whether they could have been carrying enough food and water for the journey, which must take at least 4 days, probably more.

I had a nose around the western side of the Island yesterday to see what sort of a mess our benefactors are making of the landscape. They have masses of timber and building material everywhere, so apparently have not finished their schemes yet. There is barbed wire in every imaginable place, tanks parked beneath trees, excavations and huge camps for the many hundreds of foreign labourers. Along St. Aubins Bay there are several forts being erected and some lengths of reinforced concrete wall built outside the existing sea wall some 20 feet high. The old railway track is being used for a semi permanent railway between forts. I also hear of a railway now being constructed between the airport and the quarry near Sorel. Our poor little once pretty Island is surely being mightily scarred – many of the erections will never be able to be shifted, being of reinforced concrete built on really generous lines. There will surely be a terrific amount of labour needed when eventually the time comes for us to be able to start the clearing up – may it be soon.

May 5th 1942

We note with some interest the OT (Jerry's Pioneer Corps) who have hitherto been wholly concerned in various construction schemes, are now being given military training. If Jerry is going to rely on them in the event of invasion, he might just as well abandon all hope right away, as except for some specialists, the OT recruits from those classified as unfit for military service – which in Germany means nearly unfit for anything. Or maybe the idea behind the training is to enable them to quell any trouble which might develop amongst the cosmopolitan labour they control. I fancy there will be trouble when Jerry's hands are fully engaged elsewhere, especially as many of the Frenchmen have been lured here under false pretences and will be only too pleased to get their own back.

Latest anti invasion order forbids anyone to sleep outdoors or under canvas.

My luck is in today – I am to have my motorbike out on Saturday of next week. The amount of petrol in my tank will prevent me from having quite such a good run around as I had on my last annual picnic, but I am looking forward to the occasion. Also a good friend has let me have a ration of tobacco and a genuine Abdullah cigarette – she (yes, it is a she) has let me have a little on all too rare occasions, being her brother's ration who doesn't smoke – reason, I am like her boyfriend who evacuated and has since married. More push bikes are being requisitioned for use by German forces, and there is much trepidation lest we should be the next.

During last night we were awakened by some very heavy explosions – probably the heaviest we have yet felt and certainly from somewhere close at hand.

May 8th 1942

We are all disappointed the RAF left a perfect target alone yesterday. All day there were parked in the bay four destroyers, one vessel of at least 12,000 tons and several smaller ships – a lovely target, of which we might have had a grandstand view.

Back in 1940, when we were issued with identity cards, provision was made for the addition of photographs, passport fashion. No more was heard until recently, possibly owing to lack of photographic material. Now we are ordered to have our photographs taken for affixing to our identity cards.

May 11th 1942

The recent unsuccessful escape attempt has brought forth many proclamations threatening all and sundry with reprisals. From the various notices, one can gather the 3 youngsters were not altogether unprepared, as they had an outboard motor and a quantity of petrol (German), compass, binoculars, food etc. They were also taking photographs with them, which seems to have riled the Germans properly. We are told another such attempt will result in the entire male population of military age being interned on the continent. It is possible, because of the photographs, the youngsters may be treated as spies, and their parents too look like getting some awkward questions to answer. Another result is all boats including collapsible canoes have to be registered – probably as a preliminary to confiscation. Anyway, they are not getting mine.

Gas is now cut off from 8.00 p.m. instead of 9.00 p.m. and buses only run now on certain days, owing to shortage of charcoal (now being manufactured locally).

May 12th 1942

Other orders require a duplicated list to be sent to the Military Kommandant of linen, crockery and many other sundries belonging to evacuated persons. Reason given is the military forces occupying the Island have need of these items.

I just had a good laugh, having come across a squad of 'nasties' being trained in goose-stepping in a quiet country road. It looks funny to see a crowd doing it together, but is even more amusing when one man alone is doing it – very straight back, stiff straight arms and stiff legs, proceeding along in a series of jerks – and all looking most self conscious as their turn came. Of course, I considered it my duty to make them even more self conscious by having a good laugh at them as I walked slowly past.

May 14th 1942

Yet more registrations with intent to commandeer – this time of all wireless sets extra to one per household. This is probably directed against people like me who 'bought' evacuated peoples' sets rather than hand them over without payment to the Germans. We are not being bounced into these registrations quite as easily as we were at first. Most of us realise we could have got away with a lot more evasion than we had the guts to try. In cases like these, the only check would be a house to house search (not a very satisfactory check, as well as a lengthy process), and our friends cover their impotence with threats of heavy fines or imprisonment in case of non-compliance.

ARP is having a most difficult patch. Every time a workable scheme is devised, the Kommandant finds reason to veto it. He wants it kept going for the sake of the civil population, but stated quite frankly to the ARP Controller he realises quite well in the event of invasion we would all do our best to help. The siren system is in the hands of the Germans, and no one is allowed to remain on the streets after it is sounded, so wardens will not be able to report incidents. The latest scheme is a nucleus body of us are ordered to get dressed immediately the siren goes and just wait. In the event of our services being considered necessary by the Germans (after they emerge from their air raid shelters presumably), a German car will pick up the Controller at his house and bring him to Central Control. Then Germans will come in cars and collect the Emergency Squad (about 24) at their houses. Thereafter we shall not be allowed in car or ambulance without a German being there too (it is presumed the barbed wire barriers will be across all roads and would only be moved at the request of a German. We are told unless a German is with us we are liable to be shot first and asked questions after. I presume I shall have to carry one on my pillion – if so, there will be at least one genuine Nazi brown shirt, for he will have a most hair raising time I can promise. Considering while all these things are being done houses will be burning and people suffering, it is a bit of a washout. It will be a full hour before the scheme even starts to work – but it is the best possible when we have an army of occupation which (rightly) suspects everyone. Actually the ARP is wise in trying to keep some sort of nucleus organisation going, for it is fully expected when our friends leave, they will return and give us another taste of the air raid with which they introduced themselves to us.

May 18th 1942

My annual treat is over and I managed to get a look see from a distance at most of the improvements which are being prepared to grace our Island's beauty. It is a tale of camouflage, concrete and barbed wire everywhere. Wherever there is a sandy beach, huge anti tank walls are being built. Concrete machine gun posts are built at all strategic points and heavy naval guns have been fixed in various places. I also saw many mined areas, especially along the north coast, as well as barbed wire everywhere. In general, they have made a bit of a mess of things.

The two orders relating to registration of extra wireless sets and evacuees' linen etc. have been cancelled pending the issue of fresh orders – there is some trepidation lest it mean total confiscation of these things. Rumour has it there is some friction between the civil and military commandants about certain of the recent orders, though even if true, I hardly imagine their disagreement would be broadcast.

Free vaccination is being offered, reason being an outbreak of smallpox in France. I think it would be a wise precaution to take advantage of the opportunity.

Mum had a belated enquiry from Bill on Saturday – December 9th – but still welcome as an opportunity to reply.

May 20th 1942

The RAF visited us yesterday lunch time and twice during the night, each time being treated to heavy and concentrated flak, though not in such extravagant and wasteful measure as used to be awarded to them in their passages. Each time they seemed to be very high up. Other noises disturbing our peace include the washing up and exploding by Germans of a drifting sea mine near to home on Sunday afternoon.

The requisitioning of push bikes has been carried a step further by commandeering the first 250 bikes (taken on licence numbers which our cycles carry) from town, and 150 each from three country parishes – we presume each parish will have to do the same. Luckily my cycle number is well above that specified. A development of the escape attempt is all boats of whatever size or types, including canoes, have to be brought into town. Silly twerps – obviously anyone who had the vaguest intention of evacuating wouldn't take in a boat, but find a good hiding place for it.

Plenty of anti invasion exercises are being carried on. Last night for instance all roads leading to the harbour were put into a state of defence and no civilians allowed that way. May it not be too long before their practise becomes the real thing. I learn from a friend who has been crossing regularly between here and France as a pilot, the defensive works here are on a far larger scale than any part of the coast which he has seen. This may be due to this being their one and only British possession or perhaps they think they could command any invasion attempt on the coast around from here. He tells me the attitude of the Germans with whom he comes into contact has changed very considerably during the last four months – there is certainly nothing blitz-like in their expectations now.

May 23rd 1942

The flak on Wednesday night was accompanied by the dropping of 11 small bombs at Trinity. Although they landed near an ammunition dump, no casualties and no damage beyond a few windows resulted and all landed in open fields. It seems probable they were bailed out by a plane in trouble thinking he was over the sea. Again last night there was heavy flak – up to date I know no further details. Our sleep is getting quite disturbed lately, especially now there is a risk of me being fetched for ARP after any such show.

May 26th 1942

Sunday night brought more RAF planes around the neighbourhood – more flak and a very heavy explosion followed some minutes after the planes went – presumably a delayed action bomb, but where my tame spies have not yet told me. Rumour has it the bomb fell on a barge at sea, but the peculiar thing is no mention was made on the BBC news of any RAF activity at all.

JUNE 1942

June 3rd 1942

During the last day or two, a barge lying alongside the quay was found to have about three feet of water in the holds, due to the sea cocks having been opened by the Dutch stevedores. A considerable part of the cargo is ruined, but one happy result is I have been able to get hold of about ¼ lb of wet tobacco which, when dried will avoid smokeless days for a while.

Owing to the utter disregard by the Germans, the local authorities some time ago removed one way traffic signs. Now entirely without the knowledge (except what they can see is happening) of any local authority, the town is being abundantly adorned with one way signs in the continental fashion. No official order having been issued, most people are ignoring them the same way as they used to ignore our signs, to the accompaniment of many black looks from German 'blitz' drivers. Another racket which earns black looks and sometimes a shout or even an attempt to frighten by nearly running one down, is to just not get out of the way when they hoot – which game I just delight in playing.

June 8th 1942

Following on from a series of rumours, the order has been published we are to lose all wireless sets and they are to be handed in this week. Rumour has now reversed itself, and insists the order will be rescinded. There is said to be disagreement in this as in other matters between the Military Commandant, Major General Graf Von Schmettow, and the Civil Commandant, Colonel Knackfuss. The reason for this confiscation is obviously fear of invasion and of the occupied territories rising in a mass (I understand the order applies throughout the occupied zones). Despite heavy penalties, many people will be keeping their sets where possible, although if too many try it, it will result in a careful search. I think I have a reasonable chance of getting away with my own, which I intend to keep rigged up in a remote corner of the store, to be able to hear the news and combat the many weird and wonderful rumours, inevitable with a complete dearth of reliable news. We all accept this as evidence the day of our deliverance is not far off. There is steadily decreasing numbers of garrison troops and still more rapidly worsening of the quality, the unfinished state of defences and lack of aircraft around. Combined with all this, is yesterday's warning to French people to get away from the coast. I don't see how we in these Islands can get away from the coast, but I am not worrying being convinced the invasion of these Islands will be done entirely by air-borne troops.

Some 18 of the biggest growers and farmers have been instructed the whole of their produce is to be kept for military requirements, so despite their panic, our friends do not intend to leave yet awhile.

June 10th 1942

There is news the confiscation of wireless sets is postponed for a week, until the 20th, with the comment this is not intended as a punishment to the population, but is a military necessity. Meanwhile there is rumour of one of the high-ups going to Paris to try to get the order rescinded for the Islands. Certainly there was a big noise who left here last night, as evidenced by a troop carrier escorted by fighters.

The prison is so full of people serving sentences for crimes against the Germans (in addition to those serving sentences in France) several of those condemned by the Civil Courts had to be released before time. There is no disgrace in being sentenced by the Germans, and if everyone had their due, three quarters of the Island would be in gaol.

June 13th 1942

In giving details about the collection of wireless sets, it is again mentioned the sets will be returned to their owners "when the military necessity no longer exists", which will be after the Germans have been pushed out of here.

Two Luftwaffe officers have taken a bungalow near us and are using it for their nights of love, with the brother of one of the girls acting as concierge. Also three AA guns have been fixed on the green on the coast road, with their crews installed in huts dug in, so we are seeing more Germans around the district than we care for.

Potato rations have progressively increased as the supply became greater until now we are revelling in 10 lbs per head per week. A scheme for fish rationing has been started and I have just got hold of our first bit of fresh fish for many moons.

Wireless sets are now being handed over to the accompaniment of much moaning. There are not so many people handing them over – there has been a big run on derelict battery sets and I expect quite a few will keep a set rigged up to hear the news. I have made the necessary arrangements to listen on my own set and think by taking ordinary precautions it is reasonably safe. If it isn't, gaol for such an offence is nothing to be ashamed of.

June 20th 1942

Since it was known we should lose our sets and the realisation of their value in keeping us even remotely in touch, there has been an ever rising tide of anger against the order spreading over the Island. Duplicate leaflets have appeared stressing the injustice and urging people not to hand in their sets. These have so aroused the ire of the Germans the Feldgendarmerie have arrested a very mixed bag of well known people this morning, believed to be as hostages until the writer of the pamphlet is found. There are many wild rumours passing around the town, but as I saw one of the men being arrested at 9.00 a.m. I know the foregoing is true.

Other rumours are all German troops are leaving within six weeks and garrison duties will be undertaken by the C3 OT. This certainly fits in with the intensive training being given to the OT, which has been a non-military organisation. Also it has been decided to put more work into the defences of the Island. I know of two of my customers who, forced, have been working for them and who have been told to finish the jobs they are doing and not to start any fresh work.

June 22nd 1942

An hour's firing from the heavy guns on Saturday morning, not advertised as practise as is usual, was reputed to be directed at some unidentified ships in the neighbourhood, which rumour I doubt. Throughout Saturday night up to Sunday morning very heavy explosions were heard not far away, with occasionally the sound of a distant plane engine. Last night (Sunday) many aircraft passed this way, so altogether there has been some activity around this way over the weekend.

For the first time for many months, armed patrols were around on Saturday night, probably in anticipation of some demonstration against Saturday's arrests, thus making my not unusual curfew breaking a little more precarious than usual. Although people are shocked about the arrests, they are taking it quietly. It is rumoured and sounds reasonable, the list of arrested persons is compiled from a 'black list' of people who have offended the German authorities in some minor way. They were first arrested and later released.

The threat of 20 more arrests has made many other people feel nervous. There was a proper panic on Saturday amongst a lot of the people who, until this news became public, were being brave and keeping their sets. Thanks be I don't come under the heading of 'prominent citizen', for I am, like everybody else, not anxious to spend the rest of the war and longer in an internment camp - so much then, for the guarantee of the lives, liberty and property of the inhabitants. One hears reports of frantic endeavours to trace the writer of the leaflets through the typewriter and duplicating machine used. I think it will behove us all to be careful in what we say or do, as this may well bring a flood of Gestapo agents here. It is worthy of note this harsh notice is not signed by the Feldkommandant, Colonel Knackfuss (reported to be out of the Island), or his understudy, Dr. Gasher, but by an underling with the rank of Captain. I think his name is worthy of note for the day of reckoning.

Our friends are after more push bikes – the first 1,750, taken at the rate of 100 to 250 per Parish by the licence numbers, have to be presented this week.

June 26th 1942

Life is not too cheerful without wireless. I only consider it safe to listen to the one p.m. news. Rumours are strong and, to say the least, exaggerated. One of the best is a raid of 5,000 over Berlin, with a loss of 400 planes. I do get some news, which is more than most people, but one has to be ultra careful to whom one passes it on – we are like a lot of conspirators about it all. There are reports of a couple of cases of people being caught listening – in each case it was said it could be heard from the road – if it be true, I have no sympathy, but I doubt it.

Our friends, in their efforts to get to the bottom of the wireless leaflet business are leaving no stone unturned and one constantly hears reports of men being arrested and later released.

I am wondering if our friends have evolved a new explosive, as during an intensive practise yesterday afternoon, the smoke puffs both from the heavy guns and the AA were a bright cerise colour. I cannot imagine Germans doing that just for the sake of beauty.

Nothing had been heard of Jersey's ship, S/S 'Normand', but I learn the crew was paid off at St. Malo a while ago. No one knows what has happened to the vessel.

June 29th 1942

10 hostages were released on Saturday. I gather the Germans traced the man who did the duplicating and traced two men who knew who the writer was. One of the two men threatened the writer, his brother in law, that unless he gave himself up he would split. So the writer has confessed and is in gaol.

June 30th 1942

Notices in last night's press announced the release of the 10 hostages upon the discovery of the culprit and the arrest of 5 more men as hostages in connection with a second batch of leaflets 'with inciting contents'. This is the first intimation which I or any of my friends had there is a second lot. This morning I hear at least one more hostage has been taken and it is intended to make the number up to 10 today. The latest bag is even more mixed than the last and makes one think almost anyone might be picked on.

Another notice orders the confiscation of all cameras and photographic materials – this following on the recent attempted escape when the escapees were trying to take photographs with them. Nothing has been heard of what has happened, or is to happen, to the two boys, although I understand they have been shipped away from here.

AA guns opened up yesterday afternoon when a plane passed very high up. As usual, they hit nothing, though I must admit their gunnery is pretty good – I have often watched them at nights laying a box barrage around a cloud in which they suspect a plane is hiding, and it surely is nice work. For some curious reason their searchlight crews are just hopeless. Despite the fact there are many really powerful lights now (including one blue one), I have never seen them catch an aircraft in their beams yet.

JULY 1942

July 1st 1942

July 1st is the second anniversary of 'Black Monday' when we first heard the sound of German jack boots reverberating in our streets. Another cause for misery is our friends are 'buying' our stock of pipe fittings almost entirely, which makes my principal and standing worry of how to keep afloat even more acute.

July 2nd 1942

German planes disturbed our slumbers last night, for a change, one flying so low on his return trip I was hoping to hear the sound of a crash. The passing over of German planes is now regarded as an event, and worthy of recording – how different from two years, or even one year ago. I have lost my bet the Union Jack would be flying here by July 1st and in general am disgusted at the opportunity being wasted. The Luftwaffe is nearly markedly absent, the defending troops are nearly all civilians, and the defensive works are not completed and therefore worse than useless. I know it isn't an easy job to put an army ashore in France, but it will be 10 times more difficult and expensive next spring. Unless a move is made within the next few weeks I am resigning myself to being in this mess until 1944. One honestly can't help getting a bit disheartened – I know, as I have all along known, we shall win this war, but it almost looks as if there are people who don't mind when – I am a hurry, and want it done soon. One can get a bit browned off with this Occupation racket after a while, and two years of it begins to pall.

July 4th 1942

It is now necessary to get a special permit from the Feldkommandant for any building work valued at more than £500 – which makes us laugh, as they have had pretty well all the timber and other building materials. We can no longer even get cement, except on the black market, which in the first instance is pinched off the Germans, so how on earth do they think we can do any except the smallest patching jobs. A little turps substitute was brought, for instance, and is being rationed out to painters at ¼ pint a time – which gives some small idea of the size of work which can be undertaken.

July 6th 1942

Latest example of the inquisitive nature of our friends is an order to register all car batteries, electric and other car accessories and spares, and cellulose paints, no doubt with a view to further confiscation.

I have been singularly lucky over this smallpox vaccination and have felt nothing. Others less lucky have been really bad over it, probably due to lack of resistance through the under nourishment. I take this as proof my health has not suffered very much from this two years of Occupation. I have lost no weight and feel quite fit. This is probably due to the fact we have been not unsuccessful in the great game of 'grab', even though we have not been willing or able to pay some of the phenomenal prices asked for some things. If we do no worse between now and the end of this lousy period, we shall not have a lot to moan about.

July 10th 1942

Aftermath of the 'leaflet' hostage business - time having expired for the capture of the culprit of the second leaflet. The five hostages have been released, although the culprit has not been caught. This may have something to do with the return to the Island of the Feldkommandant, Colonel Knackfuss. Despite exhaustive enquiries, I have yet to find anyone who has any knowledge of the second leaflet, so it seems even if such a leaflet ever existed, it was never circulated. Whilst on the subject of imprisonment, the two prospective escapees are supposed to be in Caen gaol, each having to serve his own sentence and also half of the sentence of the other boy who was drowned.

Rumours running around, as distortions of BBC news after passing through a few hands, include imprisonment in the Tower of London of Hore-Belisha, Duff Cooper and others for giving away military secrets to the enemy; Queen Mary (a) is dead, (b) has had a baby; the King and Queen have abdicated in favour of the Duke of Windsor and Mrs. Windsor, as well as many others of like ilk. Another rumour is it has been broadcast the USA Air Force is to bomb hell out of Jersey. These things are repeated in all seriousness. It is not easy to stop these rumours without disclosing one listens to the news oneself – a most dangerous admission to make in these days when one cannot trust even those with the best of intentions. They have only to be heard discussing the news for enquiries to be started as to where the news originated, and our friends are expert at wheedling such information. I only pass on the news to a select few friends, taking written notes to avoid the possibility of error, and we behave like a gang of conspirators. I only listen when the gates are locked to avoid the possibility of being surprised – the Germans consider no place private and go where they want. Yesterday one was standing within a few feet of my set and I was in fear and trembling least he should notice the electric wire which I had to run up to my listening studio under the roof. But it pleases me to be doing that which is forbidden, and if I should get caught, it would be a new experience and I think no disgrace to do 6 weeks in gaol for such an offence.

My hiding place for the set is more directed against many civilian eyes then against the Germans for I credit the latter with enough gumption that, wherever I hid it, if they came searching they would find it.

The RAF seems to have been around on reconnaissance today, AA guns opening up about 2.00 p.m. when the Germans' own sirens sounded. There was a plane going round but he kept so high up it was impossible to distinguish markings.

Thanks to the generosity of the French Secours Nationale the children here are being given 1 lb each of sweet biscuits.

July 15th 1942

I mentioned earlier the gaol was very full. Further proof, if that were necessary, comes in the fact G, sentenced to 12 months for not handing in his wireless set, is allowed at large pending the time when there is room in prison. This has happened in other cases and the culprit is picked up without warning as soon as there is accommodation.

We now hear the unfamiliar sound of railway engine whistles – the high pitched peep-peep peculiar to French engines – as trains go puffing along between Millbrook and the piers. Quite a lot of engines and goods trucks have been brought over, and the line runs, or will run, from a tunnel built into the side of St. Aubins tunnel, believed to be an ammunition dump, and along the old railway track bordering the sea, presumably to feed ammunition to the forts being built at West Park, Millbrook and Bel Royal. Connections also run down each of the three piers. Huge quantities of coal have been stored in the Island for driving the engines. The other railway, which I mentioned, being built from Ronez quarries to the Airport, has proceeded about half way, roads, walls, fields, trees and even houses being sacrificed to the need for a straight and level line. Jersey's third railway has been running for sometime carting sand from Gorey Village to Gorey Pier.

July 16th 1942

Funny I should have picked yesterday to write about the railway, for it was officially opened yesterday afternoon, with high officers, a band, many swastikas and eagles, flags as well as the solitary Heinkel stationed here dipping in salute. There seem to be about a dozen locomotives (French) and upwards of 100 trucks – these latter labelled 'Posen', and if they are a sample of Polish railway efficiency, I am not surprised the Germans walked all over the Poles. They look as if they hadn't had a coat of paint since they were new and many of them are literally falling to pieces with rot. I should not have thought the Germans would have considered them worth the shipping space to bring here. During my inspection I had a nosy at a job being done opposite the lifeboat shed. They are blasting into the solid rock, and judging by the subsidiary work going on around this, I imagine it is intended to place petrol tanks in the hole. I think, at the present rate of progress, the job will be finished come Christmas century, but meanwhile operations are proceeding at the expense of roofs and windows in the vicinity.

After having my prognostications of us being out of this mess by July 1st proved wrong, and as week succeeds week and nothing is done, I am tending to lose hope this will be our year of release. I just hate to look ahead to a third winter of this.

July 25th 1942

This diary has once again suffered a spell of neglect as a result of further successful experiments in the manufacturing department, but not much has been happening to record. Work on the fortifications is proceeding with all speed and our friends have been indulging in manoeuvres for the rapid movement of troops from the Island, including the collection of rations from their bakeries and depots in the small hours of the morning and rapid transit to the piers from all parts of the Island. May the day come soon when this part of the proceedings is carried out in earnest. The week's 'no wireless' rumours include a statement variously credited to Churchill and Eden the Islands will be relieved within the next 40 days. I certainly don't believe such a statement would be publicly made, but if we aren't relieved soon, we shall be in this mess for a long time to come. Generally believed are reports Alderney has been again bombed, and Guernsey had their wireless sets returned. Many rumours have been passing around about the return of ours, but nothing has yet happened – we might have had them if not for the leaflets.

Still more push bikes are being called in so that a selection may be made, but fortunately it doesn't affect me yet. If it does happen I have got a trick or two up my sleeve.

July 29th 1942

The Evening Post suspended publication last night pending the arrival of further supplies of paper. This happened on a previous occasion despite drastic economies in limiting the number printed so two households have to share a paper, not publishing an edition on Thursday and confining the issue to a single sheet on other days.

Our Feldkommandant has made a mass issue of orders and notices, some are of most awe inspiring character, with death penalties strewn all over the place. Others of less importance promise the death penalty to dogs found loose in the Military Zone, including all beaches. The reason for the last one is because several land mines have been exploded by dogs. Other notices not worthy of reproducing in full reiterate for the umpteenth time the public must clear off the streets in case of air raid alarm, doctors and midwives who may have to be out during an alarm are ordered to obtain a special permit, and cattle must be kept close to the farm buildings at night – the reason for this latter is most obscure. Another notice deals extensively with ARP, but the instructions are contrary to that ordering us to stay indoors. The Germans themselves seem to loath this multiplicity of orders. On two occasions lately I have had to ante date invoices for them to avoid an order requiring a Feldkommandant's permit for certain classes of goods to be bought. Their remarks on Bekanntrachung generally, although delivered in German, left nothing to the imagination. We unfortunately are still seeing too much of the Germans, whose stock order is for 'all' of this and 'all of that', and we have had to do some rapid wangling and take some risks to prevent them having their 'all'. Even so, I have had many thousands of their dud marks in exchange for my good British goods.

Frequently and cunningly the Germans make appeal to the terms of the Hague Convention to give justification to their various confiscations and general nastiness. Often they introduce the Hague Convention into their notices on a side issue, and people not reading through carefully, as is always the way with official notices, assume International Law is on the side of the taker every time. In the case of the confiscation of wireless sets they claim the right under Article 53 of the Hague Convention to confiscate apparatus for the transmission of news. No one has ever denied their right to take wireless transmitters, but most people, merely glancing at the notice, do not realise this attempt to justify their action is an admission on their part.

AUGUST 1942

August 1st 1942
St. Malo's air raid, as might be expected, was definitely audible from here, but curiously the planes do not appear to have passed this way either going or returning. An odd RAF plane or two have shown their noses during the past week or two but without excitement except for a little flak.

August 6th 1942
All the horses in the Island were paraded last night for official German inspection. None were taken, but it looks as though some at least will be borrowed in the near future. Once again in the small hours of yesterday morning RAF fighters adorned our air to the accompaniment of heavy flak. I rely on other people for this information, having long since become sufficiently blasé not to bother to wake unless it gets so heavy one can't sleep through it – this despite official

ARP orders we have to dress and wait to be fetched every time a warning goes or flak goes up. Last night it was German planes around the neighbourhood judging by the absence of searchlights and flak – just to prove that there still is a Luftwaffe.

August 12th 1942

We had excitement last night when breaking the rule about having lights on after 11.00 p.m. Our black out must have been imperfectly fitted for we heard a loud knock on the glass. Guessing what was up I switched off and went to the door, to be told in not-too-bad English to put the light out please – which I did until they were clear of the house and then switched it on again. I wasn't losing my supper for them and their laws. We were lucky over this as a few days back a house close to us had a bayonet stuck through the window first for a similar offence, whilst fines on the spot are quite usual.

Our local rag recommenced publication on Monday after nearly a fortnight and we expected a repetition of the mass of notices which graced the last issue. But all we had is a notice that selling spuds outside the ration will henceforth be punishable by the German authorities as well as under local law, an order for Eire citizens to report to the Feldkommandant, and the call in of another 300 cycles for a further selection. Also it looks as though recent rumours of another car buying commission to purchase all cars, lorries and motorbikes remaining, even the older ones for scrap, are well founded, as temporary car valuers are wanted to represent the States in the matter.

August 15th 1942

It is reputed several local people, as well as Irish and English conchies, are in the pay of the German authorities trying to trace the sources of news which they find is getting about. The Germans are now so closely intermingled with the population they know quite well there is genuine news being circulated, but up to date they don't seem to have been able to make an example of their first victim, although it is said one or two people have been fined for passing on news, but have not disclosed its source. It is also reported the Italians are to lose their sets – although officially allied to the Germans, many of them have lived here for many years and married locally, so some of the leakage of BBC news is credited to them. We are being even more careful about the dissipation of news – Guy Fawkes conspiracy was not carried out with greater precautions than we now find it necessary to take. Unlike one chap who was in the store this morning, and who deserves to be caught, for although he hardly knows me, he even told me exactly where his set was hidden.

The following is correct in outline, but not having seen it, I cannot vouch for the embroidery. Two or three lots of prisoners or refugees, numbering a thousand or two and reputed to be brought from burnt out Russian villages, have arrived in the Island during the last day or two. They include women and children and are said to appear underfed and certainly ill clad, many being without foot covering except for pieces of sacking. God knows what treatment they have had in their journeying across Europe, but they had to finish their journey from the pier to La Moye on foot, despite their condition, and men on the pier at the time report the guards were armed with truncheons and whips.

Yesterday I attended an auction sale when common cups without saucers were sold at the rate of 75/- per dozen – shades of Mr. Woolworth!!

All ARP battle bowlers have been collected under German orders – which make it look like as if ARP is to be even more discouraged.

August 19th 1942

Although this business has only turned out to be a flash in the pan, it has done us one bit of good – last night and again this morning there is not a German to be seen except those on duty – they are all on duty. The Forum, Germany's own cinema, was closed last night, and according to the manageress of one of the hotels, her crowd had everything packed ready to leave – the officer in charge told her it was a practise. The barbed wire barriers which normally are placed across the slipways every night (except on the not so rare occasions when they are forgotten) were still across this morning. It pleased us no end to know last night that in the teeming rain every one of Hitler's little men was out getting wetter and more miserable and more jumpy every minute – I slept happier for the thought. I expect it will be a few days before our friends get back into the jog trot happy go lucky way of doing their garrison duties.

August 21st 1942

Things have reverted to normal, and the only reminder a day or so back there was an invasion panic is a new curfew order of 10.00 p.m. till 6.30 a.m. and, of course, a detailed account of a repulsed invasion in today's paper. There was a fire aboard an oil tanker barge in the harbour yesterday, which was soon put out unfortunately, and another fire at a house they occupy at St. Saviours. This is the second within recent weeks, as another very fine house was gutted a little while back. Why should they worry?

August 24th 1942

Reports are still coming in of the panic last Wednesday. Transport marshalling depots in St. Marks Road and West Park were crowded with cars, lorries and guns, all ready for instant removal. Not much was known here about the raid during the morning for it wasn't until the afternoon the panic measures developed. The local men working for them were all sent home, without explanation or even being told when to come back, whilst the French and Spaniards were herded back into their camps under armed guards. The Russians, who have already been put to work, were also quickly taken back inside their barbed wire enclosure. Everything readily movable was got ready to go, and those soldiers who got any sleep that night had to do so in their full kit. In view of the fact a rehearsal flit was held a few weeks back, (it is supposed to have taken six hours to get the troops, fully provisioned and with all the equipment which they intend to take down to the piers), I am really wondering whether they intend to defend these Islands at all. Yet the amount of defensive works built here are out of all proportion and huge supplies of all materials have been stored as though they intended to withstand a long siege if necessary. Certainly their actions are often contradictory.

Much to his surprise, the chap who was waiting for a vacancy in the gaol to serve his sentence for having a wireless set, was sent for the other day and had his punishment commuted to a 100 marks fine. I know of at least two cases where houses have been searched on the receipt of anonymous letters, but in each instance no set was found although there was one in one of them. It does show you can't trust anyone. Apparently there are people who have only to get slightly offended with one to tell all they know (or think they know) direct to the Germans.

August 29th 1942

For several days heavy bombardment has been taking place somewhere in the neighbourhood but is difficult to know where, as the times of the BBC news giving details does not always fit in with our requirements.

Still more proof is forthcoming of the firm intention of our friends to leave us had last week's raid developed into a real invasion. One hears many confirmations of the story the seaward legs of all the cranes on the pier were loaded with H.E., ready to blow at a moment's notice, so sabotaging the cranes and filling the pier berths at the same time. It is also said a collier in the harbour was ready with loaded explosives to be blown up in the pier heads after the evacuation was complete. I have a feeling when eventually they do go they will fire the many store and ammunition dumps and generally give us plenty to fill our hands for a few hours.

I have just heard some of the recent banging was directed against a small convoy between Jersey and Guernsey. We are all pleased if this is a sign shipping is not to be allowed to go unmolested around this part of the world as it has done for the past two years. It has made our hearts bleed to see so many perfect targets awaiting coastal command. The local report is of 2 Germans killed and 3 injured in a land mine explosion, and of 3 small eggs having been laid on a searchlight unit at St. Ouens a few days ago, with good results.

SEPTEMBER 1942

September 4th 1942

The whole district of Coin Varin, St. Lawrence, have received orders to clear at short notice. The district affected is upwards of a square mile and nearly 40 farmers have to find alternative accommodation for their cattle and stock in a hurry which has caused some problems. The reason for this wholesale eviction is variously said to be – (a) a hospital is to be built there, with its base on the Catholic Convent – (b) it is to be extensively mined and (c) (this I believe to be more reasonable) it is connected with the extensive tunnels which have been dug in the neighbourhood, and which as far as the lay eye can see, would more or less extend right under the affected area.

I am negotiating to buy another animal – a young calf this time, and owing to the heavier risks to be taken, I have to pay a heavier price – 7/- per pound. I am not going to have him in one piece as I did the last pig back in January. Mum and I, with Horace the pig on the kitchen table and Mrs. Beeton's cook book resting against him open at the appropriate page, walked around with a small knife and an ordinary saw working out which way we had to start cutting him up. We must have made a fair job of it, for none of our friends with whom we shared him complained he was tough, as I am given to understand by experts would have been the case if he had been wrongly cut. I surely never thought we should be engaged buying and cutting up whole animals. Another thing that would seem amusing to anyone watching is to see me every day now perched up in a remote corner of our store right under the roof, sitting on my radio set with the volume set at just 'audible'. It is dark up there, and with that to handicap one and the speed at which one has to write, my notes on the daily news want quite a lot of deciphering afterwards. Now Britain has reverted to ordinary summer time, I am not able to carry out my original safeguard of listening only when the store is locked, and therefore have to take a chance whilst my mate stays on guard. It is not too safe, as the Germans, especially OT men, come in quite frequently and walk around as if they owned the place. I chose it as a safer alternative than being seen coming in here every night say at seven o'clock (for the six o'clock news) and going away at 6.15 p.m. knowing there is at least one spy in our street. It is rather funny to be putting all this in writing, and thus condemning myself if ever this epistle got into the wrong hands. It is said two men went on a trip to France yesterday for having a set working – supposed to have been split on.

I understand, owing to the Dieppe raid and the aversion of the high-ups to being taken prisoner, the administration of the Island is henceforth to be run from Granville, whence all senior officers have already gone. It is said there is no officer in the Island senior to a captain, and I certainly have not seen any high ranking Germans about for a few days.

September 8th 1942

Our hopes were again shattered yesterday. A very big ship, escorted by three destroyers, lay in St. Aubins Bay all day and when about 1.30 p.m. a heavy burst of AA fire went up, directed against a plane (presumably British) very high up, we all expected he must have spotted the ships and would pass on the information. But no luck, the expected bombing did not take place.

The eviction order for Coin Varin is to be held over, those concerned having been told after the 10th they must be prepared to get out at a minutes' notice. It looks as though my idea it is in connection with the tunnel is right. Our friends surely expect something to happen during the next few days, and since they have apparently got the idea of leaving us in case of trouble, it would be natural they should want to blow up the ammunition dump in the tunnel. The police tell me they have received orders, in the event of an 'enemy' landing, they are to demand shelter from the nearest house, and stay there until the alarm is over – which they are told would not exceed 3 days. Nice wouldn't it be, to have a hefty policeman parked on one for 3 days when it is more than likely there wouldn't be enough grub for the existing members of the household.

Further proof of the expectancy of our protectors comes in an order published last week end by the German authorities insisting on the completion of harvesting within 48 hours, and stating the Feldgendarmerie had orders to take the necessary steps to see it was done – which was taken to mean they would conscript anyone they saw standing idle, and many people were afraid to go out over the weekend. I spent the whole of Sunday out in the country, however, and did not see a sign of that much-loathed body.

One of the many AA shells put up yesterday failed to explode until it reached the ground, when it made a four foot crater in the road at Pontac and shattered windows – it must have made people in the area think the fun was really starting.

September 16th 1942

There have been no rumours, as usually there are preceding a vicious order, and the whole thing came as a complete surprise to us. When I first saw the deportation order in last night's paper, I was of the opinion as I am of Jersey descent; I was not affected by it. Just in case I decided to take preliminary precautions and visited the Constable of our Parish this morning. I had a shock to be shown an agenda with my name included – meaning I am on the list for one of the next deportation batches. Quite naturally my first thought has been evasion, and I am pulling all strings possible to avoid having to go. I am reticent to leave mother alone, remembering she is two years older than at the time of the evacuation, and although she has had no bad turns, is in no better health, and this might quite easily kill her. I have no doubt those thus taken will be route-marched across France to the bombed areas of Germany, there to work in war factories making the wherewithal to kill their friends and relations and to prolong this worst of all wars. Where now the so often appealed to Hague Convention, and where too the solemn guarantee of the German Government the lives, liberty and property of the peaceful inhabitants would be respected. One hears and only partially believes the propaganda atrocity tales until they arrive on one's own doorstep. Those here who have preached not all Germans are bad are indeed being hoisted on their own petard. Proof, if necessary, of the nature of the beast was shown yesterday afternoon when two soldiers were laughing loudly at the notice as printed in their Inselzeitung. They were well and truly told off by a passing woman – all honour to her. The most brutal part of the business is, I think, the abrupt manner in which it is being carried out. Until the paper came out yesterday afternoon, nothing at all was known of it. At this moment 600 men, women and children are already on the high seas en route for the unknown. Apparently the whole scheme was prepared with the utmost secrecy to the last detail. Many unfortunate souls were roused from bed last night and served with notices telling them to be on the pier at 4.00 p.m. today. A convoy of ships arrived this morning, and the streets in the vicinity of the harbours were crowded with weeping friends and relatives this afternoon when I was out on my various string pulling occasions. Many of my friends are amongst this first batch, probably more than I know about, and there is no doubt the complete scheme of things will result in greater disruption in the Island than did the real evacuation. Most of those who evacuated to England were those whose presence made comparatively little difference except to their immediate friends and relatives. Almost all who felt it their boundened duty to stay did so, as for instance, doctors and other professional men, business men whose affairs were tied up with those of others. How inhumane to include men up to 70, as well as women and children.

September 17th 1942
The first batch has gone numbering 555 and from all accounts all went with their chins up. Exemptions are all men working for the Germans, doctors, clergy and certain essential services such as gas, water and electricity employees and their families, so those who went were all real British. They were gathered on the pier from 4.00 p.m. onwards whilst the necessary red tape was gone through and were fed by the States with bread and jam, hot milk and coffee. They were also given (believed by the German authorities) a tin of meat, one of beans, one of milk and a slab of chocolate to eat on the journey. Eventually the ships sailed at about 9.00 p.m. each carrying a local doctor who will return after seeing the party in France. Certain rejections were made on medical grounds, as well as those who had more than four children – apparently our friends found the responsibility of big families too great. They went surging away from our pier heads shouting of their English affections. True British, they would not show to the German swine the grief they were feeling at leaving home, friends and everything that went to make life worthwhile, to be taken by force to a strange and enemy land, there to suffer with the Germans themselves and privations which will accumulate on the day, not too far distant we hope, when Germany is once again back where she was on November 11th 1918.

The usual crowd of women with prams who always conglomerate at weddings and funerals and so forth were there, and during the evening many other people gathered in the approaches to the harbour and the overlooking heights. Anticipating demonstrations, our friends were present in force armed with rifles and tommy guns and in full war kit. The taking up of the tune of 'Tipperary' by those on Mount Bingham when they saw the boats leaving resulted in the crowd there being dispersed quickly, with the added incentive of the guns in the vicinity being directed towards them, whilst the troops ostentatiously prepared their boxes of hand grenades and stood ready with them in hand. I did not see, the foregoing is compiled from reliable reports.

We have this evening been to visit some old friends, both white haired. The man worked in Jersey for 46 years, and his wife is Jersey and has brought up a family of four sons, three of whom are in the army. Whilst we were there, a local honorary police official and a German gendarme soldier brought papers – at nine o'clock this evening – for them to be at the Weighbridge at 4 o'clock tomorrow afternoon. Their paper requested the man to present himself with wife, near relatives and children of any age and parents, together with all the one blanket and strong boots guff. There were also particulars about exceptions, which include bakers, millers, farmers, etc as well as those previously mentioned. The event, although expected, caused some consternation in the house. Imagine it, being called on just to walk out and leave everything, especially in the case of anyone who has reached the autumn of life. The man was just on the point of being pensioned off from his job at the Boys College. I have every hope they will secure exemption on the grounds of ill health, for neither are in good health.

This opens up a new problem for me – what of mother? At 63 and with a groggy heart, she could not possibly face even the short sea trip to St. Malo, let alone the hardships which lay beyond. The small arrangements I have been able to make in the last day or so have ensured that, staying here, she would not be short of the wherewithal to live, but now all that preparation may be in vain. She, brave soul that she is, would welcome the opportunity to be with me and to share and help in whatever lies in store.

It is late, but we neither of us have any inclination to go to bed, having been present at another's 'condemnation', and having seen the officials of our Parish going around with the Germans on our way home rounding up people, for we both feel our turn may be now.

Of my own feelings in the matter I can hardly write. Since I have known, I have felt numbed, and would almost welcome the unwelcome when it comes, if only to break the suspense. It is like living on the edge of a volcano, in the certain knowledge tomorrow or next week it will erupt under ones feet. I have often said in the last two years I could never conceive a more torturing period than that between the real evacuation and the Occupation – well, we have found it now. I believe there is a way out even now – to go and volunteer to work for the Germans. But I prefer to go to Germany as a 'Britisher' than to stay here as a pro German, and to have to creep to the Germans to do so. My appeals for exemption are all based on civilian essential service – on my drain pipe making and on the storage of local grain which I have recently undertaken. I sometimes wonder whether, even in making appeal for such, I am being un-British and selfish, for even if the hundredth chance did come off and I were exempted, it might mean someone else going who might otherwise have stayed. It is one of those problems to which there is no answer. Friends all assure me, even those who have no choice but to go, that it is everyone for himself in this case. I cannot conceive I was cowardly in staying here, however much events proved me to be wrong in so doing, for I chose what was for me the harder, not the easier course. But is it cowardly to avoid taking one's medicine with one's fellow Britishers, however plausible the excuse?

Coming back to earth, at least one German officer was practising a refined form of cruelty on the pier last night by assuring people that they were only going to Germany for repatriation to England. I am told the officers were excelling themselves with their courtesy and kindliness – kindliness indeed, towards old men and women and young children whom they were evicting from their homes and planting in a foreign country with almost nothing except the clothes in which they stood, and where they would not be able even to make their needs understood, and where they will be hated even as the Germans here are now hated. Where there will be no pity, only a burning desire that they may be killed by British bombs by way of reprisal for the punishment now being meted out over Germany. Thank God those who have gone and are still to go are of sufficiently British temperament to welcome the RAF and its rain of bombs even as we here have welcomed their visits on the all too rare occasions when we had that thrill. The private soldiers seem to have been less subtle, or maybe are less imbibed with Goebbel's propaganda, for they showed their satisfaction at the treatment meted out to the British in the jeering expressions on their faces.

I bemoan my own case plentifully but how much worse for those who, through this inhuman German order, have to take wives and young families into the unknown which lies beyond the Weighbridge at which they have to gather. In perhaps two hundred homes tonight, at this moment, packing and preparation for the morrow is causing frantic efforts – everything which has to be left behind causing a heart break. A sleepless night, followed by a day of final arrangements and goodbyes to all those friends who in the stress of the moment one can remember or reach, then the long wait whilst formalities are carried out before a night on the boat en route to France – a second sleepless night this, and succeeded by the long trek to Germany, trying to carry the needs of the whole family and to shepherd one's little flock and guard it from more discomfort than need be. That is one of the effects of the so much boosted 'Kultur', and of the 'New Order' in Europe.

It grows late, and my turn, it seems, is not to be with tomorrow's batch, unless indeed I be awakened in the middle of the night or be presented with my ultimatum tomorrow morning as happened in many cases on the first batch. Staying out of bed can do no good, for I will need to be as fit as possible to face my own ordeal when it comes; and perhaps even to help some unfortunate with even greater burdens and problems than my own.

September 18th 1942

So passes another day of this long drawn out nightmare. My call has still not come, and I have spent the day in making more of the many preparations and arrangements which seem to be without end. The few days respite has given me opportunity to provide myself with the many little things which will go to make life less unpleasant. I have been able to scrounge a sweater and a pair of shoes and to get the last pair of wearable boots which I owned resoled (this is a job which normally takes some weeks and entails queuing up to get the work accepted).

Many friends and customers have been coming in and out of the store all day, either to say goodbye because they had to go or to enquire as to when I was going. I have also been advised the two appeals under essential service which I made through various States Departments have not been accepted. I am not disappointed, for I had firmly made up my mind last night not to expect any miracles, and today it seems, unlike Wednesday, there are just about no exemptions at all, and one even hears of those rejected then being issued with fresh notices – the most leniency granted today appears to have been an extra day or so grace, and that only in exceptional circumstances. Two boats were due out again tonight, and my store hand (if I can still regard myself as boss of the store) has gone to France, as a St. Johns Ambulance man with the party and will return on the same boat. We were on the coast road watching for the vessels to leave about 9.00 p.m. (they travel under full lights) when the unusual sight of a bus coming along attracted our attention, and, after it had stopped, out poured just about everyone who had been warned for today in the district, including one family of six children. They all seemed highly delighted to be home again, but it is only a week's respite, as all have been accepted and are to be shipped next Friday. Apparently it was found at the last moment that the ship in which they were to go was not fit to be used for the purpose, and so the whole party assigned to her were sent home for a week. They all seem optimistic that during that week 'something' may happen – probably their optimism has been fanned by the many wild rumours which spread through the crowd during the hours of waiting – according to one report, which might be expected under such circumstances, British troops had already landed in France and were wiping things up. For days a yarn has been going about the channel was packed with thousands of ships, an armada coming to do the long awaited job. You would be surprised how seriously people repeat that sort of thing. Other rumours which may or may not be true, but which have gained much credence, are the likelihood of evacuating all men from 18 to 35, 36, 41, 45, 51 (according to the teller), as well as the wives of all service men. Me, I am a sceptic, and like to see orders in print before I believe them.

There have been many hurried marriages during these hectic days, sometimes because a girl is anxious to be with her loved one in Germany rather than alone here, and sometimes because a girl chooses to marry her Jersey born man rather than accompany her family into the unknown. There have also been the inevitable suicides and attempts at it on the part of those whose mental balance is unable to withstand the heavy strain imposed by this horrid uncertainty.

September 21st 1942

A reaction of optimism has set in, and for no apparent reason everyone not concerned has suddenly become completely convinced no more of us will be taken. Certainly a welcome few days respite is with us, and, as far is known, next Friday's sailing of those who should have gone last Friday is the next event in this forced emigration.

As I don't believe in fairies, I prefer to keep myself prepared for the worst – as I see it, invasion is the only thing which can prevent our being taken. Last week's events include a query as to what has happened to the second of the two ships which took Wednesday's consignment. One arrived here to schedule for the second batch on Friday, but the other did not, and was to have been replaced by a coal boat which chanced to be in harbour, except that at the last moment it was deemed unfit even for the transport of English refugees – and was later used to take troops away. It was the missing ship my store hand-cum-St. Johns man was supposed to travel on, so he did not go after all. This little 'holiday' is proving longer and less convenient than anticipated. Of the ship which did go on Friday, our local pilot refused service on her, and she was taken out by her German skipper. Bad seamanship resulted in her ramming some barges, running aground and then striking the pier heads before eventually getting clear of the harbour - which performance must have been rather distressing to the sorely tried passengers.

Not satisfied with the generous system of exemptions operating on Wednesday, a different crowd of Germans were on the job, and one had to have more than ordinary disability to get away with it. Our old friends mentioned earlier were not rejected, as I hoped they might be, and I shall be indeed surprised if they ever see our once happy little island again. Their only son left here is naturally terribly cut up that his aged and decrepit parents have been taken whilst he is left. Also taken on Friday after exemption on Wednesday are an elderly clergyman and his wife, the former still bearing marked signs of shell shock sustained during the last war, as well as other obvious signs of ill health. This business of exemptions is being so tightened up German doctors have been around examining those who, confined to bed, were unable to present themselves as required. Local doctors' certificates count for nothing. I give these merely as examples of the type of treatment to be expected.

There have been one or two suicides and attempts, but apart from these isolated cases, I have been amazed at how philosophically everyone has taken this complete uprooting. No one is making a very great song about it, even though this time there really is something to moan about. I suppose that the same holds true of every British person – a little inconvenience demands a big grumble, whilst the biggest troubles are faced up to with amazing courage. As an instance of the sort of real pluck which doesn't earn medals, I would mention a chemist friend who I left but a few moments ago. He was actually aboard the boat which did not sail on Friday, with his wife and son, and at the last moment was sent home for a week. He is not so young, and has not very long started in business on his own account, so that he has much to lose. He was back at his shop on Saturday – running 'business as usual' - for one week only. He has nothing to gain by so doing, as he can only take the regulation 10 marks with him, but I suppose he feels that it is his job. With no-one to carry on in his absence, it puts an end for him on his little endeavour.

The only bright spot on the week's news is that the S/S 'Diamande' is at present firmly fixed on the Dogs Nest rocks not far outside the pier heads. She is a vessel of about 1000 tons, and is the same which the RAF claimed to have hit in Alderney harbour some time ago. She appears to be a total loss, and at high water only her masts and the top of her funnel are visible. Wreckage is being washed ashore on all the adjacent beaches and the local army and navy have been engaged all day in salvaging the flotsam. As I write, I hear frequent blank shots as the guards on our beach fire at any civilian who goes too close to the water's edge – poor souls are afraid we might pinch some firewood. This wreck has caused many smiles of happiness on faces which for the past week have forgotten how to smile. Rumour insists a number of bodies varying between 6 and 12, have been washed ashore, but as rumour always does adorn every accident with tragedy, I am not completely convinced of this (but I hope it is true).

One other item of news – a telephone wire near Samares Manor has been cut, and, starting last night, civilian pickets have been posted. Each has to do four hours duty, either 10.00 p.m. till 2.00 a.m. or 2.00 a.m. till 6.00 a.m. and I am hoping our honorary police will be honourable police too, and leave me out of it – if I have to go to Germany, they might at least leave my few remaining nights undisturbed. We have been lucky to date, as this is the first time our district has been so afflicted.

With all the excitement, I failed to report before that at least two more arrests have been made of people with wireless sets, one having been split on by his Germanite daughter and the other by a neighbour who had been in the habit of coming in to hear the news. At about the same time, a local dentist was arrested, but his offence is not definitely known, although many rumours on the subject were current before we found new and more poignant topics of conversation. He has always been a pronounced and outspoken anti German, and is known to have gone amongst the foreign labourers inciting them to go slowly. His offence may be almost anything. Report has gilded the picture of his arrest as a very violent affair, culminating in his having been taken from the house bound hand and foot. Knowing the man, I can believe that part of the yarn as quite possible.

September 24th 1942

A steady gale, after wrecking the S/S 'Diamande', has resulted in a postponement of the sailing tomorrow (Friday) of those put off from last week and of those since called for that sailing. For which extra respite everyone is duly grateful. There are those (always those not directly affected by this swinish order) where intuition gathers from these delays the certain knowledge that we unfortunates will not have to go after all. They think they are doing a kindness by optimistically broadcasting their unfounded opinions to all and sundry. I have rather pointedly and not very politely intimated to such as I have come into contact with that they are doing an unkindness by raising hopes which are probably false in the hearts of those of us who, knowing we shall have to go, have made up our minds to go with the same good courage which our friends have shown. This false optimism has just about touched me on the raw – can you imagine anything more likely to break the amazing morale shown through this most difficult period than to allow one's hopes to be raised and then dashed to the ground. Even should a miracle happen, and we be left in Jersey yet awhile, I shall never feel safe from the dark shadow which overhangs us until the Union Jack is once more flying here. The vessel being used for evacuation is at present in Guernsey waiting for the weather to abate to take a load from there, when, it is presumed, it will return here to carry on the good work. I would here mention that, whereas last week all people born in the colonies were told that they were exempt, many of them have been warned to sail on the next boat – their papers were not then made out, and yet mine, which was, has not yet been delivered to me – thanks be, for I surely don't want ever to see it again.

A message arrived today from Bill – this is the first batch which has arrived in the last six weeks.

There was some little excitement in our neighbourhood last night. One of the aforementioned Germanites had a row with her German a few days ago; or rather her husband did, with the result that said German reported to the Gendarmerie a wireless set was hidden in the house. The soldier has always been regarded as a most harmless individual for a German, and had known for some months about this illicit set – which goes to prove just how much one can trust a German. For some reason, maybe to have a companion in distress, the husband told the Gendarmerie that another of the Germanites close by had a set hidden away, but a search of the house revealed nothing. They apparently found a good hiding place for it. Not much sympathy is being wasted over the matter, for we all feel that it serves them right for entertaining Germans.

September 26th 1942

For no apparent reason except to confound trading, the rate of exchange has been again altered to 9.36 marks to the £. Hitherto it has been 9.60, making the mark worth two shillings and a penny and the halfpenny worth 1/4d, quite a workable business. I can only imagine this new arrangement, which will not balance exactly against any English denomination, is intended to induce banks and trade generally to keep their books in marks instead of in sterling. Someone put it rather aptly to me the other day that there must be a sort of Brains Trust Committee in Germany who do naught else but evolve schemes for the discomfiture of the occupied peoples – this being one of their more niggling efforts as compared with the bombshell thrown in our midst by their recent super brutal order. With their usual generosity of giving a penny and taking back two pence, it has also been promised the gas will be left turned on until 10.00 p.m. on November 1st instead of 8.00 p.m. as at present – which may be some small consolation to those unfortunates who, until then, will have to sit in darkness or go to bed.

The doctor, St. Johns Ambulance man and two nurses who left here with last Friday's party of refugees have arrived back after spending a week in St. Malo. It was originally arranged they should be brought straight back on the vessel which took them, and indeed their permit contained the proviso they were not to leave the vessel. On arrival in St. Malo they learned the vessel was not coming back to Jersey, but was to go to Guernsey to pick up English refugees from there. Left stranded it was fortunate between them they had the necessary funds to live during the period. They made several attempts to join vessels which were due to come to Jersey, but in each case sailing was postponed owing to stress of weather. Up till last night, when they left St. Malo, the boat from Guernsey had not yet put in an appearance, presumably storm bound. Notices are continuing to be served on people for the next sailing, but I am still living in a sort of fool's paradise. I can't quite make out why I have been left so long, for my papers ready for serving were at the St. Clement's Constables Office on the first day, and others whose papers were not there have since been served. There is plenty of argument about the reasons and intentions of the Germans in this scheme. On the face of it there doesn't seem much sense. If they want labour, why take old men and women and children? On the other hand, I could more easily give credence to the oft-repeated (but only verbally) statement it is for repatriation to England, if they excluded men of military age, and if they gave the reason fuller publicity. My own idea to be proved right or wrong as time goes on is someone in authority realises all is not well, and, losing his temper, conceives the idea it will be a just revenge to make English women and children share the hail of bombs of the RAF. Carrying the idea further, it is possible, though not so likely, when the evacuation is complete, publicity will be given to the fact English people are in the most vulnerable areas in the hope that it will stay the hand of the RAF.

September 28th 1942

The shipping date has now been fixed for Tuesday (29th), and a hospital ship and a big cargo vessel have arrived in harbour. It is believed quite a big crowd are to go, in addition to those sent back last Friday week – somewhere in the region of a thousand.

As it is obviously necessary to be well equipped with good footwear and clothing, and as most people's own, after more than two years of Occupation, are not so good, arrangements have been made for those going to be equipped with what they need in the way of clothing and footwear (wooden soles and leather uppers) by the States, gratis where necessary. Although our clothes ration is being run on coupons, having the necessary coupons and cash does not mean one can get the goods. I have been trying for months to buy a pair of shoes or boots, and, now my need has become imperative, have had to scrounge some.

Fortunately I am not so badly off in other respects. I cannot boast of being smartly clad as I once was but I have most of the warm clothing which I shall need – anyway as much as I can carry.

September 29th 1942

September 29th is doomsday for many. There seems to have been a lot of last minute call ups last night of all those who have been guilty of 'crimes' – and as this includes such heinous offences as curfew breaking, holding a wireless set, having a traffic accident and many other misdemeanours, it has accounted for many. A day of heavy wind and rain, it is a most inauspicious start for the journey into the unknown. I gather people will start being sent from the marshalling sheds down to the ships soon after 2.00 p.m. there to await embarkation at about 9.00 p.m. – seven hours in the pouring rain as a preliminary to a rough sea trip of some seven hours duration, with its attendant sea sickness and other discomforts. During the past two years, we have complained, and not without cause, of loneliness, hardships, privations and general discomfiture. But we are now faced with an infinitely greater degree of all these and other troubles. I am taking with me a second volume in order to continue this diary, though I have great doubt as to whether such will be possible, or whether it will be possible to get it out of Germany. This little book of mine has been a source of some consolation (and not a little pride) to me.

September 30th 1942

A reprieve - some 600 of the refugees were shipped in two vessels, and then an announcement was made at the place of assembly the specified number had been taken, and there would be no further evacuation in the immediate future. Those left, numbering about 200, were advised to go home and resume their normal occupations. It would seem some 1,200 have been taken from Jersey and reports place the number taken from Guernsey at 800. A friend who was on duty at the Weighbridge came rushing around to the store – I thought he had gone barmy – to tell me the glad tidings. I am naturally delighted at the turn of events, but still fully expect to go sooner or later. It may be a month or two months before anything further is done in the matter, but that is so much longer to be at home and so much less time to spend in Germany. This reprieve is welcomed with mixed feelings by some who were turned back, for many have eaten all their food stocks and some have even sold their homes to prevent the Germans getting them. So they are in a bit of a mess – they don't want to buy other furniture, or even to ask for their own stuff back, in case the call comes again soon. Others have got married to be together, and now find themselves spliced but unable to set up home for the same reason. There were rather larger demonstrations than usual last night or else the guards were a little less tolerant. I prefer to stay at home on these occasions, despite my wish to obtain the true facts as far as possible, and so have to rely on others for any information. It seems the places which previously were used as vantage points for shouting and singing farewells and encouragement to the outgoing refugees were closed to the public by cordons of troops, and in one or two places the crowd broke through and had to be persuaded out with fixed bayonets, and in one case a volley was fired over the heads of the crowd. It seems to have developed into a bit of a rough house, and a local parson's son, himself due to go, is supposed to have laid out the officer in charge. Bayonets are supposed to have caused some superficial damage, and quite a number of cyclists had German jack boots thrust through the spokes because they would nor or could not get back quickly enough. One result is some 15 or 16 young bloods cooled their heels in gaol last night. No official comment is forthcoming, but it is possible there may be some form of general punishment, and certainly more stringent precautions at the next evacuation. Amongst yesterday's evacuees was one who draped himself in a Union Jack and Stars and Stripes, whilst another labelled his bag 'Adolf Hitler – Berchtesgaden'. I do agree Jerry should not be shown he is getting us down by his lousy tricks, but I can't see much sense in this melodramatic and undignified way of carrying it out. Many women went away with tricolour ornaments in their hats, and the whole party showed the usual courage, although they seem to have been rather quieter – possibly lacking the encouragement from the land which was evident on previous occasions, and also probably as a result of the nervous tension of having had more time to realise things.

So ends a fortnight of plain hell. Every time there has been a knock at the door, we have thought the time had come, and it has been sheer mental torture. We are not finished with it yet – probably the next that will be heard of the matter will be notices requesting our presence on the morrow – and that may come next week, next month or in three months time. Jerry is quite capable of doing things this way in order to break our morale. I certainly don't believe his full requirements have been met by these few small shipments. They seem to have been most eager to take those with the largest families. I cannot see an adequate reason for wanting large families, with extra mouths to feed, to go to Germany. In fact, the whole scheme is beyond my comprehension. If it be labour he wants, why not take men of military age – that was one of the risks which I knowingly faced when I chose to stay. If repatriation were intended, it would hardly be wise to include any men of military age, and especially the last one to be included with yesterday's party – the ARP Controller – a man who probably knows more about the German dispositions in the island than anyone else. I think my previous conclusion of 'bomb fodder' is the only reasonable one.

As a measure of the triumph of mind over matter, it is worth quoting during this fortnight of great stress, we have been able to pass on to friends 6 lbs of the 21 lbs (over a period of a fortnight) of bread which represents our ration. This is the first time during the two years in which bread has been rationed we have not had to look at every slice twice before eating it – indeed we have been overjoyed, if not overfed, on those occasions (very rare) when an extra loaf has come our way.

OCTOBER 1942

October 6th 1942

Jerry has got the jitters again, though at the moment the reason seems vague. We heard the welcome sounds of heavy bombardment and distant plane engines yesterday afternoon, and on one occasion the guns near home opened up, though I fancy the planes were well out of range. Piecing together what little information has been available in town today, and trying to sort the wheat from the chaff, it appears a general alarm was put out at 10.00 p.m. last night. All troops were on duty, barriers placed on many of the roads, the telephone exchange taken over by the military, and guards placed on every conceivable place, even the decrepit OT being roped in for duty. Our local tanks, Jersey's protection against invaders, were out patrolling the roads, and the night made more hideous still by much marching and shouting and motor cars and lorries dashing about. This morning every soldier on his ordinary routine duty – collecting the day's provisions etc. – carried his rifle, whilst many patrols armed with rifles and tommy guns paraded the streets. Telephone communication was not restored until 11.00 a.m. and men working the ships were not allowed on the pier until that time. Naturally many rumours have been going the rounds and one which probably started as a joke but which has had many serious repetitions, is 50 parachute troops landed in Sark of all places. These alarms and excursions do some good, if only to give us something less oppressive to talk and think about and it thrills us no end to know the state of the Jerry nerves. Unlike the day of the Dieppe raid there don't seem to have been preparations made for a wholesale 'flit'.

October 8th 1942

Once again I am confounded by my own words, for the Sark landing has turned out to be a fact. This does account for the panic which has not yet completely died down. Yet the raid, according to the BBC, took place on Saturday, and the alarm was not raised here until 10.00 p.m. on Monday. Is it that the Germans anticipate the possibility a British occupation will be attempted to prevent further deportations, or is it, as some Germans believe, a rather larger scale raid was made on the district around Cherbourg over the weekend? Naturally this Sark raid, with all its implications and effects, has been the one topic of conversation today, and there have naturally been many "I told you so's".

I have received many of them, being a confirmed sceptic where these yarns are concerned. Everyone is thrilled we are so definitely in the news. I suppose the escapees from Guernsey a week or two back made things sound rather worse than they really are (not that I consider them good), hence the small raiding party to confirm reports. I guess they must have had a shock to know of the mass deportations. I am not sure this publicity is an unmixed blessing, but the proof our plight is officially known is a great comfort to us. Only about 10% or so have actually gone. The total from all the Islands is in the region of 2,000, whereas it is estimated 10,000 to 12,000 are actually affected by the order in Jersey alone, so there are many people in England being unnecessarily worried. I can imagine Bill jumping in his excitable way, and condemning me, as I now condemn myself, for staying here. Even in the case of those whose people have actually gone, the knowledge of this brutal mass deportation will not help – it is one of the cases where ignorance really is bliss. One small batch of messages has arrived during the last two months so we imagine there may be some connection between holding up of news and evacuation. I have some doubts as to whether those messages now being accepted are being forwarded immediately.

Again yesterday about midday the RAF were giving some place around here a thorough pasting, but again no mention has been made on the news. It may be the raids are on too small a scale to be worth reporting, but judging from the vibrations felt here, those in the neighbourhood must have found them not so inconsiderable. For all these signs of activity we are not ungrateful, but what wouldn't we all give for the real activity which will release us from this uncomfortable state of suspended animation. Each day our cries join those of millions of French, Dutch, Belgian, Danes and Norwegians – when, when,

when? One day our hopes rise – the weather is perfect for invasion, and the Germans seem extra jittery and to our jaundiced eyes look even less like soldiers able to stand and scrap than they really are. The next day it blows a gale, and we realise bitterly invasion at this time of year is too much to hope for. We look at the extensive defence works springing up all around and see despite the poor quality of the garrison, a landing would meet with very formidable difficulties. Thus do we oscillate between optimism and pessimism – though, except in isolated instances, most peoples' pessimism never reached the depth of 'whether' merely 'how long'.

October 9th 1942

The account in the paper about the taking of prisoners during the Sark raid and their alleged ill treatment by the landing party reveals one amusing detail – they were in their shirts only, and so must have been taken prisoners when asleep. There must be a very fine guard kept. I suppose on Sark, tucked away in the midst of the Islands, they considered themselves completely safe from such indignity (as indeed did I until it actually happened). It explains why the OT generally are in disgrace at the moment. During the panic they were on guard all night, as well as having to do their ordinary work during the day, to the great delight of the ordinary soldiery. Well, that is one little laugh culled from the paper, but it also contains a few words which spell more boredom than usual – curfew is to be shortened (or should I say lengthened) to from 9.00 p.m. till 6.30 a.m. as from Sunday (11th). Until our friends made any infringement against their laws punishable not only with the penalty of the crime but also an excuse for deportation to Germany, I was not a bit fussy about breaking the curfew, and quite regularly left a neighbour's house after an evening playing cards an hour or more after curfew. Now it behoves one to exercise greater discretion, especially as patrols have lately become very active indeed. Up to a little while ago, infractions of the curfew order were handed over to the civil authorities and almost always resulted in 48 hours clink without option. But recently I have noticed there have been no such prosecutions in the Courts, and as I am sure people have not mended their ways so completely as that, I take it the cases are being dealt with by the German authorities. The only case of which I have knowledge was of a man who actually arrived on his own doorstep as ten was striking, and was summarily fined one mark on the spot. I imagine more serious infractions would be dealt with rather more severely. It surely isn't wise to let one's name get put in the official black book if one can help it – although regulations are so numerous one can't possibly help breaking one or other every day. Life won't be so cheerful but it is a much lesser evil than being sent to Germany. We imagine there may be a reprisal for the recent escape from Guernsey, although no official mention has been made of that matter.   It is yet another proof our present Civil Commandant, Col. Knackfuss, is not such a nice man as his two predecessors, Capt. Gussek and Col. Schumacher – bitterly as I loathe Germans, I must admit we were justly, even generously, treated by these two, which is more than can be said of recent events.

October 13th 1942

We are treated in tonight's paper, in connection with British atrocity tales, to an assurance the English people taken from here are not to be used as forced labour, but merely are being interned. I can believe that as possible, in view of the fact women and big families formed the preponderance, but I wouldn't mind betting the internment camps are in vulnerable areas. One hears the trials (secret of course) of those arrested in connection with the disturbances during the last evacuation took place on Monday, as well as those of many others accused of other offences, such as disseminating news and having wireless sets. The disturbance offences resulted in sentences from three years downwards, those under 18 being fined. These facts seem to be generally agreed though it is difficult to get authentic details about this as there is so much variation in the repetition.

October 14th 1942

Another sleepless night last night – sundry loud bangs in the wee small hours awakened most people, and I gather star shells or similar were sent up off the north of the Island.   For a period of about half an hour the odd bangs merged into a continuous rattle of heavy and lighter explosions. I heard no planes, and imagined at first one of the ammo dumps on the Island had been fired, accidentally or otherwise. It eased down too quickly for that and I have heard no report today, as I certainly should have, that all the shemozzle was on the Island. So my conjecture is the explosions came from an ammo ship either through bombing or accident, hence the hectic half hour. Today's BBC news gives no clue at all to the matter, so it looks as if it will join the many unsolved mysteries of this Occupation.

ARP is completely dead having taken a long time dying. Central Control has been closed, and all permanent officials dismissed, and we have each received a letter of thanks for all we haven't done. It has at least tided the motorbike over a period when I might otherwise have lost her – I may still do so, but at least

ARP has increased my chances of still having the old soul when this is all over.

October 16th 1942

The BBC news of a convoy being intercepted by the Navy around here, even though it meant the loss of sleep, is welcome. We only wish some of the other convoys, obviously important, would receive similar attention. Maybe now the Navy knows this is being used as a back alley for Jerry shipping they will pay more attention to it.

Still trying to trace the sources of news, the unworthy Gendarmerie has started a new dodge. Two people talking in the street are accosted, separated, and then each asked to give details of their conversation. Should the two versions not agree, they are arrested and then have to prove they were not discussing the news – no easy matter. Getting wise many people are pre-arranging an innocent topic of conversation for use in case. Jerry is no mug and will soon be trying something else. Many arrests have already been made with the aid of this and other ruses, and it will be interesting to know, after all this is over, just how many people have been gaoled for minor offences. The list will be an imposing one. It surprises me I have not yet been included amongst those so honoured. I have earned the death penalty on more than one occasion by disregarding their more 'serious' regulations, whilst the prospective remaining years of my life would not be sufficient to cover the terms of imprisonment to which I have rendered myself liable. The breaking of German laws, even though there is a risk, disturbs no one's conscience. I wouldn't even mind being found out (the worst part of any crime) were it not for the fact German adjudication is the antithesis of its British counterpart – under the 'new order', it is not sufficient to be punished for one's crime. Long after expiration of one's misdemeanours, one is liable to be yanked up again and either used as a hostage or be deported to Germany even though one's other qualifications do not entail that honour. Having once been found setting a foot wrong, one's name gets put on a black list, and then you don't know quite what is going to happen. I would rather stay anonymous to the Germans, though the trouble is one hasn't much choice in the matter, as there are so many things for which one can be got. Honestly, were I not so firmly convinced the new order has not come to stay, and the day is not far off when we can look to a reversion to something like our old free and easy ways, I would feel like doing what so many hundreds all over Europe have already done in their despair, and committing suicide. Life under the present conditions, with hundreds of Damocles swords over one's head, and with all the mental agony a demented brain has been able to devise and inflict on us, just wouldn't be worth living, were it not for a hope in the future.

October 23rd 1942

I had a narrow escape from that not unexpected blessing – a term in gaol. Back in the days of the last attempted escape an order was issued all boats including canoes must be delivered in town. I destroyed my old ship, but didn't want to part with my latest one, and I parked it up in the roof of an evacuated neighbour's garage and forgot all about it. On Thursday, without any preliminary flutter, our friends decided to take away quite a few of the bungalows in the vicinity, for re-erection at St. Johns Manor. I was fortunate, on the occasion of his visit to the bungalow, the States official concerned was not accompanied, as is usual, by a German officer, and fortunate the man concerned is not a Quisling. I had (and took) the opportunity to alter its appearance so it now looks just like firewood, being just that. It didn't please me to have to use a chopper on the thing, albeit a lesser inconvenience than a spell in gaol with all the attendant repercussions of being in German hands.

Other than this, there has been little of note happening. Quite a number of more arrests have been made, including some quite close to home, but the nature of the alleged offences is not known. We have been again warned black out offences will be dealt with more rigorously, people having grown careless.

NOVEMBER 1942

November 1st 1942

After two winters being two hours ahead of the sun, with depressingly dark mornings (sunrise not till nearly 10) we are this winter being treated to an extra hour of light in the morning, the clocks being retarded an hour tonight. The first definite news we received via the BBC, when they announced revised times of overseas news to match the altered situation. Other than that, there is little to record. The barbed wire barriers and anti tank devices on slipways are being replaced on most of the slips by hefty concrete walls. Our own slip is amongst those affected, and as the grass patch alongside is wired off and contains 4 light AA guns and a search light, we go quite a distance to get onto the beach.

November 2nd 1942

We had another disturbance during last night, and judging by sounds it was the naval attack on a convoy referred to on the news. The AA gun crews near home, judging from shouts, thought it to be a prelude to invasion, and got one of their periodic fit of jitters.

Being home early in the evening has thrown us a on our own resources for entertainment, and naturally reading comes first. I have not yet made up my mind whether it is pleasant or not to read of other people doing those things which are denied to us. Heroes nonchalantly light cigarettes, whilst every time we smoke, we bear in mind it is one less to last the week. Our mouths water by mention of bacon and egg breakfasts, motor drives, and above all by the ease with which fiction moves its characters from place to place – these things make bitter sweet reading, reminders of happier days when we could do these things without being aware of it being a treat. Yet the human mind is a curious thing, for leaving aside occasional days of mental torment when our protectors spring on us some unpleasant surprise, it would be futile to say we are unhappy. Always present is the feeling of being separated from our loved ones, and there are many extra worries and difficulties created by present conditions to be overcome, but to be honest, we have been far from miserable, being doubly appreciative of the few pleasures left. Our comparative contentment with this unsatisfactory way of life may be partly explained by the fact we are kept constantly busy improvising to overcome the many difficulties, leaving little time for introspection..

November 9th 1942

Our RAF friends passed this way yesterday and stayed around the district for nearly an hour, to the visible agitation of the local flak merchants. They stayed so high the guns could not spot anything to fire at. Again this morning they came, this time diving on some ships off Noirmont with guns blazing. All the AA guns around home opened up, and for a few minutes it was quite an inferno. I hear this afternoon several scuttlers have been admitted to hospital with bullet wounds. I cannot understand the mentality of the Germans in using our hospital for such cases. They ought to realise such news travels around quickly. I have heard a firsthand account of the first of the naval actions against convoys in local waters. One torpedo boat was definitely sunk, with a loss of 170 lives, and my informant saw another which managed to reach St. Malo burnt out.

Some stereotyped postcards have at long last reached here from those poor souls who were forcibly evacuated. No mention is made of their whereabouts, but all speak of decent conditions, being together in the day and separated, men in one camp, women and children in another at night. A few have managed to get themselves sent back, on grounds of ill health, but being threatened to silence regarding their adventures.

Everyone is full of beans at the evidence of something doing. We all wish the military activity were closer to home, but realise although Egypt and Algeria are so far away, it is building up for the day when it is our turn for release. It is amazing to me, in view of the officially complete lack of radio sets, how quickly special news items like these, get passed around; which just goes to prove by no means everyone was so awed by Jerry this time as to part with his set. I fancy quite a few sets which were kept for the sake of not losing them, and were stowed right away, have since been brought into commission. Even from the biased accounts of events given in the local press, we are able to read between the lines a different attitude to two years, or even one year ago. German propaganda is far from being as cunning as it was both in a military and internal affairs sense. Inaptly enough, for instance, we have recently been treated to an article glorifying the recent increased bread ration (to 4½ lbs) in Germany and the 50 grams (1¾ ounces) increase in the meat ration. Emphasis is laid on these increases at a time when England's rations are being further reduced; ignoring the fact England is not rationed at all for the two main essentials – bread and potatoes. Another example occurred about the time when our local rag had to cease publication through shortage of paper – an inappropriate time to point out similar shortage in England resulting in reduced circulation. The various cuts in the sweets ration have also had some publicity – not effective propaganda to a suborned people who have nearly forgotten what sweets taste like.

In a military sense too, the propaganda people seem most concerned with the assurance capitulation is unthinkable and events bear no parallel to 1918. With the exception of fantastic claims of U boats sinking, even the official communiqués seem on the defensive and refer in the main to the repulse (with heavy losses) of all enemy attacks. It is said orders have been issued here, in the event of a British landing being effected and holding more than 12 hours, the troops are to be withdrawn from the Islands, whilst if the 'raid' lasts more than 7 days, the OT, all that will be left, have orders to burn or blow up all stores.

November 12th 1942

The occupation of Southern France, combined with other recent events, has led to another general alarm for our garrison. Barbed wire barriers have been across all roads every night, double guards everywhere, and many patrols carry hand grenades slung around their necks as well as rifles. I believe some 2,000 troops and a great deal of equipment have been taken away under cover of darkness during the past day or two. The Forum, reserved for Germans, has been closed. The town in the evenings is quite deserted, with the Germans and their molls out of the way – just like old times, except 8.0 p.m. seems like 2.00 a.m. There have been so many alarms during the last few weeks the individual soldier will soon be thinking the High Command is crying "wolf" too often, and will be caught napping when the real time comes along.

The appearance of a notice in last night's paper forbidding the civil population to give to the foreign labourers, especially Russians, who come begging, any food or clothing, reminds me beyond the bare mention of the arrival of these Russian refugees, I have not given any indications of their ways of life (or rather existence). The notice referred to states they are sufficiently fed. The actual facts are their whole diet consists of ½lb of bread and one pint of soup per day, plus whatever they steal or scrounge; with the results there has been plenty of stealing and scrounging. I have not seen one of them yet, but friends from the west of the Island, where these men are billeted in camps, tell me it is necessary to watch the clothes line the whole time things are drying. Those people who, on compassionate grounds or fear of the consequences of refusal, have responded to their begging appeals for food or clothing have in many cases been rewarded by being robbed – and by the men bringing along all their pals. However sorry one may feel for these poor devils, it is obviously impossible out of one's too small rations to do anything to alleviate their misery especially as helping one means having a small army of them expecting the same. Unlike the other foreign labourers, who are quite well paid, and are thus able to buy such unrationed goods as tomatoes and apples, the Russians only receive two marks per month – which in Jersey is worth just about what 1/- was before the war. Their clothing is in rags, and almost all have only rags wrapped around their feet in lieu of socks. Altogether they are a sight to make the heart bleed. I am told by those who live near the quarries where they work they are most harshly treated by their OT guards. Shootings at the least sign of insurrection are apparently quite a regular occurrence, and it seems they are knocked about pretty badly if their work doesn't meet the approval of their Nazi masters. Altogether the scheme of bringing them here is not a good advert for the much boasted 'new order'.

November 17th 1942

The excitement of the past day or two has included the passing on Sunday morning very low (so low our AA gunners did not wake up till too late) of a Yankee plane. I saw it, but it was a mile or so north of home, and as it bore a strong resemblance to the FW190, I took it to be Jerry. On Sunday evening there were sounds of heavy bombardment somewhere in the district, though not since mentioned on the radio. Yesterday a very big convoy comprising of one ship of 20,000 tons, many smaller ones and a dose of E boats sheltered all day in St. Aubins Bay. I presumed they had been bombed out the previous night. They disappeared last night, and we hope it was because the RAF was anxious to put salt in their tails, AA guns had a busy 5 minutes when some planes were around about 11.00 p.m. One in particular flew so low over the town as to be clearly visible in the bright moonlight. Elaborate precautions against surprise attacks are still being taken, and for more than a week the Germans have been subject to a 6.00 p.m. curfew. But so many false alarms will, we hope, cause less notice to be taken, and one day the high-ups will cry "wolf" once too often.

November 19th 1942
One of yesterday's fighter sweep casualties was a Spitfire piloted by a De Gaulle man which, running short of petrol, made a forced landing in a field at Maufant. The machine was only slightly damaged in landing, and although the pilot had to wait for a long time (over half an hour) for some Germans to appear to whom he could give himself up, he did not destroy it. It is said a farmer was asked for the necessary inflammables and either could not, or would not, oblige. It may be he had in mind the oft repeated death penalty threat. It is a pity the machine was allowed to get into Jerry hands practically intact.

November 26th 1942
There is a complete dearth of incidents to record, but the general exodus continues. Nearly every night troops, tanks and equipment are shipped away from town, and, if reports speak right, from St. Catherines and Ronez. I should guess there are fewer troops here than at any time since June 1940. Their general panic, with its six o'clock curfew, continues, and it pleases us greatly we are allowed out later than the troops. Instead of the bodies of 200/300 men, whom we used to see going route marching, our streets seldom are blessed with groups of more than 20 at a time, and other proofs of the reduced number have come in reports from the various provider departments.

DECEMBER 1942

December 1st 1942
During the course of my travels this evening I came across the Spitfire (less wings) which made a forced landing here, being taken quay-wards on a lorry.

It is named 'Chislehurst and Sidcup', and so is presumably one of the Spitfire fund machines. My travels were in connection with a heifer which is to give us and our friends a rattling good feed – but one has to pay for such a luxury these days, this one being considered cheap at 9/- a pound. I have not given overmuch space to the food question for some while, the reason being there has been precious little food to mention. For some months there have been no extra rations at all. It is only now the winter is approaching an occasional extra is forthcoming; with the result our diet has been even more vegetarian than usual. A secondary result has been a steady and continuous rise in black market prices.

A local man has been killed, and his sister badly injured, whilst trying to prevent a burglary at his house – believed to be by a Russian. The Russians, although officially our allies, are even more unpopular than our official enemies. We know they are deserving of our sympathy in that they have been brought hundreds of miles from home, have been ill clad, badly fed, and vilely treated by the German overlords. But the advent of some 2,000 of them has resulted in a state of affairs which may be not exaggeratedly described as a reign of terror in the west. They have been given some clothes from evacuated houses, but despite that it is necessary for clothes lines to be watched all the time on wash days. Never a night passes without several burglaries. Cattle food, seed potatoes, livestock and anything which they can lay their hands, are all considered fair game. A regular technique is for one or more to approach the front entrance and beg by signs for food, and so keep the householder engaged, whilst others enter the premises from another direction and pilfer whatever is portable.

At long last arrangements have been made for forwarding extra clothing to the poor devils who were transported from their homes to Germany. It is only from the third and last batch to leave news has been received. They were supposed to be housed in wooden huts somewhere in south west Germany but were expecting to be transferred to brick built quarters for the winter. Cooking is a communal arrangement, over which there appears to have been disagreement between Jersey and Guernsey women – even in extreme adversity, the two Islands, as always, must agree to disagree. It is a curious fact the two peoples, although of common stock and living so close together, are dissimilar just as if they were of different nationalities. Local talent has been recruited for entertainments in the camp, and, taking it full and bye, they seem to be making the best of a bad job, as we knew they would. Their continued courage, I'll bet, is giving Jerry an eye opener.

December 2nd 1942

The 6.00 p.m. curfew for the soldiers has been lifted, and there is greater animation in town of an evening than for some time past. Also there seems to be a fresh lot of troops, and more of them. I have seen one batch of several hundred route marching, and there are some storm troopers about. It is altogether more like the bad old days.

I failed to mention there are quite a few Russians at large, apparently having taken French leave from their camps. For some curious reason no effort seems to have been made to round them up until the recent tragedy made the matter imperative. It is popularly believed locally the many pilferings are at the instigation or at least with the permission of their OT masters. I can hardly see else how they would have the opportunities.

There have been many reports and rumours the Germans would be leaving here soon. In fact the first of the specified dates was today. Certainly the continual shipment of troops and equipment away from the place, the peculiar behaviour of the troops, and many little details have pointed to something out of the ordinary being in the wind. These rumours, in many cases, emanated from members of the German forces. According to these reports we are to be put under International Red Cross, who will arrange for our feeding and so forth, brought from France in a ship under the Jersey flag. A local defence force is supposed to be formed (presumably unarmed) to keep control over the Russian and other foreign labourers who would be left here. In mentioning these matters, I don't believe all I am told, but the matter has gained such credence, even amongst the usually better informed, I find it necessary, in the interest of accuracy to detail, to include a summary and gist of the thing. Even the fact each household is to have an extra cwt of coal for December (publicly stated to be thanks to the kindness of Feldkommandantur 515 in releasing it) is construed as extra evidence of their intention to depart soon.

December 6th 1942

A few minutes ago we were treated to the music of bombing in the neighbourhood, followed by the sound of a plane flying low. Searchlights made their usual ineffective sweeps, but the plane had almost gone from earshot before the heavy batteries sent up flak. The sound of bombing continues, so it looks as though our sleep may be disturbed tonight – all in a good cause.

No tobacco ration this week, or for an unknown period – the most that is promised is the possibility of a few cigarettes or cigars at Christmas. This, I take it, is a minor result of the occupation of North Africa from whence I fancy it came - something else to suffer in a good cause. I hear we were mentioned in a talk after the news a day or so back. Accurate details are hard to get, with listening being done in difficult conditions, but I gather the reference to those of us who remained was confined to a few platitudes. I am surprised, since Britain knows we have no radio, no leaflets have been dropped to keep us in touch with developments – not that it matters, for such things are liable to be a source of trouble, and it is amazing how quickly news travels. When there has been anything special, I have almost always found my efforts to pass it on to trusted friends have been wasted. .

December 7th 1942

A most exciting day so far; we were disturbed at about 2.00 p.m. by heavy explosions, and with my usual curiosity, I dashed out to see what it was. From the coast road, after wedging myself between the barbed wire and the concrete wall which has been built across the slip, I could see a convoy of 8 to 10 ships coming across St. Aubins Bay, though still well out. By this time no planes were in sight, but AA smoke bursts were still appearing in the sky over the ships. Closer inspection showed smoke was coming from at least two of the ships. As we watched (I had by this time been joined by most of the neighbourhood) one of them lifted her stern and quickly disappeared. Another of the ships was coming full speed for the harbour with smoke pouring from her, and sending out distress signals at the rate of two or three a minute. The curious part of this phase of the incident is, apart from much shouting before I reached the coast road, the four AA guns crews established on the green had shown no evidence of life at all. Someone coming past their quarters reported they were all in their shelters; tin hatted and in comfort, not even a look out being kept. Determined to be in at the death (we don't get enough excitement to be able to afford to miss any) I got into town as fast as my bike could be persuaded to go, and reached a vantage point in time to see the damaged vessel come into harbour. I should say she must have suffered a very near miss, for her bows were flattened in, and the AA gun platform was at a peculiar angle, with no sign of the gun itself. At least one corpse was laid on the hatches, and as she berthed one of the fast patrol boats came in and made fast alongside. From the two vessels at least 5 bodies were brought ashore by the cranes, as well as quite a number of scuttlers who had apparently been picked up out of the drink. Quite a crowd were there watching events, Germans with solemn interest, and we with many smiles and much rubbing of hands. Others who saw the affair from the heights overlooking the pier swear another ship was sunk. Certainly

I fancied smoke was coming from another, but was so engrossed in watching the one I knew was going, I could quite easily have missed the disappearance of the other, especially as all the ships were zigzaging all over the ocean and were well out, some 6/7 miles from us. Anyway, I will be content to claim only what I saw – one sunk and one damaged, and call it a most successful day. I was too late to see anything of the planes, which did not wait to confirm results, but the number of machines is variously given between 2 and 7 – a natural difficulty at that distance. I certainly think the number must have been small, judging by the short period of explosions, and the report they were dive bombed is true, as the guns did not seem to go into action till after the eggs had done their good work. The whole show took a very short time, not more than 10 minutes elapsing between the first signs of commotion and the up ending of the one which sank. Since then everyone is happier than if they had received an extra ration of bread. As usual with these little reminders of the existence of England, our guardians have another 'panic' on, very few being off duty, and double guards everywhere. Thus ends a show which I wouldn't have missed seeing for anything, and I'll bet it also ends the German habit of parking big convoys out in the bay. Like Oliver Twist, we shall go on asking for more, even though this interference with local sea transport may quite easily result in the temporary absence of some little luxuries, or even electricity if an oil barge should catch a packet. Whatever the consequences, it is worth it to have this direct evidence Jerry is not to be allowed to come and go at his pleasure. I have dearly longed and waited for just such a 'do' – may we get more and more between now and the time when we again see the Red Duster flying from ships in our harbour.

December 10th 1942

The RAF again visited the Island yesterday at about 9.00 a.m. and put paid to another ship off Corbiere. Another patrol boat entered the harbour bearing signs of the conflict. Six planes were in action on this occasion. Further confirmation has been forthcoming of the sinking of the second ship in Monday's 'do' – a brand new oil tanker barge; so the week's bag is 3 sunk and 2 damaged.

December 17th 1942

During the recent visits of the RAF, the guards in charge of Russian workers were apparently so worried about their own safety, many of the Russians escaped, and although some have since been rounded, many are still at large. One result has been a notice in the paper asking for public co-operation in locating these men and promising there will be no harsh punishment for them – which I doubt.

Last night's paper contained a reiteration of the threat of punishment, as published last January, for anyone refusing to supply goods or do work for the Germans, or to do it in such a way as to mar the purpose. There was also a notice about wireless sets, to the effect, knowing there are still sets in the Island, immunity from punishment is promised to anyone bringing theirs in before the end of the year. Thereafter, the punishment will be strictly imposed – fine, imprisonment, or in some cases death. So there is another score on which I have incurred the threat of the death penalty. As far as the immunity clause is concerned, knowing the Germans, I doubt it. Even if the offence were overlooked, it is pretty certain, once having got one's name into their black books, there would be a distinct probability of being yanked in for some other minor offence. Of those sets already taken, many have been bought already by German soldiers, using the threat failure to accept the offer of purchase will mean confiscation. A good number have already been confiscated without even informing their owners. Those who voluntarily wish to sell their sets have to sell to a specified dealer, who in turn must sell to Germans wishing to buy, thus removing the threat. A surprising number are selling, apparently believing they will be taken anyway, and therefore they might as well get what they can for them.

December 23rd 1942

There is to be an extended curfew on Christmas Eve, Christmas Day and Boxing Day till midnight, and on New Year's Eve and Day till 1.00 a.m., with corresponding extension of gas and electricity hours. A curious feature is the order has not been published in the press, but only posted at Parish Halls and Churches, as was the old custom. It is believed this is because the local paper gets checked after publication by a German censor in Paris.

Extra rations are even less than last year. A few sweets for the children, a small ration of cocoa, a quarter pound of chocolate for adults, coffee substitute, double oat flour, an extra four ounces sugar, plus a small ration of cheese represent the full extent of official expectations of our overeating. Not being content with that I have another half pig for us and our friends. Last year's worked out at about £45 for 236 lbs – this year's has meant an outlay of £57 for 110 lbs. God knows what price it will reach if this goes till another Christmas. By much digging around, I got this animal comparatively cheap, fifteen shillings a pound. We have not been much affected by Russians down our end of the world, but one was around on Monday begging – a huge chap, over six foot. One of our Germanite neighbours promptly ran to her friends for help (the fellow seemed quite harmless) and when I came along, one poor little soldier was holding the Russian at bay, and it looked as if his gun was likely to go off any second. Of the two, the German looked the more scared, the Russian being quite unmoved by the threatening rifle and refusing to move. A few seconds later another six soldiers came along with tommy guns, and after a short palaver, the Russian sauntered along with them – quite unconcerned. If such be a sample of the average Russian, I am not surprised we hear tales of German reluctance to go to the Eastern Front.

December 28th 1942

That's Christmas, that was – our third under Occupation - may it be the last. For ourselves, we have kept a long way above starvation level – despite the absence of fruit, sweets, nuts and Christmas pudding, it was still a time of over eating. I fancy that most people had quite enough to eat and made the best of things.

December 31st 1942

We had a small ration of fireworks at about 8.00 p.m. last night when the RAF favoured us with a brief 'pass over', followed a little later by the sound of bombing. No mention of the matter has been made on the news, so we presume it only to have been a small raid. This is the first night show for some time, and the first I have seen from the coast road, from whence it made a pretty sight. As usual, the searchlights wandered around aimlessly and failed to find their targets, whilst the guns just blazed away, distributing their ammo over the whole sky. The whole show lasted for very few minutes.

The Germans march in and soon become a familiar sight
around the island

A photo with some of the locals

At a bus stop in the Parade, St Helier

T. F. PIROUET & SON

PARKSTONE STORES,
UNION STREET, JERSEY.

Having been called up for active service. I beg to advise customers and the public in general that the Firm of T. F. PIROUET AND SON will be carried on with MR. P. LE SAUTEUR as Manager.

T. LE B PIROUET.

Prop. T. F. Pirouet and Son.

The *Evening Post* advert to advise that Phil will be managing the business and the business premises below

STATES OF JERSEY.
DEPARTMENT OF LABOUR

Requisition of Services by the Occupying Authority.

Under Article 52 of the Hague Convention, dealing with requisitions in kind and services, a demand has been made for the services of some 150 men and women. These services are required, under the Convention, to be of a non-military character, and an assurance has been given that these requirements will be observed.

It has also been agreed by the German Authorities that persons performing the services mentioned will be employed, as far as possible, in the Island. For the services requisitioned, the wages will be the same as those paid to men employed locally on construction work. If, however, some of the labour is temporarily required for work in another Island, a separation allowance of 25% will be paid in addition to the above. Again, men employed under this requisition will be supplied with the same rations as those supplied to nationals of the Reich.

This circular is being addressed to you, in order that you may ascertain if, from amongst your employees, any will be prepared voluntarily to offer their services for this work.

Will you kindly inform us by Friday next, March 26th, of the names, addresses and occupations of any of your employees who offer their services.

EDWARD LE QUESNE,

President.

19th March, 1943.

The notice sent trying to requisition staff for the Germans

186

Phil on his beloved motorcycle

His favourite lookout post
on top of the roof

Eine RM - **20** fr. Nº 20

STRAFE

für eine Ubertretung im abgekürzten Verfahren.

AMENDE

pour non observation des règlements de circulation (immédiatement exigible).

8/12/42 a reward for being
caught cycling two abreast

Der Militärbefehlshaber in Frankreich

The fine ticket for cycling two
abreast

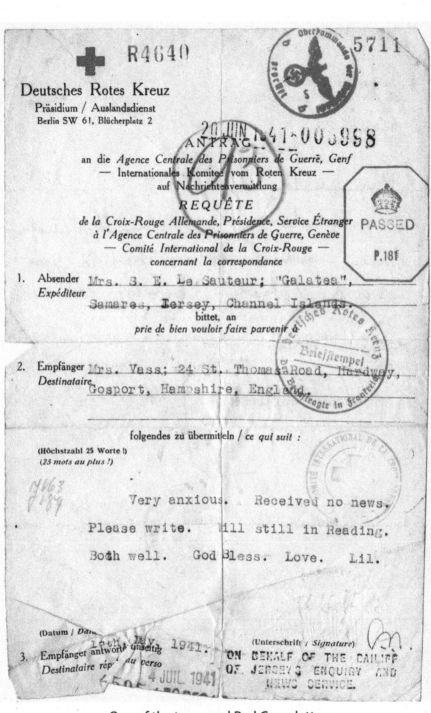

One of the treasured Red Cross letters

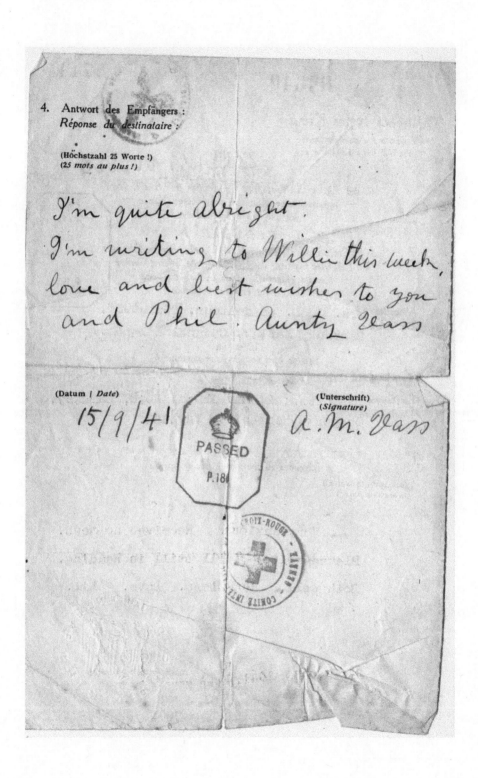

4. Antwort des Empfängers:
   Réponse du destinataire:

   (Höchstzahl 25 Worte!)
   (25 mots au plus!)

I'm quite alright.
I'm writing to Willie this week.
Love and best wishes to you
and Phil. Aunty Vass

(Datum | *Date*)

15/9/41

(Unterschrift)
(Signature)

A. M. Vass

PASSED
P.18

189

Phil and his mother's ID cards

INSTRUCTIONS FOR REPLY.

8 DEC 1941

TO ANSWER THIS MESSAGE:-

(a) You may write up to 25 words on the back of the enclosed form.   Place it
     in an envelope, addressed to:-

                    Comite International de la Croix-Rouge,
                         Palais du Conseil General,
                              Geneva,
                                   Switzerland.
     Mark your envelope clearly on the front "Red Cross Postal Message Scheme",
     and post it in the ordinary way.   (3d. stamp or 5d. Air Mail)

                              or

(b) Should you wish to keep this form you may go to a Red Cross Message
     Bureau which is generally at a Citizen's Advice Bureau, and have your
     reply copied on to another Red Cross form.   This will cost 1/-.

     NO ADDRESS MAY BE GIVEN WHEN REPLYING ON THE BACK OF THE ENCLOSED FORM.

     If you have changed your address, take or post the enclosed message to
your nearest Red Cross Message Bureau, which will despatch it and record your
new address for you.

     You should take a stamped (3d. stamp) envelope with you to the Bureau,
addressed as above (a).

     The address of your nearest Bureau can be obtained from the Post Office.

Instructions on how to reply to a letter

A red cross parcel sent to the family in 1945

Orginal copy

Kameraden,

Der von Hitler entfesselte Krieg geht seinem
Ende entgegen.
Amerikanische Truppen haben einen Brueckenkopf
auf dem rechten Rheinufer errichtet und sind
auf dem Vormarsch ins Innere Deutschlands.
Das OKW sieht keine Moeglichkeit mehr, den Ansturm
der Alliierten aufzuhalten, sie wollen den
ungleichen Kampf aufgeben, im Gegensatz zur
Nazifuehrung, die auch noch den letzten Deutschen
hingeschlachtet sehen wollen. Es ist nur noch
eine Angelegenheit von einigen Wochen, dann wird
der Krieg in Deutschland zu Ende sein.
Zu Ende?
Die Nazioffiziere der Kanalinseln sind fest ent-
schlossen, auch noch nach Beendigung des Krieges
in Deutschland die Inseln weiter zu halten, nur
um ihr armseliges Leben noch etwas zu verlaengern.
    Aber es wird soweit nicht kommen. Der Tag
der Abrechnung rueckt naeher. Schon kuenden
Braende und Explosionen, dass eine grosse
Opposition gegen den verrueckten Vizeadmiral und
seine wahnsinnigen Mithelfer vorhanden ist, bald
werden die ersten Nazileichen euch den Weg zeigen,
wo die groessten Verbrecher gegen die gesamte
Menschheit zu suchen sind.
Noch einmal ergeht unser Aufruf an Euch:
Organisiert den Widerstand, sprengt Munition,
brennt Unterkuenfte von Offiziern, die jetzt noch
den Nationalsozialismus verherlichen , ab, merkt
Euch gut die Nazis unter Euch, es wird keiner
vergessen.

Artillerie und Flak, wartet auf das Zeichen, es
kommt bald.
Infanterie und Marine, unternehmt keine Einzel-
aktionen, wartet auf das gemeinsame Signal.

Kein Nazi verlaesst diese Insel labend.
 Alle Kriegsverbrecher an den Galgen.

        Es lebe ein freies Deutschland.

Comrades.

The war let loose by Hitler is coming to its end. American troops have secured a bridgehead on the right bank of the Rhine, and are advancing towards the interior of Germany.

The German High Command sees no further possibility of halting the Allies. They wish to give up the unhappy struggle, in contrast to the Nazi Government who wish to see the last German slaughtered. It is now only a matter of weeks till the end of the war in Germany. The end ?

The Nazi officers in the Channel Islands are firmly determined to keep the islands even after the end of the war in Germany, if only to prolong their miserable lives. But things will not fall out thus. The day of reckoning is drawing nearer. Already fires and explosions show that there is great opposition to the crazy Vice-Admiral and his senseless assistants: soon the first Nazi corpses will show you what the greatest criminals against humanity have to expect.

Once more we summon you: -

Organise resistance, destroy supplies, burn the billets of officers who still glorify National Socialism, and note well the Nazis among you. None must be forgotten.

Artillery and anti-aircraft men: wait for the signal. It is coming soon.

Infantry and Naval men: Do not carry out isolated actions, but wait for the general signal.

No Nazi will leave the island alive.

To the gallows with all war criminals.

Long live free Germany.

The note calling the troops to mutiny

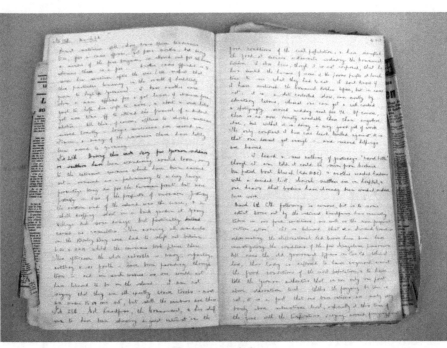

The original diary

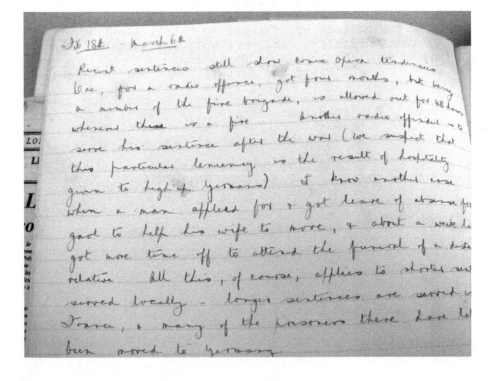

Fri 18th – March 6th

Recent sentences still show comic Opera tendencies. One, for a radio offence, got four months, but being a member of the fire brigade, is allowed out for 48 hours whenever there is a fire. Another radio offender is to serve his sentence after the war (we suspect that this particular leniency is the result of hospitality given to high up germans). I know another case when a man applied for & got leave of absence from gaol to help his wife to move, & about a week later got more time off to attend the funeral of a distant relative. All this, of course, applies to shorter sentences served locally – longer sentences are served in France, & many of the prisoners there have lately been moved to germany.

British troops retake control of the Island on 9th May 1945

A British troop escorts German prisoners of war to waiting boats

Sah ein Knab ein Röslein stehn....

A postcard found by Phil in a deserted German bunker days after Liberation

Phil and Nell Atkins' wedding day 3rd June 1948

Fred Hedouin, trusted Occupation friend and confidante,
Phil and mother Sarah

Fred and Georgina Crumpton, close friends deported to
Germany September 1942

Centenary of 'Pirouets' showing Amos Burt and Phil with
their Occupation building experiments circa 1960

Dad with Susan and Peter circa 1957

Brother Bill, Mum Sarah and Phil July 1967

Sand racing at St Ouen's Bay

CHANNEL REPORT
18th August, 1967.

A tragic boating accident on Wednesday claimed the life of a
popular Jersey resident.

Philip Frederick Le Sauteur was born at Southsea in 1911 and
came to Jersey in 1923. He leaves a widow, a son and daughter.

"Phil" Le Sauteur was well known in the islands both in business
and his hobbies. A quiet, man, he had a quick sense of humour, a
ready wit, and the ability to turn new acquaintances into
friends at the first meeting.

His voice was known to tens of thousands of visitors who never
saw his face by his commentating at sand reacing and hill climb
meetings of the Jersey Motor Cycle and Light Car Club.

He loved boats and fishing and he was elected Secretary of the
Bouley Bay Owners Association.

I remember best the closing statement he would make at each hill
climb. He reminded spectators that Bouley Bay was one of the
most beautiful bays in the island and asked them to leave it as
tidy and as beautiful as they found it.

Tragically it was from this bay of which he was so fond that
Phil Le Sauteur sailed for the last time, and now, Bouley Bay
and indeed Jersey will be a sadder and lonelier place without
him.

GY/DW

Verbatim copy of Channel Report, Channel TV August 1967

Phil commenting at sand racing event for Jersey Motor Cycle and
Light Car Club with companion Lady Coutanche 1960s

1943

JANUARY 1943

January 6th 1943

So to 1943, our year of great hopes. To summarise at the end of 2½ years of this everlasting Occupation, would be a waste of time. Conditions are much as they were at the end of 1941, except we are even shorter of what we always considered the necessities of life. My own problem at the moment is cycle tyres. In common with other people, my tyres have long since passed their best, and I am unfortunate in the few being brought from France are the wrong sizes. The last two long rides I made have both finished as long walks, one of 12 miles and one of 6 miles, followed by weary hours of sewing leather patches on dilapidated tyres.

1943 has not had a very auspicious start for our guardians. On Sunday a small convoy approaching the Island saw four planes approaching, and being ultra nervous since the recent RAF activity, opened fire and succeeded in shooting one down. Unfortunately, (for them) the plane was German, we presume to have been sent out as escort. This happened off La Moye. Then on Monday evening after dark a ship leaving here, believed to be the 'Schokland' struck a rock off Corbiere and sank immediately. The casualties are given differently by everyone who tells about it, but it seems those on board exceeded 300, whilst the rescued did not exceed 150. Certainly quite a few bodies have already been washed ashore here and equally surely the States have been ordered to arrange for the immediate supply of 175 coffins.

January 12th 1943

An RAF bomber passed about two miles to the south of the Island this morning, and every gun, heavy and light, went into action. As many of the shells were bursting over land, whilst the plane was well out to sea, I imagine the gunners' excited state of nerves defeated their aim. Apparently no hit was scored, and I am told by those who saw it the machine, still flying low, headed south.

Indefinite rumours have been rife about a further impending deportation. Those affected are said to include undesirable characters, men of military age, more English born, Freemasons, and, daftness of all daftness, Nonconformists. Light on the subject came with a special mail delivery on Saturday to those who had held commissions in the British Forces, requesting them to appear at the Feldkommandatur (Victoria College House) for interview. After individual questioning, they were given a sketchy medical examination (just the pulse felt) to decide whether they were fit for deportation to Germany, then told to watch the press for further instructions. I now hear some at least of those who have been in gaol for various offences have been notified to appear for a similar interview. Each of us is worried on his own behalf by this spate of rumour, which has at least some truth. In the case of the officers the option is being given as to whether the man takes his family with him to Germany.

January 13th 1943

One hears five only of the ex-commissioned officers have been warned to expect to go to Germany, undesirables are now being interviewed, as well as the leading lights of such secret societies as the Freemasons. What it all means possibly the next few days will show.

During the early hours of this morning, our AA batteries put in half an hour of sleep disturbing fire against the RAF – as usual with no results. Further details of the day visit on Tuesday, from several who were fortunate enough to see the incident, show the plane, said to be a Sunderland with American markings, approached the Island from the south east so low it had to rise sharply to clear South Hill, passing over the AA gun there. After proceeding westwards a little way, still low and travelling slowly, it headed out to sea. Whether on this excursion or on last night's visit I don't know, but it appears mines have been laid. Therefore the port has been closed to shipping for three days whilst sweeping operations are carried out. Jerry seems to believe the mines are close to the harbour, for the sweepers are this morning working between the Oyster and the Dogs Nest.

January 16th 1943

Local flak batteries were in action twice during last evening, and one could hear the melodious noise of heavy bombing in progress.

The interviews of prospective evacuees continued up to yesterday including retired officers, officials of 'secret societies' (Odd Fellows etc), undesirables and Jews. There seems to have been a high proportion of rejections - only 5 officers were selected as fit, and it is generally accepted the local German officials are against any further deportations (possibly in their own interests should they lose the war), and the whole scheme will flop. News is coming through from the last batches of deportees more freely now. They seem to have had a very thin time in the food line which is now to a great extent alleviated by regular and marvellous parcels sent by the British Red Cross, containing many items the taste of which requires a good effort of memory to us here.

January 25th 1943

In preparation for the building of a railway to the east of the Island, a number of people with their houses built on the site of the old Jersey Eastern Railway have had notice from the German authorities to quit. We have often heard rumours of this proposed railway, usually after surveying work has been done, but this is the first official news of their intention.

Flak was again in action two or three times during Saturday evening against the RAF en route for L'Orient'. With frequent doses of this and the sound of distant bombing, we get 20 times the evidence of the existence of the RAF to that of the Luftwaffe. It is only on rare occasions a couple of ME109s go round and round trying to kid themselves (and us) that they are whole squadrons.

Consequent on 'contagious diseases' (diphtheria and VD), all dances have been banned and children under 14 barred from the pictures. There is a good deal of diphtheria about, even amongst adults, whilst TB has grown to such proportions another hospital has had to be prepared and is already full.

It is only recently it was made an offence in Guernsey for foodstuffs to be sold at higher than controlled prices (I can't imagine why the German authorities, usually so hot on that sort of thing, didn't step in before).

FEBRUARY 1943

February 5th 1943

The Evening Post, for the umpteenth time in recent weeks, has ceased publications owing to shortage of necessary materials. Other local news is all those rejected by the German doctors as candidates for deportation to Germany have again been examined by another doctor, apparently sent specially for the purpose. It appears to us College House is anxious to accumulate evidence of their kindliness to offset the bad mark made against them last September, and hence the previous rejections on such a grandiose scale, apparently putting excuses on the candidates' lips. Whether because of professional etiquette or because the second doctors are of minor rank, it seems all the rejections have been upheld. After a lull of a few weeks, more people have been arrested for wireless offences and for passing on news. Like all other military offences, no publicity is given, so one can get no more reliable information than hearsay as to what punishment is implemented.

Last night's raid on Dorset was both audible and, incredible as it may seem, visible from here. Our local flak birds had quite a busy night, and wasted much valuable ammo trying to pick out one of the many aircraft which passed this way.

Even here the mourning for Stalingrad is in progress, and the Forum was closed on Wednesday evening when the order came through without completing the performance.

February 13th 1943

After several postponements, some 60/70 deportees were assembled yesterday afternoon at the Forum and later put aboard a ship. Once again the affair was postponed, and they have to present themselves today. These put-offs, one presumes, are mostly with the idea of breaking down their morale. This batch is comprised of 'undesirables' and the few Army officers not exempted (less one who committed suicide rather than go). The 'undesirables' are a mixed bag and includes habitual drunkards; a few serving sentences or waiting to be sentenced for civil crimes; a local dentist who let his feelings get the better of him and punched a German in the nose and who had to be restrained from repeating the performance at yesterday's gathering; several illicit wireless listeners; an indiscreet chap who used a camera and was seen by a German officer, another who, working in a German hotel, peeled the spuds too thickly (sabotage) and many others who in one way or another have offended against the myriads of petty regulations which hedge us in. There are a few going who insist there is no reason to their knowledge to account for being picked on – one presumes the pin method was used to make the requisite number.

There is ample evidence locally of the changing tide of events – all the younger OTs are being pressed into the Army, to their annoyance, and scuttlers are being given intensive military training, whilst the last few batches of arrivals have been 16/17 year olds, replacing the more mature men being taken away, one presumes and hopes, for Russia. All of which augurs well for the forthcoming invasion..

February 17th 1943

Recent blitzes on L'Orient have resulted in vibrations of such intensity to make it almost unbelievable we are over 120 miles distant, and last night, our gunners made one of their usual 'ineffectives' against passing aircraft. Even now, after nearly 3 years of constant disappointment, I am still hoping the RAF will get fed up with this constant pin pricking and will silence a gun or two.

Except for one or two comparatively modest attempts, there has been nothing much in the order line for some while. But the Evening Post of the

15th is a most awe-inspiring document, with death penalties, and gaol splashed all over the place. It covers a lot of ground already dealt with in the many orders it revokes – fresh provisions make VD a punishable offence, legalises the system of general confiscation as a punishment (rather late), and rather vaguely promises retribution for insults to a member of the occupying force, or one of its employees. The resemblance of our present life, in its unreality, to Alice in Wonderland, grows every week, and we have the parallel to the Queen's edict "off with his head" in the "off to Germany" which rewards such dire offences as breathing in when one should breath out.

February 20th 1943
More people, believed to be 'offenders' are being interviewed at College House, foreshadowing yet another evacuation. Further orders have been published relating to black out and lighting regulations, the only change being black out now extends from sunset to sunrise, instead of an hour after and an hour before.

In the last flak outburst, there appears to have been some miscalculation in the fuse timing of one of the shells, as two people whom I know, have seen one of the AA guns nicely opened out like the petals of a flower where a shell exploded prematurely. Rumour has it 10 of the guns crew were killed.

February 24th 1943
The practise of small fines for such heinous offences as cycling two abreast has been altered – now the culprit's Identity Card is taken and he has to apply to College House to get it restored. By this means one's name is obtained for the black list, probably as a future excuse for deportation. Another practise puzzling people, but probably in the same connection, is of taking ciné films from a car of any small group of people talking in the street. It is mostly surmise at the moment this is connected to deportation as, up to date, I know of no sequel to such incidents. I cannot imagine it to be entirely without purpose.

MARCH 1943

March 1st 1943
There was another small scale deportation last Thursday. 27 people went, including a few men and girls who volunteered to work in Germany; some more 'undesirables', some of whom assume their deportation to be due to their names being taken many months ago for cycling two abreast.

A new German order insists on us handing over our electric fires – they suspect (quite rightly) most people ignore the order banning their use. We in our turn suspect they prefer to pinch our fires to getting some from Germany. Of interest is a States appeal to those having excess stocks of potatoes to sell to the States as present stocks, it states, will only last till April, between which time and June the Island will have to go without spuds. I am amazed at how nearly self supporting the Island has become. I learnt today from an Agricultural Inspector we grew about 2,800 tons of wheat last year, against our requirements for rations of 3,500 tons – a far smaller deficit than I would have believed possible.

The RAF sustained activity, whilst not including us in the schedule, has been heard and felt, and our lads passed low last night on their way to and from St. Nazaire. Except for two isolated shells they were allowed to pass unhindered.

Our friends have been going around to shops enquiring as to numbers of employees and hours worked. One presumes this to be in connection with the general mobilisation of labour going on all over Europe. Presumably to trace sources of pilfering, some people have been stopped in the streets and questioned as to where they got the petrol in their lighters – which makes us laugh. A third spot of unpleasantness is during the last few weeks German lessons have become compulsory in all schools for elder children, certain of the local teachers having taken the necessary course in the lingo.

March 13th 1943

Arrangements are quietly being made for a 3 day 'curfew'. Those engaged on essential services (gas, electricity, water), will have to stay on the job, and the only ones allowed out between certain hours will be milk and baker rounds men. These are being issued with special permits. The rest of us will perforce have to stay indoors and twiddle our thumbs. The reason for this is obviously connected with invasion, and is apparently an aftermath of the recent visit of upwards of a 100 'high ups'. But the real intentions in the matter are a matter for surmise. It may be the 3 day curfew will be used for full scale anti-invasion exercises, or more probably, the curfew is intended to operate in the emergency of a real invasion. There are two alternatives to this latter, too. The 3 days may be considered ample for completely repelling all invasion attempts, or may be in order to evacuate the military and equipment from the Island without the probable sabotage interference from the civil population. Time will show which of these conjectures is correct.

March 19th 1943

In contradistinction to the optimism of the New Year, a pessimistic wave seems to have spread over the Island. 9 out of 10 people one speaks to believes there will be no invasion this year and we have another winter of occupation. The more confirmed of the dismal jimmies see 3 or 4 years more. Although I have not joined the ranks of the doubters, I must admit to a state of severe depression – so bad indeed I stayed away from work for a day just because I felt that way. I know one's mental and physical resistance is normally about its lowest ebb this time of year, and one also has to allow the aggravation of this being our 3rd Occupation winter, with a steadily decreasing amount of food in one's belly. A subsidiary cause of the deep depression is the mental agony of never knowing whether it will be your turn next. Recently a clergyman, his wife and daughter were caught and sentenced for news distribution, and another case now under inquiry has resulted in quite a few being held in custody. Altogether getting on towards 50 people have been questioned in connection with the affair, which started with the grave digger at St. Saviours being caught copying out the news. Now, several prominent people, including the Deputy and the Acting Rector are in gaol. The result of this is people have become extra careful about telling the news. This week's meat ration won't help either – there just isn't any. One is constantly hearing we should be without, but until this week supplies have always arrived just in time.

March 23rd 1943

For the first time in weeks, our local flak went into action 3 times last night against not very high flying aircraft. These are about the first planes, German or British, we have heard for quite a while. There is a notable decrease in the barrage put up now, compared with last year. I should say not more than 6 to 10 heavy batteries were in operation last night, and I am sure that at one time we had full 100 AA guns of various types – and all went into action at the least possible excuse.

March 29th 1943

No meat ration again this weekend, though some is promised for next. Our 'in lieu' ration this week was a tin of tunny fish, which is just about as good as the 4 ounce meat it replaced – not like last week when 2 ounces of smelly Camembert cheese was the alternative. However, a pig obligingly lay down and died in time for this weekend, so we and our friends have done quite nicely thank you.

APRIL 1943

April 14th 1943

An RAF machine made a forced landing in the sea off Corbiere early Sunday morning. Local AA batteries had a smack at her, but apparently had nothing to do with the destruction of the plane. The crew bailed out, and were picked up, one dead, 2 injured (now in our local hospital) whilst the pilot was quite OK. But we don't need this extra reminder our pals spend quite a lot of time in the district. There is regular aural evidence of their activity.

The new eastern railway proceeds at high speed – not because the Russian workers are rushin (pun) but because so many are on the job. Three miles have been prepared to receive the tracks, following the course of the defunct railway, but deviating where necessary to avoid knocking down houses. To date, nothing worse than walls and trees have suffered, but as they approach town it becomes unavoidable. There seems some indecision which way they will run it, several people turned from their houses at short notice have been told they can go back. I am no engineer, but the new line being prepared doesn't look safe to me. Crossing fields the top 6 inches of soil is moved and the sleepers laid on the ground – no hard core foundation is put in. At Pontac slip, where lines leave the original track and come along the road, the necessary embankment to ease the gradient is made just from sand brought from another part of the track. A good wind or a heavy shower of rain could easily shift it.

At a States sitting reported in last night's E. P. after quoting a deficit of nearly £3m, it was announced yet another registration would take place, this time of men from 16 to 50 and single women from 18 to 35. It was emphasised the measure is solely a civil one, although it bears a striking resemblance to conscription measures all over the occupied territories, and follows so closely on the appeal by the States for volunteers to work for the Germans. Regarding that appeal it seems to have been met easily in the case of the women, who are eager for every opportunity to get into contact with the Greenfly. In the case of men, the requisite number were rounded up from the Labour Department and ordered to present themselves to the Germans who kindly informed them, whilst they could not be forced to work for the Germans, if they were ordered to do so they could not refuse. Which sounds to me heads I win, tails you lose? From what one can gather of this latest order it seems to design sufficient labour for the essential services (harvesting etc). I fancy it may also entail civilian guard duties against our Russian allies who, brought hundreds of miles from home and left with little food, are pinching all they can. They are so 'adequately' fed they grab amongst the potato plants and eat the half rotten seed raw.

I mentioned earlier many people are parting with their £1 English notes for 30 to 34 shillings worth of marks. They cannot see further than the end of their noses – first, in making 10 to 14 shillings profit, they are putting themselves and the Island 30 to 34 shillings in debt, by parting with what will have tangible worth in exchange for a currency which will buy nothing except in Jersey, and will therefore be a liability as soon as this comes to an end.

The trial by Court Martial of the offenders in the recent wireless case was held in the Royal Court in camera, but in some cases local Advocates were employed for the defence. After appeal the 16 accused were given sentences between one month and 3 years. Incidentally all those who are now completing sentences in France are being transported, with their families, to Germany. Two elderly ladies involved in the above radio case have had their sentences deferred until after the War.

April 27th 1943

For several weeks little in the way of vegetables have been available, owing to a new Jerry dodge of waylaying farmers on their way to market and commandeering all their loads except for swedes and maybe a few leeks.

Two developments of the recent order passed in Court - firstly, the lack of response to the appeal for volunteers has resulted in the Germans doing a comb out of the building trade, taking some from each firm for work in Alderney. They are due to go today, though I do not know how many are involved. The second event is, in St. Clements Parish at least, the area where Russians are working is patrolled by 3 civilians (it seems we all have to take a turn at a 6 hour stretch) to prevent the Russians going off from their work on begging expeditions. We are also expecting to have to do night shifts guarding the new camp being built for them at the top of Grouville Hill, but to date that is rumour.

April 28th 1943

Another spasm of air activity started about 5.30 p.m. yesterday when about a dozen planes descended on a convoy approaching from Granville. I unfortunately missed seeing the incident, which offered a grandstand view to those lucky enough to be at a good vantage point. It seems two ships were sunk in St. Aubins Bay, one of them carrying 800 tons of coal for Guernsey, whilst a 3rd sank in the harbour after being helped in by tugs. A 4th is also believed to be damaged. 3 of Guernsey's buying commission in France were aboard one of the vessels which was left out of the bombing but which received a share of machine gunning – fortunately they suffered no casualties. Ambulances were busy during the evening bringing up wounded and killed – the latter, according to all accounts, seems to reach quite nice proportions. Also last night, more planes passed quite low, presumably on the mine laying operations mentioned in the news. 10 minutes after their engines faded into the distance our flak guns let go a few rounds.

MAY 1943

May 1st 1943
Curfew goes back to 11.00 p.m. tonight. Shaky writing is due to excitement – an RAF fighter has just passed over town quite low, the first I have seen for some time. AA batteries went into action, but the smoke puffs appeared a long way from the plane – hardly surprising in view of the terrific speed at which the plane was travelling when I saw it. I fancy our audacious friend did some machine gunning in the harbour area. Tame spies tell me Mont Orgueil Castle, used as an observation post, was machine gunned Thursday afternoon, whilst a barge loaded with horses was sunk off Gorey. Also last night one of the barges leaving here was machine gunned off Corbiere and had to put back pronto to bring in casualties. May the blitz continue – we love it. A show like this afternoon's makes my eyes shine more than a whole case of bubbly.

May 4th 1943
Saturday's excitement has, as usual with such events, brought much conflicting evidence, but it appears an RAF bomber and a few fighters passed en route to or from L'Orient. They apparently shot up a big ship laying in the roads and some of the flak positions which opened fire at them. An ME109 came up from the Airport and joined in the fun, but I gather there were no casualties amongst the aircraft engaged, but I don't admire their choice of battle ground for a dog fight – about 200 feet above the town.

There are many rumours about reduction of the bread ration (they started before Jerry found the excuse of British interference with supplies). The position is as follows. We grew about 2,800 tons of wheat last year towards our annual need of some 3,500 tons on present rations. This local stuff is only now being used, so there is ample till this year's harvest comes in, hence no reason for the States to consider reduction, which would come as a real hardship to all. It is said the proposal, or rather order, came from the Germans, who want the basic ration to be 2 lbs 10 ounces, or 2 lbs 12 ounces a week, instead of the present 4½ lbs. The report says our States stood on its hind legs and threatened first, resignation and then to take the matter to the International Red Cross at Geneva. Rumour continues the unwelcome publicity which would be entailed, deterred the Germans from pressing the matter.

May 8th 1943

In town today is a mixture of pleasure and chagrin. The former is at the news of the fall of Tunis. People are so delighted about the good news as to be terribly indiscreet in openly discussing it. The chagrin is the natural result of the reduced bread ration which comes into effect forthwith. It is a sad blow to all, for I know of no-one who has hitherto found their bread sufficient, especially on occasions when jam is issued. Although it is a matter of discomfort to us, and could mean something approaching starvation to people already under nourished, there is general optimism our days of occupation are getting well towards the end.

The same German police who were responsible for rounding up the Guernsey police some while ago have been active here. No details have been published, and one has to make due allowance for the rumour mongers licence, but it seems lightning raids on certain premises by these police have revealed quantities of sugar, the import of which, by underground channels, has been one of the biggest money making rackets of all. Some 20 civilians had sugar confiscated and were released after questioning – they hope to hear no more, which I doubt. Three tons were found in one butcher's premises. As the price to the consumer was about 16/- to the lb, this represents considerable money. I gather the raid was carried out primarily to get at the Germans who were at the head of the racket. Many of their sailors, including some of the higher nobs of the German Harbour Commandant's staff, are under arrest. It is said some of the Feldgendarmerie were involved. Whether or not true, it is a fact there is more graft in the German forces generally then one would consider possible.

RAF fighters passed this way low about 7.30 this forenoon and apparently shot up the patrol boats stationed at intervals around the coast, for casualties were being brought ashore from one of them later in the day. Rumour has it one of them was sunk off Corbiere, but there is no confirmation. Owing to the difficulty of getting authentic facts about all these happenings, my epistle would be more sketchy if I did not take the rumours into account and accept those which fit in with known details and common sense.

There are numerous indications of greater expectation of bother in the future. A high up flak General has been staying at Lady Trent's place. Before his arrival the house was subject to a tooth comb search, presumably for time bombs. Whilst he has been here, a solitary Heinkel has been circling the Island during the day – to keep away the RAF I suppose. Big convoys of ships have arrived on several evenings, and many big HEs and aerial torpedoes have arrived, so it appears possible the extensive work which has, and still is, being put in at the Airport will be justified. Also today's EP contains lengthy orders relating to black out, fire precautions etc. So we may well expect sparks to fly before too long.

The black market sugar racket seems to be an extensive affair. The stuff has been brought from France in German patrol boats, showing connivance in high quarters. This sort of money making graft seems quite common, and I have had cognac and tobacco which I know to have come from members of the Feldgendarmerie. Those involved in the racket have so far not been arrested, and it makes one wonder whether the repercussions of the affair reach so high and involve such officials as to merit it being hushed up.

May 17th 1943

Mock invasion exercises were carried out last evening around the piers and the Esplanade, to our amusement. When about 2.00 a.m. planes in great numbers started passing over, some high and some low, I started to wonder whether the real thing had come, especially when several light AA batteries opened up. I got up and went into the garden, and could actually see some of them in the moonlight, but the AA fire had caused the indiscreet to show their lights, proving them to be Germans. Later news shows them to have been en route for South West England and Wales. Rumour has it one was shot down in St. Aubins Bay, and whilst I can't confirm it, one of the low fliers certainly stopped his motor abruptly. For the next 12 days local flak is going to practise against aerial targets – 3 hours every morning and afternoon. We are warned to get indoors if shrapnel starts falling in the vicinity – that could quite easily be too late.

After the hurried laying of a gas main to the electric power station, followed by a delay, part of our electric supply is now being produced by gas plant, with the result gas is sometimes left turned on at the verboten hours, to everyone's great joy. The gas hours have again been altered, and the supply is now available from 7.30 a.m. to 3.00 p.m. and from 5.00 p.m. to 8.00 p.m. I am afraid the illicit use of gas will soon cease, as one hears it is intended to extend the special main laid from Rouge Bouillon to the Power House and make it independent of public supply.

May 22nd 1943

Some RAF activity early this morning, which may be connected with the pleasant sight which greeted my eyes as I came to work, of a ship of some 2/3,000 tons perched on a rock off Noirmont.

I am getting considerable trouble with my eyes – lack of some vitamin or other, I suppose. But I consider myself lucky to have suffered so little compared with others, although I have never hesitated to spend money in order to prevent malnutrition, as far as my pocket and available goods allow. I have spent considerably more than my earnings, especially the last 6 months, when the need has been greater and the prices higher as well as opportunities being more frequent.

May 26th 1943

Noirmont is now lit, in addition to the Greve D'Azette and Le Hocq lights, when shipping is about – a victory for Jersey's rocks, for it worries our friends to have lights on, though it would worry them still more to use daylight. They have also adopted a hitherto scoffed at British idea of barrage balloons on their ships. The first two ships wearing them came in over the weekend, but as usual Jerry was unlucky with his weather. Heavy winds blew one amongst barbed wire with which our piers are so liberally decorated, whilst the other got tangled up in a crane, and had to be shot down – exit two new balloons.

JUNE 1943

June 5th 1943

The dreaded Colorado Beetle has put in an appearance, probably brought with potatoes imported from France. It is a matter of some wonderment we have been so long free, when one compares the elaborate precautions taken before the Occupation and the complete lack since. Farmers have to spray with arsenate of lead.

Those working for the Germans were supposed to wear a white armlet with the inscription (in German) 'on duty for the German Army', but I gather there has been a general refusal so far.

The body of a British Airman has been washed ashore here and was due to be buried from the hospital at 7.30 a.m., but after some hundreds of us had got up early, the event was postponed. It was said another body had come ashore, and both are to be buried tomorrow (Sunday). It may be fear of a demonstration made them bury him like Sir John Moore – 'quietly, at dead of night'.

June 7th 1943

The double funeral of Sergeant. D. C. Butlin (547514) and Sergeant A. Holden (597390) took place yesterday. Despite it being at 7.00 a.m. and half an hour before the time unofficially given, many hundreds were outside the hospital, and again outside the cemetery to pay their respects and something in the neighbourhood of 200 wreaths, mostly red, white and blue were sent. The Germans gave them a military funeral, with Union Jacks over the coffins, and a firing party. Four civilians were mourners, the coffins being borne by flak men of the Luftwaffe. I must give credit to the Germans for being decent about this show, showing their respect and allowing us to show ours even to the extent of red, white and blue flowers. The public were not allowed into the cemetery during the internment, but were able to file round the graves and lay their flowers later. The service was carried out by the Dean and a local chapel preacher, and they even left the control of the public in the hands of the local police, although their own Gendarmerie were there if there had been any demonstration or trouble.

June 10th 1943

Invasion mania goes on – several anti invasion exercises have been held, and on Tuesday there was an alarm which brought the Wehrmacht on its toes and made us laugh. There seems to have been a decided thinning out of troops and I gather departures during recent weeks have considerably outnumbered arrivals.

Following on from enquiries made amongst larger shops a few weeks ago as to numbers of employees and hours worked, the Germans have selected a few men and women from each shop who, it seems, are expected to work for them. Another German activity, which causes some doubt as to their intentions, is the search of bank safe deposits. The reason is ostensibly to 'freeze' gold bullion, raw diamonds etc. which might be used on black market. I fancy they won't find much. Fortunately the banks were prompt about sending to England all securities at the first sign of impending bother, or our friends might have had the equivalent of some millions of pounds worth of foreign currency.

I draw attention to the German's invasion mania, but must admit there is an almost parallel state of nerves amongst civilians. After 3 long years – a longer period than even pessimists forecast – and with no concrete reason (except hope) to expect an early release, we are all getting to the end of our tether. Tempers are more easily frayed as month follows month, and the various dates forecast for our release pass. Fortune telling in various ways has secured a much bigger hold on peoples' minds than ever before. One method of spelling out answers to questions by means of a glass on a polished surface has become quite a craze. This latter gag does really work, and some remarkable answers have been 'received' by it, though I would not like to lay money on its accuracy. With few exceptions it does seem to spell reasonable answers. The first questions asked are always – the date of the invasion, our release, and the end of the War. Whilst the answers are not always the same, the usual replies are June, July, and October respectively.

When, nearly 3 years ago, I started writing this epistle, I never expected it to develop into such a book as it has. Even if no-one else ever reads any of it, it has served a useful purpose to me in giving me occupation, as well as being a source of reference whenever there has been any argument as to an order or a date. Possibly when I grow old and have grandchildren (if ever I get spliced and have children first) I will want to refresh my own memory before spinning them the yarn.

June 12th 1943

This week opens with the news of another panic. Everything was normal at 7.00 p.m. yesterday, but by 7.30 p.m. all Germans had been roped in from cinemas, cafes etc. and sent to battle stations. Freed of meandering soldiers, the town represented a more lovely sight than I have seen for many moons. This morning things were 'normal' again. I don't know what lies behind these panics – rumour naturally gets busy with reports of Commando raids – Cherbourg and Calais were mentioned but there is no sort of confirmation.

June 15th 1943

Another little panic Sunday evening – it seems to be quite a game they are playing at. I only hope these false alarms happen so often that, when the real thing comes, they will think it is only one of these 'phoney' rackets.

A German flying boat picked up a British airman in the region of the Paternosters reef, after he had been afloat in a rubber dinghy for some days. He is presently in the General Hospital suffering from the effects of his ordeal – another of the incidents to which Jerry gives no publicity, but which become public knowledge in very few hours.

June 19th 1943

We had a double potato ration this week, thanks to Jerry returning with those they shipped away, neighbouring French ports being closed. Nothing exciting seems to be happening, unless you call frequent artillery and flak practises of importance. Our RAF friends seem to have left us alone, so we become more and more browned off with this uncomfortable state of affairs. If only we knew just how long we had to wait, we could tick off days and weeks. Our hopes are all centred in the near future, with an oppressive background of fear that maybe after all we have an unconscionable time to wait.

Our wireless sets, confiscated over a year ago, are being taken away from the Island. This is despite the repeated statement the sets would be returned to their owners as soon as the military need ceased to exist.

New laws to stop black market meat trade have been recently introduced, and certainly complicate matters somewhat. I imagine the order must be at the instigation of the Germans, for it is to my certain knowledge some at least, and probably nearly all, States members get black market meat whenever the opportunity offers. Actually the new law leaves quite a big loophole in the case of pigs, but I don't quite see how we can get around it in the case of heifers. Hitherto, the farmer was allowed to have the heifer providing he killed it within 14 days. By a bit of wangling, this was stretched to 3 or 4 weeks and quite a useful amount of meat became available. In a way I am hardly sorry – being convinced of the need for such extras during the winter, and being in such a state of mind as not to worry about money, I have since Christmas spent more money on food then I have earned, despite the fact, in the case of meat, mine doesn't cost as much as most folks. Now summer has come, it doesn't matter as much, but, in partnership with my radio shop pal, we had a hectic 6 months handling 13 heifers and 4 pigs, a few odd pieces and some butter. I only hope next winter there won't be the need to indulge in under cover rackets. Naturally, I will stop all black marketing as soon as our friends leave.

June 29th 1943

Contrary to early days, when a 5 minute infraction of the curfew order if caught out resulted in a few days in gaol, no notice seems to be taken of it now. In view of the increased possibilities of invasion, one would expect an increased number of patrols about at night, but it is a long time since we heard any around our way and longer still since I heard of anyone being caught for curfew infraction. We in the country have become increasingly careless about it, and I believe even in town it is common for civilians to be about at 11.30 p.m. On Sunday at about 11.30 p.m. mother and I came face to face with two flak blokes (not on patrol duty) but they said nought. As a matter of fact, the 11.00 p.m. curfew also applies to them except if they are on patrol or sentry duty, so maybe they couldn't very well do anything about us being out.

JULY 1943

July 3rd 1943

July 3rd is the commencement of the 4th year of Occupation. The occasion was marked by a special edition of the 'Deutsche Inselzeitung' and an inspired editorial in the local press about how kind our friends have been during the past 3 years compared with what they might have been. Maybe they could have been even worse than they have been, but they have done plenty to earn my perpetual enmity and that of most people. I entered on this lousy period with an open mind, prepared to find propaganda tales were just propaganda, but gradually it has been borne in on me just what a rotten crowd Germans are. Polite – oh yes, polite alright, which virtue is construed by many to mean they are nice people. I prefer to judge by the many broken promises and guarantees, by their unconstitutional treatment of many minor offenders, by the taking of everything of value, including radios, our one small comfort, rather than by their superficial politeness. Also to celebrate this 3rd anniversary of this, their first and last 'conquest' of British soil, there has been a big parade of troops about town this forenoon, with bands. This culminated in a march past in the Parade of some thousands of troops (more than I thought were in the Island), hundreds of horses, guns and everything else. I did not go to see it, though some of the procession passed me in Bath Street, but I am told the march past took 25 minutes. Dr. Goebbels's fixing of invasion day for today (per radio) does not seem to have been taken seriously by the local High Command – maybe they too are discovering how truthful the good man is.

July 10th 1943

Although we have recently had no evidence of RAF or surface craft activity in these waters, 5 minesweepers have been busy for 2 nights on the outer part of St. Aubins Bay. Judging by the many loud explosions, their efforts were most necessary. It is curious the sweeping should have been done at night with the aid of searchlights. With few exceptions, ordinary shipping only moves at night now, but one would imagine, both from the point of view of mines and planes, minesweepers would find it better to work by day.

I have been trying without success to get a copy of the 3rd anniversary edition of the Deutsche Inselzeitung. I had sight of one and it contains an order from the Military Commandant, Major General Graf Von Schmettow, referring to the Islands as the outpost of the German Empire which must be held to the last man, and comparing the resistance which must be offered to that at Stalingrad.

July 13th 1943

Local flak units had their first bit of active work for a long time in the early hours of this morning, putting up a heavy dose for the benefit of some of our RAF friends in the neighbourhood.

An order has been issued banning all public assemblies; the reason being is the still prevalent diphtheria. As this is not as bad as previously, and as they are not doing the obvious thing as a preventative by closing schools, most people believe it to be just another bit of nastiness to stop what little pleasure we still have.

The French Red Cross sent a present of 1 lb of biscuits to all children in the Island, received with grateful thanks by those who get them. The women are registering their usual moan – men get their regular tobacco ration and children a treat of chocolate, whilst they get nought and have the most difficult task of all in providing meals out of nothing.

I hear, together with a few recently convicted for such offences as robbing from the Germans, several people connected with offences against the occupying troops (not the accused themselves) have been taken to France or Germany at short notice. One case in particular is Advocate Ogier, whose son was found to be taking notes and sketches of all the fortifications here. Father and son were tried in Paris, the father later being allowed to return whilst the son remained.

The Germans had a great round up of curfew breakers this week and got about 30 people who were after mackerel which, regularly at this time of year, swarm around the bay at Archirondel on the evening tide. For a few evenings, fishing had been going on there till later than 11.00 p.m. often watched by the Germans stationed in the vicinity. Such a state of affairs was too good to last, and I understand the unfortunates suffered at the rate of a mark for every minute over time.

July 19th 1943

On Saturday evening the Gendarmerie visited various cafes in town, and took the identity cards of the civilians, ordering them to be at College House yesterday (Sunday) forenoon to get them back. Quite what lies at the back of this sudden raid I can't imagine, unless it is to make a list of people sufficiently friendly towards the Germans to fraternise with them at cafes. Our friends seem to love statistics on all sorts of odd subjects.

July 21st 1943

Further information about the raid on cafes - apparently it is part of an intensive campaign to try to cut down VD. All females rounded up in the cafes were taken to the Merton, the German Hospital, and examined for VD. Rumour has it some 20 of the 150 or so examined had it.

Another wireless case was tried a day or two back. Quite a few were involved, accused of having a set and listening or disseminating news. Sentences from 21 months to 14 days were imposed, but the culprits (or victims, depending how you look at it) are still allowed free, there being no room in gaol for them yet. No doubt they will be called at a moment's notice a later. Unless as we hope, the Germans here receive an urgent message from Adolf the real invasion has started, and all hands are wanted elsewhere. Another victim of this mass trial, was a man who preached a sermon to a girl he had known all her life, and who had been going out with Germans although her husband was in the British Army. He got 6 months.

A case for a future Court Martial, likely to prove disastrous to the offenders, concerns 5 men who have been accumulating German rifles, ammo and gelignite in a shed in Pier Road, presumably for when it may prove possible to use them against the Germans. I don't know how they managed to get hold of the stuff, but there must have been considerable daring and ingenuity to get the considerable quantities they did. The crowning piece of bravado was a notice on the shed –'Entrance forbidden – by Order of the Feldkommandant'. Probably they hoped any section of the Wehrmacht would suppose it to be the work of another Department, and leave it alone.

Everyone is most amused at the latest batch of boots for the Army which were taken into the German stores (late Woolworths) a day or two back. Surely it must be a decided sign of shortage these are fitted with wooden soles, especially as hitherto German Army boots have always been one of the best parts of their equipment. I wouldn't mind having a pair of jack boots for motor cycling when this is all over. A friend of mine the other day had the pleasure of watching a German soldier fall asleep in a horse carriage at the F.B. fields after removing his boots for greater comfort. Some kids, with their eyes and wits about them, took the opportunity of pinching his boots. I am amused to see quite a few civilians going around in German jack boots. It is possible these may have been salvaged in one or other of the low water visits to the S/S 'Diamande' which still lies on the Dogs Nest.

This is only one of many contrasts with the Germany Army of 2 to 3 years ago. When first they came, they commandeered 30 horse power Fords and other big Yank cars in sufficient numbers for just about all the officers. Later they were allowed nothing bigger than 14 horse power. Now, it is only the very important ones who have cars, and I think the Feldkommandant himself is the only one with a big wagon, whist the Military Commandant (Befelshaber) uses an M.G. Midget. Most other officers have to use horses, cycles, or their big flat feet. In transport the Army has to use more and more horses. It is no exaggeration to say they have thousands of horses here, and latterly many of them have been driven by local commandeered labour. Almost all the lorries the Army use are adapted to charcoal gas. The consumption of petrol must be small indeed. I mustn't exaggerate about the officers' transport – a few have little 'pipsqueak' motorbikes to run around on. The OT, more favoured than the Army, seems able to get petrol in sufficient quantities to keep plenty of vehicles on the road. Whilst on the subject of transport, our new eastern railway is completed but has never been used except for shifting earth as required in its own construction. An engine and a few trucks have been left unmoved at the Dicq for over a month. When I say it is complete, it doesn't yet link up with the western railway, there having been considerable trouble with collapses in the tunnel which is to run from La Collette to the Victoria Pier. Maybe it will be used if ever it connects with the harbours, but we are amused a separate pair of rails is being laid for the astern (2' 3") alongside the western line (3'), instead of laying an idler line between.

29th July 1943

Having reached the point of being short of every mortal thing, we sometimes discuss what we would take first of the many amenities and luxuries we previously took for granted. My own choice runs in the direction of a bath with real soap giving lather. Except for those fortunate souls who still have a stock of pre-war soap, none of us have had a real wash for ages. The stuff we get called toilet soap has a gorgeous smell (for them as likes it), but being made with whiting and pumice powder, it gives no lather at all. One craves too for something sweet to eat, though no doubt most of the pre-war confections would make us very sick. Food features largely on the horizon of the future when we can again choose a bit. Greasy concoctions like fish and chips are high on the list. I look forward eagerly to the day when I can have my motorbike on the road again, but meanwhile my idea of heaven includes a pair of bike tyres with a reasonable chance of not requiring constant sewing and patching. A great proportion of spare time is used this way. Although I have never taken a great interest in clothes, I find after 3 years of nothing new and gradually getting shabbier, I really would appreciate a new outfit. When one comes down to it there is nothing which we do not want, and little we do not badly need.

In the small hours of yesterday morning, the big guns in St. Brelades' area opened up to seawards at a British destroyer which was some 8 miles out. No doubt fearing invasion, a general alarm brought tanks and everything else out, but apparently it was part of the Navy's little 'do' against minesweepers mentioned on today's news.

At one today our heavy flak had their biggest outing since the night of the St. Nazaire raid. Planes were passing by the score for about 20 minutes and shrapnel from AA was falling just like the first heavy drops of a thunder shower. No searchlights were used, and despite the intensity of fire, it fortunately did no damage to our pals. But the funny thing is no mention was made on the news of any activity around this way, neither did the planes return this way.

AUGUST 1943 TO OCTOBER 1943

August 3rd 1943
Bread rations have gone back to the old basic 4½ lbs, with 6 lbs for manual workers, which is a relief. The official reason given is there has been no enemy interference with the food supplies of the Islands since rations were cut; so we may expect to be cut down again next time a ship is sunk in these waters. It was emphasised at the time of the cut it was not intended as a reprisal against us for RAF activity. If it isn't just that, I would like to know what it is. With a bit more bread and some local tobacco available one is able to be more cheerful.

August 7th 1943
Heavy flak batteries went into action during the forenoon, as usual without results, and a few minutes later the pompoms on the pier had a go. But the plane must have been pretty high. I only faintly heard their engines about midway between the two outbursts of firing.

August 13th 1943
I thought we were in for excitement yesterday afternoon when flak let go a few rounds. Being Thursday, I was home and able to dash on to the coast road in time to see a couple of planes, probably fighters, disappearing southwards.

Several ships were crossing the bay, outward bound, and I was disappointed they were left unmolested.

Another series of some 20 arrests have been made in another wireless case. Or rather I should say 20 interviews were held, the gaol being always overfull, and often not able to take those sentenced. As none of us has a chance in a million of decamping from the Island, it is pretty safe for suspected persons to be allowed such liberty as the rest of us get.

August 20th 1943

Extensive anti invasion exercises are going on every night all over the Island. It may be in connection with these Organisation Todt people are patrolling town and country in groups of 3 with rifles, or it may be some of the foreign workers have escaped in preference to being taken away. Some 500 were taken away last night. Quite a few Russians have, during recent months 'evacuated' from the camps and gone into hiding on farms, working just for food. A little while back the Germans rounded several up on the Mont Cochon district.

August 23rd 1943

We hear some folks have escaped from Guernsey to England – good luck to them, and I hope they have taken useful information with them. I expect it will mean reprisals on their relatives and on the whole of Guernsey, and maybe of Jersey. Water is the latest item of economy, being now shut off from 9.00 p.m. till 6.00 a.m. Not so terrible, but one has to plan one's needs, even to lavatory requirements, in advance.

It now becomes necessary for me to discontinue my writings for a week or two. This would be most incriminating if my worst fears of the moment were realised. I received the tip through a friend who is often at College House on business, the store and a place adjacent are suspected of being news distribution centres. On the principle it may be true, we have had a hectic afternoon disposing of wireless sets. These volumes and other dangerous papers I am leaving with a friend. So, for a while, I like most people, will have to rely on second hand information, and to store in my head the necessary facts to keep this up to date.

October 21st 1943

At long last it seems safe enough to resume this effusion. Although I had no visit from the Germans, a few days after the warning was received from our mutual friend, the other chap in the nearby property (J. B. Pool) was visited by the Gendarmerie. They told him they had come unofficially about tyres and oil which should have been handed in, and about several cars which had not been registered. No mention was made of a wireless, though Pool had got rid of his set on being warned. The Gendarmes advised him to get in touch with the local petrol controller about the various items, but before Pool had time to change and get down to the Petrol Office, a phone call came from there asking him to call. The Gendarmes had already been down and arranged the various illicit items be disposed of without fuss. A few days later, they returned, officially this time, and making no pretence of a search, noted matters had been put right, and went away. It would seem, whilst one hates Germans in the abstract more now than 3 years ago, there are one or two exceptions to the rule.

After a delay of some 4 weeks, during which our fears gradually evaporated, I made arrangements for this and other incriminating papers to be returned.

Through the good offices of my friend Bartlett, to whom I was indebted for the tip about the Gendarmerie, I was lent a small French wireless. For various reasons we did not consider it wise to keep the two sets at the store, and I devised a fairly good hiding place at home. For the sake of those concerned, greater secrecy was kept about this than about the other sets, about which quite a few people of my little circle knew.

For a few days all went well and once again we had full and reliable information. Then there was another scare. I gather one or more sets which Bartlett had repaired and delivered to the Commandant (Town railway station) had been stolen (probably by Germans). Bartlett and the chap who delivered the sets down there were suspected and the shop and each of their homes searched thoroughly. This was by a different branch of Gendarmerie to that which so kindly passed on the tip before. Fortunately nothing of an illicit nature was found, though it would not have done for them to search his town garage. In view of my friendship with Bartlett, regarding which the Germans would almost certainly have found out, I thought it advisable to 'farm out' my little box of tricks to another member of the gang of good friends which this Occupation has proved.

The Germans had already taken away many empty wooden bungalows from around home and from all over the Island, using them in St John's Manor and Trinity Manor grounds for ammo storage. They came again about 8 weeks ago, looking for more, so I decided it was time for our place to be no longer wooden and transportable. My good friend Joliffe is foreman for a building firm doing a lot of German work and, acting on the 'go slow' principle, has time on his hands. Much of his spare time he has been in the habit of spending with us at the store, lending a hand when necessary and giving valuable advice and help in my various experiments in concrete work. Having duly introduced the good man, I must record his offer to help me to cement the bungalow. So for 3 or 4 weeks I have been taking off afternoons and, with his help, getting on with the job, now duly completed. The Germans have unknowingly supplied everything for the job except the expanded wire – cement, wood, nails; even his labour is on the German bill. I had to pay black market for the materials, but that isn't for Jerry's benefit.

Now for a summary of events during this period - on 21st August, a barge went on the rocks west of Demi des Pas, in a sudden squall. Her cargo of flour, onions and other flotsam, was washed ashore the following day, and almost everyone on the east coast had a supply of onions gratis.

German patrols were on all beaches preventing the many beachcombers from getting away with their finds, but in most cases did not object to onions being taken. Subsequently frantic attempts were made at salvage, and she was got off the rocks only to sink in the fairway. Some weeks later another squall caused the loss of two more barges near the Dogs Nest, as well as a tug sunk and another run ashore at the back of the castle. The latter was later got off and sank again in the entrance to St Aubins Harbour. It is getting quite a habit for barges to get into trouble when there is any wind. Hardly surprising, for, being designed for river and canal work, they must be a bit of a handful in a squall.

With the exception of about four firms, the OT are leaving us, and for weeks now ships and barges have been leaving every night loaded with heavy equipment, foreign workers etc. The Eastern Railway, only used in its own construction, has already lost its locomotives and rolling stock. A huge stone crusher, built near L'Etacq, has been blown up, and there are many similar instances all over the Island. On Route Orange a huge fire relieved them of the need for shifting huts, workshops and stores. Probably in order to complete works started, the interviewing of young men of 18 to 25 at College House goes on, and many are already working for the Germans.

Local flak batteries, reduced now, have been in action several times by day and night, including one happy afternoon when they chucked up everything they had (they would have sent up the guns themselves if they could) at a big US bomber which passed over the Island from end to end at little over tree top height. I saw part of the episode, and thought at first it was AA practise from the fact shell bursts were to the rear of the plane. Uncle Sam replied by machine gunning at Grands Vaux, causing casualties which included 6 killed. I could just imagine that plane's crew put their fingers to their noses at the AA, for it didn't bother to alter course or increase speed to avoid the flak.

After several weeks in the water, the body of a US airman was washed ashore near Bonne Nuit, being buried early the following morning. No civilians attended the burial, as it wasn't generally known until afterwards. An epidemic of whooping cough is raging here, especially amongst children, and I must also record this year's grain crop is only half of last, whilst potatoes too are very short, so the latter part of the winter looks as though it won't be easy. The 4 ounce meat ration is occasionally missing too. There is no doubtif we had been brought right down to our present pass in 1940, many of us would have starved. As it is, our minds and stomachs have become gradually used to the food shortages and so we manage to carry on. I am a couple of pounds heavier than at the Occupation and with the exception of my eyes feel no ill effects, although like everyone else I have not the same amount of energy. Many people are not so fortunate and many, especially young ones, have developed consumption.

October 30th 1943

Some 200 Italian soldiers arrived last Saturday (23rd) complete with their band, and at least one more batch has come since. I gather these are the 'betwixt and betweens', who won't fight for Jerry, but don't mind working for him in preference to being taken prisoner – though it would appear they are very much prisoners. The action on Saturday night in which the cruiser 'Charybdis' and a destroyer was lost, did not disturb my sleep, though many people heard the explosions and saw flashes. This with a short burst of flak on Wednesday evening completes a quiet week.

NOVEMBER 1943

November 6th 1943

The only thing worth recording this week is I stood in a queue from 7.30 a.m. till 11.40 a.m. for a permit to buy shoes – then got none, so the performance will have to be repeated later if and when more supplies arrive. Getting a pair of shoes today entails a scramble to get a permit, then to be signed by a Parish official to confirm you have no other footwear, then another queue to return the signed permit, and yet another queue to buy the shoes. You get a pre-war 12/6d pair for 50/- and many lost hours. We 'exhumed' Phillips and Ekco this week, but both have suffered badly from 10 to 11 weeks internment. Ekco is being dismantled until a more suitable time, being rather large, whilst the other is to be done up for use here at the store, so with our little friend at home we shan't miss much.

November 13th 1943

One hears of other arrests for wireless offences – one man, manager of an erstwhile ice-cream factory, was found to have 3 sets, 3 cameras, a revolver, 50 rounds of ammo, photos of gun emplacements etc. As usual, the search was the result of an anonymous letter by some local 'Britisher'.

All local horses are again being paraded for German benefit this week, though I am afraid our underfed and overworked nags will not reach up to German requirements. No meat ration this week – no, I don't mean this is connected with the foregoing about horses. Flak batteries had a couple of 'excitements' on Wednesday evening, but we heard much other RAF activity here this week. A few more crocked up evacuees have been sent back from Germany.

One of the leading German officials, Oberleutnant Zepernick, was killed in a French train accident recently, and brought here to be buried (he had been here for 3 years). Presumably for propaganda reasons, the public was invited to attend the funeral, and 3 special buses were filled to go to St. Brelades. Some, no doubt, went for idle and foolish curiosity, and no doubt a few officials, who had come into contact with Zepernick, had to go. Many well known locals have earned the scorn of all 'Britishers' by their attendance and floral tributes to an enemy. It compares badly with the last funeral of the US airman washed ashore at Bonne Nuit, which took place before curfew the following morning, and which no-one knew about till after. Comparative photographs of the two funerals would show up the Jersey people in a bad light. Incidentally, I wonder just how many of those who showed their sorrow for Zepernick managed to get out of bed early enough to pay their respects to the two airmen who were buried a while ago.

November 15th 1943

In high winds over the weekend some 29 British naval ratings have been washed ashore – presumably from the cruiser 'Charybdis' which was lost around these waters a fortnight ago.

November 20th 1943

The funeral of the above was held on Wednesday at 9.00 a.m. without publicity, although local officials and representatives were present. The men were buried in a common grave at Mont a L'Abbe, many having lost their identity discs. There were hundreds of wreaths from Germans and local people, and the ceremony appears to have been carried out with great respect.

November 23rd 1943

The paper last night published a German notice and photograph relating to one Hedwig Bercu, a girl of no nationality, said to be missing since November 10th and badly wanted by German authorities. Severe penalties are promised to anyone harbouring her, so it seems she must have done something pretty drastic to incur the German wrath. Good luck to her, though I am afraid she will not be able to lay low in an Island like this, neither is there any chance of getting to a safer district.

More RAF leaflets were dropped on Thursday or Friday night. It appears there have been quite regular deliveries lately, though none ever seem to come around our district. I am indebted for one of these to a friend who knows I want such things for posterity.

DECEMBER 1943

December 6th 1943

A part of the Howard Davis Park has been set aside for a war cemetery, and the bodies of the sailors and RAF men transferred there, whilst other bodies from the 'Charybdis' since washed ashore are being buried there. Heavy flak opened up several times yesterday against big crowds of planes passing over in waves, but low cloud prevented us or the gunners from seeing anything.

I must correct an earlier statement the new German/Jersey Eastern Railway is not in commission – an engine has appeared on our line, though to my amusement it seems to run without trucks and without doing any real work.

December 11th 1943

Amongst recent arrests by the Germans are 10 Dockers, now in gaol awaiting trial on charge of stealing or damaging radio sets being taken away from the Island. Just about all sets left after the various purchasing and commandeering rackets had the pick are being taken to Germany, and so another promise is liquidated. One remembers how insistently it was stated 18 months back the sets were being taken into safe custody, and would be returned as soon as the military necessity no longer existed. Some 4,000 sets have already gone, and of these probably more than 100 have found a resting place at the bottom of the harbour, whilst most of the others will never be usable as radio sets without considerable servicing.

Extra Christmas rations are not so thrilling – 5 lbs potatoes, 2 ounces butter,

4 ounces sugar, ½lb sweets for children, whilst our tobacco ration (men only) is increased to 50 cigarettes and 2 ounces tobacco for Christmas week. The reduced supply of rationed goods has resulted in increased black market prices – 10 marks per pound for pork or sugar. In order to pay these enhanced prices, we have sold some tea at £8 a lb which is cheap today. I have just had a pleasant surprise – a packet of 10 fresh English Players sent by a friend who has just received a parcel of chocolate and cigarettes from his mother, amongst the internees in Germany.

December 15th 1943

Following an outcry in the press Guernsey women are to have 40 cigarettes for Christmas, a special ration of 20 each is to be issued for women – the first since the Occupation. The £1 note racket is again in full swing, and the exchange is now 20 marks per £. I seem to be almost unique in my refusal to take advantage of this get-rich-quick scheme, most people doing so in order to be able to buy on black market.

In addition to no meat ration last week, the salt ration was suspended, and it would appear there is no prospect of any of the latter for some while to come, as arrangements are being made for sea water depots around town, selling it at a penny per quart for cooking purposes.

December 29th 1943

Exit Christmas number 4. Each has become progressively worse, until it really is about time this lousy business came to an end. I am not moaning on my own behalf – at the expense of a reduction of bank balance, we had enough to eat, though no luxuries. Officially, no luxuries at all were imported, and the previously mentioned extra rations were our sole aid to overfeeding. You could get one or two things if you felt like disregarding the value of money altogether. I refused toffees, marie biscuits and cognac. Meat was only black market; our ration was the usual 4 ounces. Our little coterie of friends as usual helped each other. For instance, in anticipation of several promises of black market butter, we sent 6 ounces of our 8 ounce ration to be made into a cake, and found ourselves likely to be completely without when one of the gang managed to get hold of a ¼ lb for me. Another came along with 3 lbs of bread on Christmas Eve, thus enabling us to stuff the pork. We say goodbye to 1943 without regrets, and look forward to the coming year with high hopes it may be our last. Judging by recent news, there seems more and better reason to have faith in 1944 seeing us out of this mess. I nearly forgot to mention the hours when gas and water supplies are available are extended as well as curfew hours, whilst it is not an offence to keep ones electric lights burning after 11.00 p.m. over the holidays. Our RAF friends gave the local flak one or two day excitements during Christmas week, but unfortunately they missed coming on the day that mattered, when a huge cargo ship, with its escort of 7 destroyers, sheltered all day in St. Aubins Bay.

December 31st 1943

Flak batteries had their first nocturnal show for a long time last night, when the heavy stuff put up a terrific and wild barrage. It is notable for a long time now they have given up using searchlights, although the lights are still there and manned. Maybe they realise they just don't know how to use them. I imagine the intensity of fire last night was due in no small measure to the panicky state which the second Commando raid on Sark (December 28th) has left them. For a few days after each affair double guards come out and all approaches to beaches are wired.

1944

JANUARY 1944

January 8th 1944

This, our first week of what we hope and believe will be our last year, has opened quietly. Our RAF and US friends passed this way once or twice during their daylight assaults on Northern France, some people claiming to have counted up to 80 vapour trails left by the extremely high flying planes Thursday afternoon. There was an intense barrage put up for a few minutes during Thursday forenoon, but we could not see what it was directed against.

At some time during the New Year holidays a German soldier put several revolver shots into one of his officers and went into hiding. I fancy he has been caught, but the whole matter has been kept secret and one only knows about it because the soldier, reputed to be an anti-Nazi, went to several civilians with whom he had been friendly, for help. As far as I know it was refused in every case.

One hears a 'demolition squad' have arrived, presumably to put all the essential services out of action in case of a hurried flit. I have always expected such to happen and whilst it entails some nasty possibilities, it is nice to know our gaolers officially contemplate leaving us.

January 15th 1944

We have again been playing general post with the wireless sets, following on a warning from the Feldgendarmerie, friend B's shop, house, and employees' places are to be searched. These things are a bit of a nuisance until cleared up. Curiously 2 other people told me yesterday of having to do a quick clean up – one had his next door neighbour's house searched (without result) while he himself was listening to the news. The other has already been questioned by the head of the secret police about the man who shot his officer at Fauvic and is afraid a search may follow. We all feel we can't afford to take risks now the end is in sight (we hope). It appears the latter, an honorary police official, was told by one of his employees the missing soldier had been to him for help, and his 'crime' is for not reporting the matter to the German authorities, even though the shooting affair has been kept completely in the dark. German police methods could well serve as a plot for a comic opera, with 'secret' police who advertise themselves and their addresses, and police who, if in a good mood, send preliminary notice of impending searches. At the other end of the scale are super third degree methods and all the nastiness general to Nazism. Rumours have been going around for days about preparations for deporting all men of military age –

this one has whiskers on it by now. Adding 2 and 2 for a reasonable answer, I imagine there may be a further deportation of 'undesirables'. There surely seems to be a general drive to sort out as many offenders as possible, curfew breakers and minor traffic offenders are all having to hand in their identity cards pending their 'trial' and sentence. Until recently, it was the habit to fine on the spot and forget about it, but it looks possible another 'black list' is being compiled most assiduously.

Big day activity has been audible lately. Yesterday during the whole afternoon people could see flak bursts and hear bombs in the Cherbourg area. Twice last night our boys were around, the first time not being audible to us though all the heavy batteries to the west of the Island had a smack at them. They came again in the small hours of the morning, many machines being heard droning high overhead; but this time the flak merchants slept through it all.

Acting on German orders, local police have been finding out particulars of 190 girls who learnt typing at school in fairly recent years; whether with the intention of conscripting them for work, or in order to trace any possible sources of typed news sheets we don't know yet. If the latter, it is an inefficient means. It could also be an attempt to trace the source of a typed circular occasionally issued by the 'Jersey Democratic Party' whose underground activity is chiefly directed against the States.

January 18th 1944

A big fire on Sunday night wiped out the new portion of De Gruchys and damaged the older part. After a period as the biggest German bake house, the new wing has been doing duty as a general store for the German Wehrmacht, and they must have lost a considerable amount of clothing, small arms ammo, cellophane-wrapped bread and general stores. We await an accusation of sabotage.

After many moons of constant patching my front tyre, I have had to resort to a solid one, cut from a lorry tyre. It's not exactly comfortable, but better than walking. Nil desperandum – I am busily devising a means of springing the front wheel to avoid part of the inevitable vibration.

January 29th 1944

Jerry has peeved me considerably by insisting on taking a big proportion of lorries, cars and motorbikes at present on the road for civil purposes and those on civil reserve. Following the close down of ARP, my motor bike was put on this reserve, and I have been duly advised I may expect a visit any day from the

Nazi 'Buying Commission'. My only hope of saving the motor bike is the lousy big end which I have so many times cursed. I will make sure, if she does go, she won't carry them very far. It would break my heart if they take her, especially if for use here. I don't fancy seeing a lousy Jerry promenading on my motor bike. More leaflets arrived on Thursday morning, but though some came down in Samares district I have not been so lucky as to secure one. They were dated January 20th.

FEBRUARY 1944

February 2nd 1944

Unfortunately I completely missed the little bit of excitement in St. Aubins Bay on Saturday afternoon, when the RAF sank one patrol vessel, and left another burning. The latter managed to reach our harbour nicely damaged. That is as much as I have managed to find out, most people having got rather blasé about that sort of happening, and not bothering to find out details. Me, I still get all het up when any such event happens, and I surely would have given work a miss to see it.

The food question seems to be receiving more attention now, and for the past 2 weeks there have been such extras as macaroni and margarine which have been missing from the table for many months. The reason for this more generous distribution of food is the subject of many rumours. Some say it is the result of British representation through the Red Cross, others we are now considered as a danger zone and therefore our morale, through our bellies, must be maintained. A third surmise is the German authorities have protested against the paucity of rations hitherto issued by the States. Whatever the reason, extras are welcome, especially at this time of year. New gas restrictions are causing long and loud moans and everyone is busy working out how thoroughly inconvenient it is. The new hours when gas is available are 7.00 a.m. to 8.30 a.m., 10.30 a.m. to 1.30 p.m. and 6.00 p.m. to 8.00 p.m. Those who rely on it for light suffer most. I am told the revised hours are due to sabotage in France causing coal shortage.

February 10th 1944

On Tuesday (8th) at about 1.30 p.m. we were disturbed at dinner by heavy flak directed against a solitary US fighter plane. I gather the plane had developed engine trouble and was looking to land when it was fired on. I think as usual the flak was as ineffective as it was concentrated, and after circling once or twice, the pilot set fire to his plane before bailing out by parachute. The plane crashed on the sand banks along the Five Mile Road, whilst the pilot landed on a farm at St. Peters, suffering slight injuries. I am told within a minute or two of his landing some 30/40 German soldiers were on the spot with Tommy guns.

Another body has been washed ashore from the 'Charybdis' and is being buried in the British War Cemetery in Howard Davis Park tomorrow.

February 12th 1944

A solitary RAF machine crossed the Island yesterday afternoon and received a full share of flak, as usual without result.

The domestic affairs of certain friends bring proof, if any were necessary, of the fact that 3½ years of occupation have left most of us anything but normal. We do things now which viewed in the cold light of reason, would qualify us for a mental home. Business and work are about non-existent, with worry increasing, and all our nerves are very ragged. Hardly surprising, for in one sense we have all been 'living on our nerves', whilst in another, this has been a period of mental stagnation. I wouldn't face another such period for a £1,000 and would give every penny I possess to undo the decision which June 1940 thrust on to me.

February 18th 1944

A German patrol boat blew up on a mine on Saturday night off Corbiere, since when no shipping, except minesweepers operating by night, has been using these waters.

On Tuesday, for hour after hour, the adjacent districts of France were subjected to the heaviest bombing which we have yet felt. It must have been hell.

Recent sentences still show comic opera tendencies. One, for a radio offence, got 4 months, but being a member of the fire brigade, is allowed out for 48 hours whenever there is a fire. Another radio offender is to serve his sentence after the War. We suspect this particular leniency is the result of hospitality given to high up Germans. I know another case when a man appealed for and got leave of absence from gaol to help his wife to move, and about a week later got more time off to attend the funeral of a distant relative. All this applies to shorter sentences served locally, longer sentences are served in France and many prisoners there have lately been moved to Germany.

February 25th 1944

During this week few German soldiers or scuttlers have been wandering around loose, owing to the extensive exercises which have been carried out – rumoured as a preliminary to a large percentage being due for the Russian front but more probably in view of the prospects of invasion. Yesterday the eastern end of the Island was the venue, and a shell dropping short in a back garden at Gorey Village did some damage but fortunately caused no casualties. This morning all residents in the Bouley Bay area had to shift out between 6.30 a.m. and 11.00 a.m. whilst exercises took place there. This afternoon the whole caboodle – Navy, Infantry, Artillery have been parading through town – and in such numbers as one would not have believed to be in the Island. Most are under 18 or over 45, but still the numbers are there.

February 28th 1944

Colonel Knackfuss, the Commandant, and his staff have been showing a great interest in food conditions of the civil population, and have sampled the food at various restaurants including the Communal Kitchen. I also heard, though not confirmed, he has visited the houses of some poorer people at lunch time to see what they had to eat. The Communal Kitchen is a state controlled show, run mostly by voluntary labour, whereat one can get a well cooked and appetisingly served midday meal for 7d. There is no more variety available there than anywhere else, but it is doing a good job of work. The only complaint I have ever heard levelled against it is one doesn't get enough and second helpings are barred.

I heard and saw nothing of yesterday's 'naval battle' though I am told it could be seen from Corbiere. One patrol boat blew up (via BBC) and another reached harbour with a decided list. Several scuttlers are in hospital and one hears bodies have already been washed ashore. Nice work.

MARCH 1944

March 6th 1944

The following is rumour, but is to some extent borne out by the interest Knackfuss has recently taken in our food conditions. It is believed a Swedish Countess representing the International Red Cross has been investigating the conditions of the few Senegalese prisoners kept near the old Government Offices in Pier Road. Whilst here, this lady is supposed to have enquired about the food conditions of the civil population, and told the German authorities we are only one pint above starvation level. Whether the foregoing is true or not, it is a fact our bare rations are surely barely above subsistence level, especially at this time of year with temperatures around freezing point. One also hears 'good authority' rumours Knackfuss and his staff are going, or have gone to St. Lo to control the Islands from there, local administration being undertaken by a Major. If so, look out for new niggling orders. We have been left quiet in this line of late, the only exception being a full page reprint of the orders relating to the movement of currency between the various countries occupied. I gather from the mass of wordage it merely restricts the currency one can take away to 10 marks. The only point of interest is Jersey and Guernsey are grouped, whilst Alderney is regarded as part of France.

Another development is the pending arrival of large numbers of foreign workers. Most of the thousands brought last year were taken away again some months back but now one hears they are liable to take West Park Pavilion and other places for housing the new arrivals.

The store at the moment represents no work and plenty of worry. I am coming to the end of my 'brainwaves', having made many things in concrete – pipes, bends, double collars, junctions, gutters, chimney pots, cowls, land pipes of 4 and 6 inches, bird baths, floor tiles, manhole covers and ridge tiles. The lousy Jerry cement won't set in this weather, so we are unable to get on with the job of replenishing our low stocks. Whilst last year we managed a small margin over and above keeping our heads clear of the water, this year seems completely hopeless. What will happen at the end of this year and can still see no daylight ahead? Well, I refuse to consider such a possibility. Even if we do, as I expect, get out of this muck this summer, the store will lose money plenty, for it will be many moons before stocks start rolling in. But in that case nobody would mind so much.

March 18th 1944
Some 17 internees have been returned from a German camp for health reasons, and I gather they have seen something of the recent big day raids on Stuttgart and the neighbourhood – from what they say Yankee figures of Luftwaffe fighter losses are by no means exaggerated. The escorts from the camp, contrary to usual practise, are not returning, but have to remain and work for the Germans.

New gas hours give us 7 hours a day instead of 6½ but as the extra half hour is at 6.30 a.m. it doesn't help most people. I notice this order is signed by Major Kratzer as Feldkommandant, so the rumour of the departure of Knackfuss and other high up officials seems borne out.

March 25th 1944

Great RAF activity has been audible on adjacent coasts. Yesterday afternoon local flak batteries put up the usual ineffective barrage against what must have been a considerable number of high flying aircraft. Others have passed unmolested, detectable only by sound and a smoke trail.

According to reports, Jerry expects the invasion April 16th/18th and has made arrangements for all civil lorries left on the road to be regularly kept in certain garages with petrol in cans alongside, to be ready for immediate use in case of a hurried flit.

March 28th 1944

It was unpleasantly like the bad old days last night when many German planes passed over en route for South West England and South Wales. Probably arranged to coincide with this flight, fake propaganda leaflets were strewn all over the roads during the night. The passing of so many planes would make it appear the leaflets were dropped by the Allies, but unfortunately all of the leaflets dropped on roads, and not, as would be the case if dropped from the air, all over the place. The leaflet is a Yankee soldier's protest at the Allied under valuation of the fighting qualities of the Germans and no doubt calculated to instil in our minds the impossibility of invasion in face of such military valour as caused this pseudo US soldier to have printed a filthy and disgusting leaflet. Unfortunately for Jerry the Germans who earned the high praise quoted in the leaflet does not seem to be here for the invasion. Our defence is to a large extent in the hands of White Russian volunteers, Italians and C3 Germans.

APRIL 1944

April 8th 1944

There was a nice excitement on Thursday night I unfortunately missed, though I heard the plane pass over low. It seems a Dornier, apparently in trouble, failed to give the recognition signal, and the poms poms opened up and set it on fire. It crashed in an orchard near Five Oaks, only one of the crew being alive who has since died. I believe there are 4 casualties.

So much for good news. The gas hours now are cut to 4½ hours a day. On Sundays we get an extra half hour to cook our 4 ounce 'roast'. They must have known I had a bit of black market for Easter, as it is to be on from 6.30 a.m. – 1.30 p.m. this Sunday or maybe it is because some States members had their own black market to cook. It appears the Gas Works are operating from hand to mouth with coal, and one constantly hears unless coal arrives we shall be without in a fortnight, but up to date some has come along each time – just enough to keep us going for another week or so.

April 15th 1944

Joke – my black market pork didn't turn up after all, so the extra gas hours didn't matter. There is a general moan about the gas. The hours are so short and the quality so poor that, with everyone using it at the same time there is hardly any pressure at all.

I have been with my friend John Wright to a country concert this week. I mention this for these amateur entertainments have been a valuable contribution to the good spirits of people during this difficult time. The thing that struck me most was the amount of fun which the performers derive from it. These amateur shows range from the ambitious efforts of the Green Room Club, including Opera, Comic Opera and plays through the rather weak variety shows put on regularly in town, to the completely and genuinely amateur shows put on by various country parish concert parties. My remarks are more from hearsay than my own observations. However critical the mood in which one watches these shows, it cannot be denied they do a whole lot of good.

Our RAF friends have been around a lot. One plane has been buzzing around quite regularly day after day, high up, and there has been conjecture as to his nationality, though most people think it British. Thursday evening, several RAF planes skirted the south coast, skimming low over the water, and early this morning there were several concentrations of bombing in the neighbourhood of such weight and intensity as to make one wonder if the invasion had actually started. The Germans here have been warned to expect it any time after this weekend. My own forecast, made many moons ago, is May 1st, but remembering the fate of my prophecy last year – well, it ought not to be put in writing. In preparation for the long expected event, there has been much intensive training going on. Our friends are amusing themselves digging in old iron girders in every field in which it would be conceivably possible to land a plane or glider. This is much to everyone's disgust, as this work is making a mess of crops now coming along nicely. The holes they have dug to receive the irons make my after-curfew passage through fields in the dark more hazardous.

April 19th 1944

Owing to a big procession, ending in a torchlight tattoo in the Parade this evening, the curfew is extended to midnight so the civilian population may attend. No doubt many of the Germanite section will do so. One presumes this to be a preliminary celebration of Adolf's birthday.

One of the empty OT camps at Grouville was burnt down last week, and one hears reports of riots in the troops at Portelet, over a cut in food rations. This latter may not be true but is partly confirmed by the removal of wounded a few evenings ago from the Merton to a hospital ship under a strong armed guard.

April 20th 1944

I cite the following definite incident as proof of how easy it is to earn a prison sentence. A young insurance agent named Journeaux was at Wests Cinema with his girl some weeks ago, sitting near a German officer and his lady friend. Being fond of music, he beat time with his feet, as many people unconsciously do, and after the show his identity card was taken by the officer, with the order to be at College House the following morning. He presented himself there, and receiving his card back, thought the incident closed. After a week he was again sent for, and has just completed 10 days in prison. Probably if ever another batch is sent to Germany, this episode will label him as 'undesirable'. This sort of thing is constantly happening, and is the reason why the prison is always overflowing and with a waiting list. You don't have to do much to earn a 'gaol bird' reputation these days.

April 22nd 1944

Thursday seems to be visiting day for the RAF or Yankees, for this week over 80 passed to and from some objective close by which they well and truly bombed. Bundles of fibre were dropped here, and I presume it to be an antidote to radio location, though some allegorical minded people seem to think it is meant to signify the silver lining.

April 25th 1944

Jerry planes passed this way Sunday night en route for South West England, and many of them landed on the Airport afterwards. One hopes they were too badly damaged to proceed further. One crashed near St. Georges Chapel, St. Ouens, in flames, so one more could be added to the RAF tally for that night.

I had sight of a letter from Guernsey from which I gather a Guernsey fisherman working for the Germans in Alderney got away in his boat one misty day about a week ago. If he has reached England safely, he will be able to give useful information. The letter also contains reference to black market there –

butter is £4 a lb and everything else much higher than here. Tea is going at £20 per lb and rabbits are sold at a £ a lb.

April 27th 1944

Tuesday night was another disturbed one, with German planes passing at almost roof top height on their way to and from England. It seems it was not only the Luftwaffe about, for many copies of 'Courier de l'Airs' were scattered over the Island. All day yesterday there was heavy bombing going on, with local flak batteries in operation during the early afternoon. Again last night they opened up against planes flying south of the Island, so we are once again becoming a centre of activity. I must correct my statement of a plane having crashed on Sunday night at St. Ouens. Apparently it was some sort of bomb which came down aflame, making a big crater in a field, and looking from a distance just like a blazing plane. Fortunately there was no damage or casualties.

April 28th 1944

The air offensive continues. All day yesterday the rumbling went on, and during the morning several batches passed over. More silver paper was dropped, and I hear fairly reliable accounts of boxes of Rowntree chocolates and English cigarettes, as well as English leaflets having come floating down. Not having been lucky with any of these latter 'windfalls', nor any of my friends, I cannot vouch with any certainty for its authenticity.

Curfew goes back to 11.00 p.m. from May 1st. Not that I pay much attention to curfew, but it is necessary to get off the coast road before time.

MAY 1944

May 2nd 1944

The air offensive has eased off somewhat, though we still often hear bombing going on, and see our friends weaving vapour trail patterns in the sky. The penny squeaker air raid alarm recently installed by the flak-cum-coast-defence unit installed on the strip of grass overlooking Samares beach is constantly going – 3 times in 2 hours Saturday evening, and at least 7 or 8 times on Sunday.

May 6th 1944

There is little to report this week. Bad weather, no doubt, accounts for much reduced air activity. Our friends indulged in a heavier than usual artillery practise on Thursday, clearing all inhabitants in many districts. One dud bit of ammo exploded prematurely, spreading shrapnel about the Mont a L'Abbe area, causing some material damage. In anticipation of the possibility of no gas at all being available at some future date, arrangements are proceeding for the adaptation of some country farm ovens to provide some type of communal cooking.

May 12th 1944

The air offensive has been resumed on a very big scale, and by day and night the rumbling of heavy bombing on adjacent coasts goes on, with spasmodic bursts of flak from here as planes come within range. Our lads are around very high up much more often than they are fired on, as evidenced by frequent sky streaking and an occasional dose of silver paper. Yesterday afternoon the big artillery practise, in preparation for which many districts of the Island, were cleared of all civilians, was interrupted several times by passing Allied machines. Our friends had their own back on us this morning at 5.00 a.m. when just about every gun, heavy and light, machine gun and rifle at our end of the Island suddenly opened fire. The artillery kept going for 30 minutes, during which time we all thought the invasion had come at long last or at least a Commando raid was in progress. Machine guns and rifles kept us awake till 8.00 a.m. and it would seem to have been only a very violent anti invasion exercise. Plenty of rumours insist some British E boats were operating in Grouville Bay, or many planes were skimming the water to the South East, but I am fairly sure it was only practise. The Navy were operating around this way in the small hours of Monday. Our only intimation of anything afoot was a terrific bang, a not unusual happening. I gather since that a 900 ton ship was torpedoed between Corbiere and Les Minquiers, half the crew, including many Dutch, having lost their lives.

Gas hours are still further reduced, and are now 3 hours a day.

Our friends are today taking away from the banks all gold, valuables and securities from the Safe Deposits. Two branch managers are supposed to be under arrest for refusing to sign authorisation for the confiscation. This follows the taking a few months ago of all bank notes from the banks. The 'solemn guarantee' given when they arrived seems completely forgotten.

May 15th 1944

The sky the last 2 nights has belonged to the Luftwaffe, flying low and singly on anti-invasion raids on the south coast. To turn to the other side of the picture, the Germans are so annoyed at the RAF sinking one of their ships off St. Martins

Point, Guernsey a few days back, with the loss of a crew of 40, they have billed the Guernsey States for £60,000.

May 20th 1944

Business worry is increased by the resuscitation and enforcement of an order that no building job of over £5 may be undertaken without first obtaining a permit from College House. Jobs of urgent nature under £5 may be done, but a permit must be immediately applied for. This would seem to be yet another attempt to jamb everyone into working for them. Another snag is the small amount of cement being imported by them is now conveyed onto their jobs direct from the ship by train. Before, when taken by lorry, many a load never reached its destination, and civil work has been helped along a lot. I anticipated some such difficulty in getting illicit supplies and kept well ahead of requirements.

An indication of how well off we are for everything - long queues waited 2 hours before the shops opened on Tuesday because boot polish (on ration) was available. Many people went away empty handed.

I have just heard British light naval forces sank at least one patrol boat between Corbiere and Les Minquiers early this morning. Many rumours are going about as to the number of bodies recovered, varying between 44 and 124. It is definite 7 wounded are in hospital.

Feldkommandatur 515 has become extinct, and is replaced by Platzkommandantur 1, whereby the civil administration of all the Islands is done from Jersey. This seems to be merely a change of politics, and will have no direct effect on us. The office of Platzkommandant has been taken on by Major Heider, who has been here for some years as an underling to the Feldkommandant, and who, when acting as deputy, has been responsible for many niggling little orders.

May 23rd 1944

Many folk were late for work this morning following a disturbed night. First there was the sleep disturbing low flying Jerry planes on their way to and from England – not many but they spread themselves out over a long period, flying singly. Then early this morning light artillery and machine guns gave us half an hour of their music. Many star shells were fired and there is a rumour British E boats were off the south coast, but lacking confirmation I am more inclined to believe it to be another anti-invasion practise. Unlike the last noisy affair, when I dressed and went out ready and hoping for the arrival of the real thing, I stayed put in bed and cursed the Jerrys for disturbing my sleep.

The casualties in Saturday's naval action are still unknown. The 7 wounded in the General Hospital are not all, others having been taken to Ladies College and Merton Hotel (both in use as Jerry hospitals). It seems unlikely we shall know how many bodies are washed up, as the undertaker who usually does the German funerals tells me they have just imported a lot of coffins to do their own 'clearing up'.

I have since heard 15 of the crew of 40 were rescued intact, the remaining 25 being killed, wounded and missing.

May 26th 1944

There may after all be something in the yarn of British E boats being the cause of the great noise on Tuesday morning. Certainly a barge was sunk not far from the pier and is visible at low water. Also on Tuesday night about 11.00 p.m. planes were seen to descend on a convoy off Corbiere, at least one disappearing in a cloud of smoke.

May 31st 1944

Announcing a reduction in the electricity ration to a basis of 2½ units a week per household, we are officially advised no more fuel oil is to be brought here owing to shortage, and the steam generating plant erected in St. Peters Valley is not yet in operation. Therefore, the existing fuel oil must be eked out until the new plant is working, or else we shall be without power. A small concession is given in the gas, it now being turned on at 11.00 a.m. on Sundays instead of 11.30 a.m.

Referring to the confiscation of gold and securities from safe deposits a week ago, this seems only to have applied to the property of French nationals.

There is continued air activity, including disturbed nights caused by the Luftwaffe proceeding low and singly to England. There are many more indications of the RAF and Yanks, though the local flak batteries do not seem as anxious to waste ammo as they have been.

The building restrictions have resolved themselves. There are no permits for jobs less than 10 marks, States permits are OK for jobs up to 50 marks, and jobs over this amount are to be authorised by College House. The chances of them giving permits are remote. No painting is allowed, being regarded as unessential, whilst jobs requiring cement will not be allowed, as the States have bought none for 10 months. This just about puts the kibosh on the building trade generally and on the store. No doubt there will be some wangling around the order, but many of the smaller concerns are closing down, whilst most others are sacking all hands, just leaving the boss to do small repairs as necessary.

JUNE 1944

June 6th 1944

From midnight onwards, with only short intervals, a stream of aircraft have been, and still are (9.30 a.m.) passing over, and being greeted by heavy flak. Roused out at 6.30 a.m. by a specially heavy dose, I went to the coast road, and found barbed wire barriers across the road, and the 3 guns stationed there elevated and manned for immediate action. Several men working for the Germans told me they had been sent home, as the invasion was on, and many big guns were being got into position around town. On my way in half an hour ago, I saw nothing of this, nor of the ambulances and other preparations said to be ready. Certainly there are no 'spare parts' wandering around this morning – all the Germans I have seen are on cycles, with full equipment, going to their posts. The question everyone is asking – is this the real thing? The high west wind and rather conflicting radio reports make me tend to believe it is not the invasion proper, but more probably a sort of suicide squad landing to carry out various demolitions in preparation. The weather conditions and tide are not what I should have thought would be selected for the job – a strong west wind, thick cloud with only an occasional break, and no fog plus a spring tide. It is also cold, though that would have little effect on operations. There is more gossip than work, and our committee (Bartlett, Hedouin, Burt and I) have just been sitting, discussing possibilities. The other member of our Occupation mutual aid and entertainment society, friend Joliffe, has not been in yet. Without these good friends, this Occupation would have dragged interminably, but having them come in regularly for a gossip each day has shortened the time and helped all of us from suffering too much mentally, whilst materially we have helped each other a lot. Before the war we were each too busy with our own affairs to be more than acquaintances, but during the last few years it has grown spontaneously into a true circle of friends with myself, I suppose, as the hub. No doubt with the intention of stiffening the great majority of young and old troops here, a few Afrika Corps has been here the last few days. They are rather a nuisance, as except for the lettering 'Afrika', they wear identical armbands to the Feldgendarmerie, and so cause many a minor heart fluttering when committing such heinous offences as cycling two abreast, or failing to halt at a halt sign. It isn't fair for them to be so easily mistaken for German police, there being quite enough of the latter about for our liking.

Later – It looks as if I once again, for the umpteenth time, have to eat my words as to the probable time and tide for the invasion, though not entirely as to the place, as I have always put the Contentin peninsula high on the list of possible landing places.

Since 9.30 a.m. there has been comparative quiet, with a few planes passing either high or well out, some distant bombing, but no flak. People have been congregating in cheerful groups around town, especially in the square at 11.00 a.m. where it was rumoured a proclamation was to be read. That rumour was wrong, but copies were posted at the Town Hall and Town Church, containing the expected threats of death penalties for any interference with German troops. The telephone exchange has been taken over by the military, and no civilian calls can be put through. Fire Brigade and ambulances have also been commandeered. There has been gathering of vehicles at various dispersal points, presumably ready for evacuation.

Whilst on the subject, may I venture another, and I hope final, forecast – granted the landing is successful (I have infinite faith it will be), Jerry will evacuate these Islands within very few days. I hear German nurses have already been down to the quay about getting away, and I am told a lot of soldiers are outside the Standort Kommandant (Town Station) ready to go. At the moment no ships are available, though possibly a convoy will have a shot at it tonight. I am told the ration strength of troops here, including OT, is 4,200.

During last night's great noise, a gun post at Green Farm, Maufant, was shot up by one of our planes, and I believe, several Germans killed. Another reassuring fact which I have learnt is, with recent imports, we have sufficient flour in the Island to keep us going until November, provided our German friends leave it alone. Anticipating, as I always have done, a flat patch in the grub line for a week or two after the Germans leave, this fact relieves my mind. The weather by now (3.30 p.m.) has improved considerably, the wind has eased, and the clouds cleared so, whilst still affording ample cover for planes, visibility for bombing is very good.

June 7th 1944

I am at a loss to understand the extreme quietness prevailing. Throughout the latter part of yesterday and last night, we heard many planes pass and some distant bombing, though not as much as we often have before. The local flak guys seem to have gone out of business. All the Germans are still on guard everywhere as yesterday. Many nurses are wandering around town, each carrying bag and blanket, so it looks as if they have been trying to get away. Four of the dozen or so barges which have lain unused in the pier for sometime have been emptied out preparatory to sinking, one supposes in the pier heads to block them. There are rumours all the high officials have already left here but not confirmed. All the phone exchange girls were sent home yesterday and told to report again in 4 days – meanwhile, we are without phones.

It looks as though our long ordeal is near its end but the complete lack of incidents up to date make it hard to believe. Maybe we shall get a bellyful of trouble before we are through. However bad it is, it cannot be worse than a continuation of the nerve wracking, soul destroying, and constant down grade we have been on for 4 years. However bad things become, one can now look forward to a more or less definite near future. Our hopeful anticipation is modest, judged by pre-occupation standards – lathering soap to wash with, sufficient bread so we have not to think twice about that extra slice, enough fats and sugar to keep our energy from daily getting less. I think above all, direct news and letters from England is the hardest thing of all. Freedom from irksome restrictions will certainly be nice, though as far as curfew is concerned, most people's lack of physical or mental energy render it almost unnecessary. We do look into the more remote future, to new clothes and little luxuries. I could fill a complete volume with all the things we need. Many children have forgotten or never known what it is to be able to buy sweets with their pennies, and worse still their feet are becoming ruined by having to wear wooden solid boots. No one who has not had a basinful will ever realise how constant ersatz and improvisation in all essentials – food, clothing, transport, cooking, heating, work, everything you can think of – gets on one's nerves. To keep a common push bike going today costs more than a car in happier days, and entails more upkeep work patching tyres and improvising.   Imagine the housewife's task cooking with gas only available for 3 hours a day, and cold meals out of the question because needs must make the black market potato the basis of all meals; washing and cleaning with precious little of the putty like ration soap. Shopping is done in shops with nothing, and what there is at many times pre-war prices; trying to make a pre-war wage stretch to paying the exorbitant black market level of prices as the only alternative to going without; clothing a family out of nothing. Working conditions are much the same, presenting difficulties, worries and risks in all directions.   At least I have done what I set out to do 4 years ago, and have kept the store open.

June 8th 1944

German nurses were still wandering around like spare parts this morning. Except for those on guard, with rifles at the ready and hand grenades strung around their necks, and those going around in horse wagons on various errands, we see little of the German soldiers. Also wandering around like lost sheep are many of the Germanites – lost without a pair of uniform pants to rub against, though I have no doubt they will be happy in the near future when British and US soldiers arrive here. Numerous guards are about to keep one well away from the vicinity of the piers, but I was able to see several ships have come into the harbour during the night. Many planes passed over during the night and forenoon, and once again no opposition was offered by the AA. People here are taking it all quietly, and I have heard of no instances of trouble. It is only the absence of any Germans wandering around that makes the town any different to what it was a week ago. I have been helping in the matter of fitting up reliable people with sets – a risky job which I have frequently done in the past, but one well worth doing. The hospital is being cleared of all patients as far as possible, on German orders. Even hating Germans as I do, I have to admit in fairness that, although many of them have sour faces just now, they are individually and collectively up to date behaving very correctly.

June 9th 1944

Despite the continual audible presence high up of the RAF, there has been much coming and going of ships, I think without interference, and it hasn't been confined to night movements only. To our surprise, our friends carried out their usual Thursday afternoon artillery practise, including a shoot from the not-yet-finished concrete fortification on the site of the old Gorey Pier station. It certainly doesn't seem possible there is heavy fighting less than 40 miles away.

June 10th 1944

At last there is an incident to report. At 6.00 a.m. today, several low flying planes and heavy AA fire once again roused me from bed. It took me a few minutes to dress and get to the coast road where I arrived in time to see 3 destroyers, which had been anchored in the bay, beating it for the pier. There was smoke coming from the foremost one, where it had been damaged by the planes. I think this was by cannon fire but the fire seemed to be out before she got into harbour. The planes were gone by then, but I saw 2 big jobs before I dressed, flying fast at about 2,000 feet.

All beaches except Havre Des Pas bathing pool and the immediate vicinity are now banned, being considered dangerous because of artillery and rifle practise. Thus again do our friends try to minimise the invasion. 4 Germans came to an ignominious end at La Rocque yesterday. They left Seymour Tower where they were stationed to come ashore, and got marooned and were drowned as the tide covered the rock they made for. The Germans took out one of the La Rocque fishing boats to rescue them, but damaging the boat, returned without reaching the men. A 5th met a sticky end in a motor bike crash. In addition to this morning's schemozzle, large numbers of planes were passing all night, but there was no flak to greet them. Our friends seem to realise it is not much use wasting ammo which will be impossible to replace, though I imagine there are vast quantities stored here.

I gather this afternoon some casualties of a machine gun attack at St. Ouens were brought in to the hospital.

June 12th 1944

Yesterday was a day of poor visibility and generally unsuitable weather for the job in hand. It was enlivened only by the radio report of the attack on minesweepers. The BBC term 'wave after wave' should be superseded by 'continuous stream' in describing the aircraft which passed this way early forenoon, following a night disturbed by many plane engines. There is also to report much artillery and general practise amongst our garrison.

The RAF alarm, which seems to be getting a regular habit, roused me again at 6.30 a.m. today. It was too late when I got to the coast to see much except a cloud of dust rising from Elizabeth Castle. I gather 4 RAF planes dropped eggs near 5 ships lying just outside the castle, apparently without getting any hits, and gave them a good dose of cannon or machine gun fire. They appear to have tried for AA positions on the castle, but as far as I could see from the Esplanade, there is no damage to the Castle. Several windows along there were blown out by the concussion, whilst all flak positions in the vicinity had a busy 5 minutes. The Germans seem to be making no preparations to flit – quite the contrary. No German is now seen without rifle and full equipment, and one is not allowed to walk on the pavement near the various HQs. Men working for the Germans have resumed work, after all being sent home the 1st day.

June 13th 1944

Yesterday's fine weather was taken advantage of, many planes passing over. Much bombing was heard, but quite ordinary stuff except for one particular 20 minute raid late evening. Every house on the Island literally shook with the intensity of the explosions, the worst we have ever felt. The raid was somewhere south of here – maybe St. Malo or Granville. We heard a few planes above the clouds at midday, but that is the only sign of a war being on. Telephones are still cut off; though from 8.00 a.m. to 8.00 p.m. doctors and certain essential services (fire, hospital) are able to make calls. After 8.00 p.m. your house can burn, or you can die, but it will be without aid. This doesn't mean one can call a doctor or fire brigade by phone during the day. Their phones are working, but ordinary civilian ones aren't.

June 14th 1944

Following a night of great air activity hereabouts, with local flak in operation and explosions coming from the French coast, we enter on the 2nd invasion week. By order of the Platzkommandant, new restrictions are placed on bus travel. Henceforth, only one bus each morning and evening will be run on each route, and priority tickets (up to 60 per route) are to be issued to regular long distance travellers.

There appears to have been an action against Jerry shipping off the coast during the early morning. Two of the minesweepers in harbour now show signs of damage. One has a bare space forward where all the others have a gun, and the damage to the other is not apparent, but she has been run right up under the slaughter house where she will ground at low tide, and has many men working feverishly aboard. One cannot go close to see – the road is banned, and I risked the wrath of the sentries by going through the barbed wire barrier to get over Mount Bingham to see. It is said two other patrol boats were sunk in the action. Certainly charabancs brought up the survivors, and there are quite a number of wounded. I am awaiting the BBC report, if any, on the affair. Probably connected with the action, an RAF bomber crashed near a farm at St. Peters. I am indebted, as usual, to hearsay for the information that the pilot bailed out by chute before crashing, but was himself killed. The fate of the rest of the crew is unknown.

Later - I have gathered the following authentic facts about the plane. It was a 2 seater fighter bomber, and crashed at 9.10 a.m. on a farmhouse (Amy, Le Marais, St. Ouen) after flying at roof height across the Island from St. Brelades. When crossing near the Airport, the pilot seemed to be trying to open his roof, and must have been in trouble. It seems probable some of his controls had been shot away. The woman in the farmhouse got out of the front door with her children as the plane struck the back. Both house and plane were burnt out. This happened at about the same time as the minesweepers were beating it for the pier, and so is probably related to the same scrap.

June 15th 1944

Many thanks to the BBC for information, and to 'Ashanti' and Polish destroyer for good work in sinking 3, leaving 2 afire and stopped, and damaging the others before reaching cover of Jersey's coastal batteries. The 7 were mentioned as M class minesweepers, and it fits in with local accounts and with the fact 2 only came in damaged. Many people living in places overlooking the sea say it was like daylight with the many star shells.

Great air activity continues. Two of our lads obligingly popped out of the clouds at about 3,000 feet while I was on my way home from work, having a look before buzzing off south. A large number were using our air about midnight, but flak was spasmodic. They only seem to fire when planes come so low they are expected to attack. That is the conclusion I have drawn from recent flak activity. I am almost sure one solitary egg, a fair size one, was dropped on the Island during last night's great Passover, there being a mighty flash, followed a few seconds later by the big bang and judder. I wait for confirmation.

Today is again one of good visibility and we can hear the air offensive continuing. I guess we shall soon be so attuned as not to be able to sleep except to the accompaniment of the buzz of plane motors and the occasional burst of flak. In fact, several people to whom I have spoken heard nothing of last night's many noises. It is surprising what one can get used to, and how quickly. Usually too late, I had a change this morning, being a few minutes too early at 9.00 a.m. to see one of our lads dive low to drop a bomb on Elizabeth Castle.

June 16th 1944

I hear there are so many wounded some have been taken to the prison, as well as the hospital, Merton, and the Ladies College (used as a naval hospital).

Further about the plane that crashed. It was a Tornado, and its single occupant was buried this morning in the Davis Park Cemetery. Since recent naval activity in these waters, there has been much less shipping about, though 450 tons of spuds were loaded yesterday for the German garrison in Guernsey. I have been told one of the barges coming here was stopped the night before last by the Navy, and on finding it carried only essential foodstuffs for the civilian population, were told to carry on but not to return. Whether or not this is true, we are certainly in a state of siege.

June 17th 1944

"Owing to the Military situation on the Continent, it is not possible to guarantee supplies during the next months". I quote from the official notice announcing reductions in bread and meat rations. It will be noted the 9 hours it was going to take to throw the Allied armies back into the sea is now extended to an indefinite number of months. The basic bread ration is now 4¼ lbs a week so we shall get 2 lbs less in our house. Infants get 1½ lbs, children 3 lbs and adolescents 6 lbs (male) and 5¼ lbs (female). The meat ration (4 ounces) will only be available fortnightly, with an extra 2 ounces (making 4 ounces) of butter on the alternate weeks when no meat is to be had. The salt ration is cut to one ounce a week – a worse blow than usual as we cannot now get sea water for cooking since beaches are closed.

The weather again today is not good. Despite bad weather, we heard many planes and explosions during last evening, and again this morning. It is hardly surprising if we are hearing things, with the fighting now less than 25 miles away. Hardly believable – since this schemozzle has been on, I have not seen a Luftwaffe plane, though possibly not all those passing during the night hours have been allied. One would have expected to see fighters especially operating by day at this distance from the battle zone. From St. Martins, the flashes of guns firing in France were plainly visible last night.

June 19th 1944

With a marked improvement in the weather later on Saturday, and with the fighting rapidly getting nearer Jersey (now only 14 miles away, and as close as it can get), the planes passing, bombing and gun fire have been incessant. I am not sure of all the facts of what has been happening around here – accurate information is not easy to get. It is reported a party of US airmen drifted ashore at Grouville Bay on a raft, and whilst being taken for internment were yelling "OK buddy, we will soon be here". This is supposed to have happened on Saturday, but I have not yet found anyone who actually saw it. It is always 2nd hand information. Therefore, with my usual scepticism I doubt it, especially the part of them being allowed the necessary freedom to shout encouraging remarks.

It does seem to be a fact several ships were sunk or damaged from a convoy coming this way from Cherbourg, and many survivors (about 140) were brought ashore here on Saturday. Private nursing homes were commandeered to accommodate the wounded, many of whom could not be taken in the hospitals.

Early yesterday morning, we could hear the sounds of another engagement, which again turned out to be against a convoy. Again, details are lacking, though I hear two barges just managed to get to the pier heads in time to sink in the fairway. A naval vessel was towed in minus bows, and other ships are said to have been sunk. Rumour reports one of our planes came down off Corbiere – the AA fire was so intense it wouldn't be surprising.

Again this morning we had a few seconds thrill at about 8.00 a.m. when 3 planes circled the town and dropped at least one egg on a flak position at the top of Mont Cochon, while every AA gun around was in operation against them. Immediately on top of that 2 twin fuselage planes came over near home quite low. Again there was heavy flak, another heavy explosion, and a big cloud of smoke from somewhere in the direction of Le Hocq - very satisfying.

The lot of the historian at such a time as this is an unhappy one – to sort truth from false reports and to decide what is relevant and what isn't is far from easy. Despite constant effort, including getting out of bed at which, in normal times, I should consider ridiculous hours, I have managed to see very little, and so have to rely on other folks not too reliable eyes. Yesterday afternoon, for instance, I went out to Anneport to see if anything was visible from there, but I might have saved my energy, or used it to better purpose by coming to town to have a look at what ships were damaged. Even there, I expect one would have been allowed to see precious little. Jerry doesn't seem to realise the service I am rendering to posterity, or he would give me a pass to go where I like, though I am rather shy of asking for it and telling him why. He might want to read it, and having done so, have some awkward questions to ask. I notice Anneport is decorated with triangle tank traps, the top of each being mined. They are also mining the tops of the anti-air-borne-landing-piles dug into most flat beaches. I am surprised Greve D'Azette, one of the most perfect for air landings, is left unadorned. Also, while pillars have been stuck in many smaller fields around, Samares Marsh has been left untouched and comparatively few defences are in the neighbourhood. There is no doubt for an inexpensive landing, ours would be the district. The German soldiers here have had no time off for a fortnight, and must be getting fed up. I notice there is just none of the "aye, e aye oh" singing. I have heard only one group of a dozen scuttlers singing since this has been on and the soldiers are seldom seen in groups now. They are mostly doing single patrols, except one sometimes sees a batch of cyclist troops.

It is exactly 4 years ago the evacuation panic began. There is excitement again in Jersey, but with what a difference. Our whole horizon, which bucked so abruptly that unhappy day when we were told measures to evacuate the Island were afoot, looks like straightening itself out a bit in the near future. Optimistic as one might be, there was a time when this day was in so remote and so uncertain a future as to be almost a dream never to be realised; when all one could do was wish 'roll on time'. Now every day is worth living. Only those who have gone through this demoralising period will ever know the difference in mental outlook the past few days have brought.

Another plane has just passed (11.15 a.m.). I didn't see him, but should judge from the noise he was not much more than roof top height. He appears to have indulged in machine gunning either at the fort or harbour. One can still hear them buzzing around to add to that 'keyed up and expecting something to happen' state of mind.

The 2nd egg dropped this morning, reported above as Le Hocq district, actually landed near Platte Rocque, the German post at the top of La Rocque pier. I believe the egg landed on the German shelter between Platte Rocque and the next house, and there were some civilian casualties from glass splinters. I must congratulate the US airmen (they tell me the planes were Lockheed Lightnings) on spotting the place, which was beautifully camouflaged. A few weeks back when I passed that way, I had to look twice to spot the anti-tank gun which is camouflaged as a pump and this was from a few yards away.

I now gather the report of private nursing homes being commandeered is untrue. This emphasises my earlier remarks on the difficulties of myself imposed task. If one waited to confirm everything before entering it, many things would be forgotten. Keeping notes and transferring later would be a bore, and would lack all spontaneity.

The affair at 11.15 a.m. was a big 4 engine US machine which dived over the piers and sprayed them with lead before disappearing at sea level. Two barges are reported to have returned to harbour all nicely riddled, but whether from this part of the proceedings or the earlier episode I know not.

June 20th 1944

A further amendment to the La Rocque incident; it seems at least 5 civilian houses are uninhabitable and many others damaged by the blast. The weather overnight has been particularly bad. Despite bad flying conditions, we heard some planes about, plus the usual dull (and not so dull) thuds of distant explosions. Not all of it is bombing – a great deal is caused by artillery bombardments. It is peculiar, since the landings on D day, heavy rains have several times been reported on the battle front yet we, only 15 to 60 miles west, have had only light showers and drizzle. Whilst we should naturally prefer ideal weather for the fighting, we certainly need rain badly for the crops.

Later - I have just had a look at the damage at La Rocque and had some interesting lessons in the curious effects of the blast. I am amazed no-one was killed, for several houses are beyond repair, and more will want a lot of work to make them habitable – more than can be done with available material. The bomb, a 560 pounder, landed just off the road, some 50 yards from the German occupied Martello tower at which it was no doubt aimed, and left a crater about 25 feet across and 8 feet deep. The damage extends from the top of La Rocque pier to the post office, but as far as I could see Platte Rocque itself escaped. Many people suffered minor cuts and scratches, but there was only one hospital case, a woman who got a glass splinter in her eye.

The other egg dropped yesterday morning came down at St. Annes, Tower Road, another German occupied place and flak site. I have no further information, so apparently there was no great damage to civilian property in the vicinity.

June 21st 1944

A plane crashed in flames in a field behind L'Industrie, Samares Lane at 3.15 a.m. today. It is said to be German, but I cannot quite reconcile this to the fact that a 2nd plane circled around after quite low and dropped something attached to a parachute. I imagined the 2nd plane, realising the occupants of the other could not have escaped and would be unrecognisable, might have dropped a message giving the names of the crew. The burial will prove the nationality of the men. It is the first time I have seen such an incident and I cannot hope to give any adequate description, even though the horror of the crew being inside that blazing inferno created such an impression on me. The plane blazed for over an hour, with ammo and petrol tank exploding at frequent intervals, the blaze being fanned by a strong north east wind. Fortunately the fire confined itself to the plane, and did not touch the several houses nearby. More anon when more details are available.

I must revert to Sunday's little affair – another incident of which I have just heard is the dropping and exploding on contact of an AA shell just outside the gates of the Palace Hotel. The windows of those houses were shattered, but Jersey's reputation for bearing a charmed life was maintained and there were no casualties.

Another excitement just before curfew (10 p.m.) happened last night when 2 barrage balloons, set loose by the high wind possibly from the direction of Cherbourg, passed over. One was shot down by the local defenders over Samares Marsh and came to earth on the beach, whilst another was last seen drifting seawards.

Last night's Evening Post contained an article of local interest, reputed to emanate from Berlin, in which the single air attack on the Islands were referred to. According to this, 12 planes had been shot down over Guernsey and 6 over Alderney, whilst damage was confined to civilian property. No doubt Guernsey was told many planes had been shot down over Jersey. Reference was also made to the strong defences of the Islands, and to the fact it would be possible 'in case of being cut off' for the Islands to hold out for a considerable time.

Later - I have seen the plane from a good vantage point, despite the presence of armed guards stationed to prevent such a happening, and am glad to find it definitely was German. The tail section, complete with large swastika, is still undamaged, but the remainder is just a smouldering heap of twisted metal strewn over two fields. I should have been a whole lot less unhappy last night had I known it was Jerry's. Piecing things together from my own observations and other people's reports, it seems the plane, a Heinkel, burst into flames after being fired on by light flak batteries at Fort Regent. The bodies of 4 of the crew have been recovered from the wreckage, and a 5th is supposed to be in hospital after landing in a field of tomato canes at the end of a parachute jump. If Jerry were wise, he would learn from this the value of bamboo as an anti-paratroops weapon. I am still intrigued about the other plane which circled low (and was not fired on) and above all about the parachute which it dropped. I don't suppose I shall ever know the answer to that. It is a miracle no one was injured by the engine, which landed at least 200 feet from the fuselage, a twisted mass but still in one piece, in a space some 20 feet wide between 2 houses on the coast road. How ironic this twisted wreck, shot down by their own guns, should be the first German plane we have seen in daylight for many moons.

June 22nd 1944

The gusty north east wind continues with considerable cloud most of the time. Despite unfavourable weather, 2 of our boys came and had a look at us at about 9.00 p.m. last night, passing over town at about 2,000 feet. I only saw 2, but the flak was so intense and immediately overhead where I was for the first time I got under cover of a wall.

Coming back to the previous night's episode, I understand the parachute I saw come down was by no means the only one, for many others came down, especially St. Martins way. Attached to each was a canister about the size of a 5 gallon drum, believed to contain ammo. The local thesis is the 2 planes took off from the Airport loaded with ammo to help out a decided shortage in Cherbourg. It is contended the 2nd plane was also in trouble, hence the bailing out, and later came down at sea. It could be thus – the planes may have been overloaded and just able to get off the ground but not gain height. My own theory is the ammo was being brought here from France, and was intended to be landed by parachute – probably as an experiment against the possibility of a long siege. I know long since the Germans have rendered the Airport unserviceable by dragging tree trunks across it. I must find if these still remain. If so, it bears out my idea. During last night other German planes were flying around low. One presumes they were repeating the performance. My theory seems to fit in with the known facts. It seems to me unlikely Cherbourg would be supplied from here, however short they were. It may well be our garrison will need all the ammo they can get, and would be glad to get an airborne supply. The reason for the parachute business could be Jersey's Airport is being kept permanently out of commission to prevent Allied landings. It seems to me, if Cherbourg were to be supplied by air, the machines would land with their loads on the airfields they still hold. It must have been intended to land the stuff by parachute, or whence the reason for carrying so many of them?

June 23rd 1944
There was a steady improvement in the weather yesterday bringing the expected increase in air activity, though none locally. The assault on Cherbourg and air onslaught on Alderney was very audible. Today the wind has dropped, though the sky is too overcast to make for perfect flying conditions. During the early hours of this morning there was a naval engagement south of here. Various numbers of ships between 2 and 7 are said to have been sunk, though the BBC say one sunk and several damaged. I heard and saw nothing, but I do know there were plenty of star shells about, and one ship was afire off St. Brelades. Later in the morning a US Thunderbolt, crew one, made a safe forced landing near the bottom of Jubilee Hill, being escorted right down by several others. It was lucky enough to pick out a stretch which wasn't mined.

24th June 1944
It is an almost perfect day, with evidence the RAF are taking full advantage somewhere around. There seems to have been another naval engagement south east of here during the night, with more star shells and banging. I await details. There also seems to have been a few Luftwaffe about during the night, flying low. The BBC says one escort and one ship have been sunk off here. A Dutch acquaintance (a barge skipper) tells me to his certain knowledge 22 ships have definitely sunk in these waters since the invasion began – an average of better than one a day.

June 26th 1944
There was sound of a naval action around here last night. There was no report

on the news, but I hear one boat was sunk off the Paternosters. Things have been unusually quiet over the weekend, the only thing to enliven matters yesterday being the passage over of a Fortress which flew sedately at a height of some 2,000/3,000 feet completely ignoring the heavy flak as though it were beneath his dignity. He did fire off one or two verey lights, which I took to be his way of saying good morning. The wind remains low, now south east, so even though flying operations must be reduced, the beach landings can go on comfortably. That won't matter for so long, once Cherbourg is usable. I should like to spend a day at the docks there after the mess is straightened out. It would give us heart to see stuff powering ashore for the job.

June 27th 1944

Yesterday was a day of steady rain, and passed without incident. Today the weather has cleared and the wind has veered to west. Another naval engagement took place in the early hours of today off the south east coast. The only things I know about it are two ambulance loads of wounded were brought up the pier this morning, and a stray shell landed in a private tennis court at 'Salthough', Samares, and, with Jersey's usual luck, failed to explode, although it forced its way well into the ground.

June 28th 1944

The Germans don't seem quite so keyed up and in a state of expectancy as they were, although they are still not allowed time off. There are quite a few scuttlers wandering around lose – probably survivors from the many ships recently sunk. They seem to be getting a bit out of hand, and quite a lot are seen drunk which is unusual among German forces. Yesterday afternoon, two of them were restrained with difficulty from 'commandeering' the Bailiff's car, whilst another pair indulged in a scrap in the market, and there was another melee in the Parade the previous evening.

Local authorities seem to be awake to the possibilities of the present situation, and St. John Ambulance has published a list of places where first aid will be available after any incident. The Constables of the Island are now appealing for volunteers to accommodate temporarily anyone rendered homeless by war action. I would like to see iron rations issued, and also advice to everyone to keep a supply of water available. As far as possible glass should be stuck over with paper, though it would be very little use offering such advice, as sticky paper is amongst the many 'ungettables'.

Some 4,000 French men and women (OT workers) arrived here last night en route to France from Alderney. I understand several hundred political prisoners, hitherto kept in Alderney, have been brought here. According to a Frenchmen, 900 of these prisoners have died or been killed there. Those who have seen them say physically they are in a pitiable condition. The local men who were forced to work in Alderney have also been brought back.

June 29th 1944

The BBC confirms yesterday's early morning battle that 2 destroyers sank 2 German patrol boats, the 3rd one escaping, but believed damaged. The weather these days is neither good nor bad, but we get very little air activity. I think it must be a week since the flak batteries opened up. Every night one or two German planes pass over at roof top height, but no more parachutes seem to have come down.

I have just had sight of a letter from Guernsey and got confirmation about the raid by Rockheeds on the harbour on June 19th. They tried for a U boat which had put in there, but unfortunately missed their target. It appears U boats often spend the daylight hours lying off Guernsey's bays, coming into the harbour each night. With the town so closely gathered around the harbour, there was considerable damage by the blast, but fortunately the raid was carried out early morning when few people were about. Guernsey seems to share Jersey's luck and not a single person was hurt. Practically all the shop and house windows in the vicinity were shattered.

June 30th 1944

We had a little excitement this morning, with a mock invasion-repelling exercise around home. Three small, and I should judge, very ancient tanks took part, and quite a number of troops. The result of the battle was a few shattered windows and many shattered nerves. Apparently in order to repel the imaginary landing, it was necessary for them to have the troops and armour at the exact spot waiting – unless it was regarded as a stage show rather than an exercise.

A 2nd attempt was made last night to ship away the several thousand French OT workers and foreign political prisoners. They left harbour at 10.30 p.m. but returned at 2.30 a.m. so there must have been something about. We have heard many tales of leaflets dropped on Alderney, supposed to be an ultimatum to surrender, but the most reasonable story I have been told is the leaflets offered safe passage away from Alderney to the civilians over a period of a certain number of days. The Germans intended taking the Senegalese prisoners of war, who have been here some time, and civilian prisoners on more than two months sentence (those on German sentences).

JULY 1944

July 1st 1944

July 1st starts the 5th year of Occupation. I hoped not to include such a statement, but even now I blame the unsuitable weather we are not already free.

A big change has come over the Evening Post. Dr. Wolken, late of College House, and a BA of Edinburgh, has been given the job of censor. A radio has been installed there set to a German station and sealed in a room with the speaker and switch outside. (Thus do the Germans trust even their own officials). From German broadcasts the Editor can publish what he likes, together with local news, provided it is neither anti-British nor anti-German. The result is details of the Guernsey raid were given last night, and the raid at La Rocque was, for the 1st time, referred to, as well as the presence in the Island of the French workers from Alderney. Hitherto such items of news have been completely ignored. I don't know whether one can make any inference from this of official policy and intentions, but this same Dr. Wolken brought two radios to friend B the other day with the request "should they lose control" the sets were to be delivered to a certain address, so from the Germans' point of view, he doesn't seem too hopeful. .

July 3rd 1944

Despite heavy rains over the weekend we heard a few planes passing and distant bombing. The French from Alderney left here on Friday night, but one boat load went aground somewhere and returned so a few of the poor devils are still wandering around. BBC reports the sinking of two and probably a 3rd ship off St. Malo and we wonder whether it was some of these. The weather is improving, but the only excitement is the passing of many planes out of sight about 1.45 p.m. The relaxing of tension amongst troops becomes more evident with the reopening of the Forum, which always closes at the 1st alarm. One does sometimes come across an odd German soldier off duty during the day time, plus many scuttlers, often attired in mixed clothing; survivors from the vessels sunk around here, have been fitted out with whatever clothes were immediately available.

July 5th 1944

The weather improved yesterday for flying, and quite a few planes passed this way without interference. Four fighters ended the day for us at 9.50 p.m. as we were hurrying home to be in for curfew, by diving from very high to about

50/100 feet along Greve D'Azette beach, and had a good look see at our local guns before zooming seawards at sea level. The battery on Elizabeth Castle fired two rounds, at least two miles from where the planes were – the worst miss I have yet seen. A report has come from local harbour officials the Navy sunk two and damaged other vessels carrying the Alderney evacuees and our political prisoners, after they failed to stop when called on to do so. They were battened down under hatches before leaving here, and so would stand a poor chance if anything happened. The same report says over 300 Frenchwomen lost their lives. Some shipping must have come, for coal was being carted to the gasworks over the weekend, and Jerry has been bringing up more cement for the concrete bunkers he is hurriedly building at St. Catherines, Greve de Lecq and elsewhere. We have been informed to expect no supplies of gas after mid-August, by which time arrangements for communal cooking. One of the centres is to be the Fish Market and the Old Market and stall holders have been given notice to quit in preparation.

I thought the shooting yesterday morning was the usual practise, but the BBC says the Navy chased some ships under cover of Jersey's coast batteries, damaging one.

July 6th 1944

Many planes passed during the night, but we were not disturbed by more than the drone of engines. This morning there have been sundry distant rumblings – presumably from gun fire in La Haye du Puits region. It seems a long time since we had our sleep disturbed at night. I hope it won't be long before we get that very noisy night for which we have waited, perforce patiently, for four weary years. I realise quite well it will be mighty bad medicine, but on that account too, the sooner it is over the better.

The town is fuller of rumour than I have yet known and that is saying something, but there certainly is something behind it all. One is the Germans expect their spot of trouble on the 12th, and another version is they are negotiating to declare this an open town. Both are not unreasonable especially the latter, provided they could get the 20/25,000 men and equipment now in the Islands safely to France where they are more needed. It is conceivable the Germans might use the safety of the 70,000 inhabitants as a bargaining point to get safe passage. It is also possible they know something which indicates trouble next week. Meanwhile, on their orders, the following arrangements, which might point to either of the two alternatives, have been made. The Bailiff and other officials are to sleep in the Court in the event of an alarm, and the Parish

Constables will stay at their respective Parish Halls. Paid Police have orders to be prepared to stay at the Police Station, whilst the Drains Department and Fire Brigade have also to be prepared to stay at their headquarters. It is presumed the idea of having various officials easily accessible is to hold them as hostage in case of trouble with the civil population. The period of alarm could be either Allied landing or whilst evacuation is being affected. Unconfirmed rumour expects a complete 4 to 7 day curfew. A week's ration of bread is being issued free to all, and it is believed rations of butter, flour, sugar, tinned milk and tunny fish are also to be issued. Those are the facts – meanwhile we just wait and see.

July 7th 1944
I am told that yesterday the smoke from bombing or gun fire was clearly visible from Gorey. There was surely an almost continuous rumble. A large contingency of aircraft passing during the forenoon were greeted with a short and sharp burst of heavy flak, with usual negative results.

Today's rumour is men from 18 to 45 are to be interned in the various camps erected around the Island for OT workers whilst whatever is going to happen does.

July 8th 1944
The Germans seem ready for whatever is coming. Amongst their recent preparations are extra Red Cross markings and flags for every building which could conceivably come under Red Cross protection, and all approaches to these areas are labelled with German notices strung across the roads, which I think forbid fighting in the area. Another instance of their readiness is the many small pits dug in hedges or roadsides, covering cross roads – everywhere where they could be used by snipers.

July 12th 1944
Due no doubt to the strong winds and poor visibility, there has been just about nothing to report. Some planes have passed our way without being molested, a few clearly visible. There is more rumour this morning, and some of it is reasonable and borne out by available data. Colonel Knackfuss, late Civil Commandant, is here again, and supposedly a meeting was held yesterday at Hotel Metropole, the Military H.Q. at which the Bailiff and other local officials were present. I am given to understand many German orders for vegetables, milk etc. have been cancelled for this weekend. There are many rumours in like vein, all indicating the possibility our friends intend a moonlight flit during the

next few days. I don't know whether any negotiations have been made with the British Government, but if so, it could account for the lack of flak opposition. Last night, for instance, 4 planes passed along the coast over Demi des Pas light, not more than 100 feet up, a good target one would think, but they were not fired on. Again this morning, two fair sized batches passed without interference. One chap says they numbered 42. There is a yarn, which may only be a yarn, 2,000 troops left last night in 5 ships.

I have just realised, whereas one never sees a German soldier without arms since D-day, I have never yet seen one of the Italians armed. I have asked many friends, but they too cannot remember seeing the Italians with rifles. It rather looks as if they do not trust the short arsed little twerps either. I fancy their duties are confined to being general housemaids to the German forces – rather degrading for poor Musso's henchmen.

July 13th 1944

There are several contradictions about the facts which might be relevant to the possibilities of our friends leaving us, the chief topic for discussion these days. Several ships, including a small hospital ship, have been in harbour for some days, and during last evening a convoy of 7 ships of assorted sizes came from St. Malo or Granville direction in daylight, apparently without interference. Against this one hears the cancellation of orders for vegetables etc. has been countermanded. You can take your choice which you believe. I imagine it suits Britain quite well to keep 20,000 soldiers locked up in the Islands, costing only a few air and light naval patrols – less effort than to keep a like number in prison camps. The commanding position of Alderney has to be taken into account, and the use of Guernsey for U boats, so maybe they would like to mop up the Islands. Assuredly Jerry would have everything to gain and nothing to lose by abandoning the Islands – if he could.

There has been another series of wireless arrests, the work of our notorious Quisling, Mrs. B, the concubine of a most repulsive looking German captain, and from accounts, due for a rough time as soon as this is over. One hears she hopes to go with the Germans, and maybe that wouldn't be an unsuitable punishment. I have reported few of these cases, but there must be a hundred or two who have served or are serving sentences in this connection. Our just friends are not content with getting the man with the set, but must collect all the friends and relations who could possibly know about it. The great majority of these cases, I am ashamed to say, are the result of anonymous letters.

July 15th 1944

13 ships left here last night – contents unknown, but we heard nothing during the night to indicate they were intercepted. 8 planes passed along the coast low just before 9.00 a.m. this morning, I don't know whether Allied or German, though I don't think Jerry has that number left – no guns were fired. The Opera House has been stripped in readiness to serve as an emergency hospital.

These last 5 weeks have dragged more than the previous 4 years. Before, one just carried on with the remote prospect of something happening in the indefinite future. Since D Day we have been expecting our release almost from day to day, and every day has seemed interminable. Neither our nerves nor minds are normal now. I find the best solution is to keep busy. We have prepared the store for post war re-stocking, and more recently by making radio cabinets also for post Occupation.

July 17th 1944

My remarks about a possible truce in the Islands were, as usual a little premature, judging by the heavy barrage put up for a few minutes on Saturday evening against 6 bombers passing over the centre of the Island.

I went out to Gorey last evening, the weather having cleared during the afternoon but the French coastline was shrouded in a haze. It was apparent the boys were taking full advantage of the better conditions. I saw dozens of formations, groups of little silver dots, very high and out to sea – out of range of local flak – whilst the explosions coming from the direction of the fighting literally made the earth shake. I don't think it was imagination that made me feel the tail end of the blast effects.

July 18th 1944

Yesterday's finer weather resulted in intense, but from our point of view, negative air activity. Many planes passed, some visible, and there was heavy distant bombing, but no local incidents, not even flak. It continued throughout the night, and at least two explosions were of such intensity as to suggest an ammo dump being destroyed.

July 21st 1944

The heavy bombing seems to have been the great RAF preparation for the advance south of Caen – 65 miles away. Six heavy bombers crossed the Island on Wednesday, so low they looked as though they were intending to attack. There have been rumours of bombs having been dropped, but they remain rumours.

I hear from someone who has seen a copy, British news, printed in German, is being distributed locally to the troops by throwing copies into lorries, cars, etc. It is in the form of packets of cigarette papers, the top leaf is blank, whilst subsequent leaves contain the news printed in red. This, one presumes, is part of the general upheaval of the conspiracy in Germany, now trying to carry out a coup d'état. Other than this there appears to be no local reaction to events to date, though it is raining heavily enough to deter any revolution.

I believe, soon after the Allied landing in France, the buyers in France for Jersey and Guernsey were interned, for fear no doubt they might try to contact the Allies. In their stead, a man named Kirchaer was sent, and he now seems to be missing. The German police have several times interviewed his British wife, but no one seems to know where he is.

July 24th 1944

Saturday evening the heavy batteries gave a few minutes concentrated effort against planes passing through thick cloud. They probably showed zeal because of the largish convoy which was just leaving, the presence of shipping being usually a signal for greater flak activity. Throughout yesterday planes were passing and distant bombing was heard.

A piece of AA shell, during Saturday's little blitz, penetrated the roof of my workmate's house, causing slight injury to his wife. A few weeks ago, another pierced the roof of my next door neighbour's place, who said I was courting disaster because I just can't stay indoors when there is any fun?

Much increased air activity today, especially at lunch time when, shortly after many planes passed, a stick of bombs was heard to explode not far away, followed later by some machine gunning. One presumes shipping just out of sight was being attacked. Heavy flak had just sent up a few ear splitters against high flying planes, but the planes were out of sight.

July 25th 1944

A big 4 engine bomber, possibly a Liberator, has just gone over town, flying straight, not fast, and at not more than 1,500 feet. One would imagine a perfect target for flak. Everything opened up at it, and gave a demonstration of lousy shooting, not one of the hundreds of rounds fired coming close enough to disturb it on its imperturbable course.

Yesterday afternoon's little flak exercise was, I am told, principally directed against two US fighters which came low enough for markings to be recognised. One big piece of shrapnel came through the market roof, without causing casualties.

The solitary plane was something in the nature of hors d'oeuvres, for he was followed half an hour later (about 10.45 a.m.) by hundreds (possibly 1,000 or more) of others. I lost all count, there being a bewildering number of formations. Flak was not as heavy as against the solo bird, and was concentrated only against those formations which were nearest overland. The great majority kept south of the Island, though easily visible, not high, and well below cloud level. The procession took over half an hour to pass, and has thrilled and delighted us all no end. It is surely the biggest group of aircraft we have ever seen, and makes the Luftwaffe in its heyday, when we used to get fleets in the region of 80 to 100, look very small.

Our guardians are faithfully obeying the new anti-revolution edict of their Fuhrer, and giving the "Heil Hitler" instead of the military salute, though many must be thinking "To hell with Hitler".

During the lunch hour, a solitary fighter has been doing aerobatics. He may be the representative of the Luftwaffe, showing it still exists, but being weak publicity as a show of air power after the morning's display by his competitors. Or it might be one of our own lads, figuratively putting his fingers to his nose to the local flak.

July 26th 1944

My guess as to yesterday's number of planes was conservative. The BBC says 1,500 heavy bombers plus a like number of fighters doing a softening up west of St. Lo.

Last year, when isolated Colorado beetles were found here, (on each occasion by Germans) the Germans insisted all our crops be sprayed. Although most people believed the finding was faked, the order was duly obeyed. It turns out the Germans did not carry out their own order, with the result their farm at Verclut, Grouville, is now infested, the crop being eaten down to bare stalks. This is the worst time for the pest, for as it can now fly, it cannot be localised. Most of us believe it is deliberate and not just gross carelessness on the part of the Germans. Everywhere else they had to leave they have done the maximum amount of damage possible, and they know the Colorado beetle can do a good share of their destructive work for them. It will mean no agricultural exports to England for the next 5 years.

There has been a relaxation of the beach ban order, and short stretches of beach at West Park, St. Clements Bay and La Rocque are now open for bathing up to 6.00 p.m.

I understand certain local people put profit so far in front of patriotism they are buying property in their own names on behalf of Germans, thus evading the law that no foreigner may own property. From the German's point of view this is a good arrangement – knowing his own country to be finished, he will want to invest his worthless paper money in a stake in a place which will, by comparison, be a much more pleasant place to live – and be willing to pay for the privilege by a generous amount to the patriotic Britisher who makes it possible.

July 31st 1944
There have been more wireless arrests, at St. Brelades this time.

About a dozen ships – minesweeper escorts, barges and cargo boats came in this morning, apparently from Granville (now cut off) seemingly without having been molested by the RAF or Navy. We were disappointed they got through, though I cannot see the sense of them coming here instead of (say) St. Brieuc or St. Malo.

AUGUST 1944

August 1st 1944
A very disturbed night; better weather brought heavy bombing during the evening, and about midnight there were several explosions of the sort that make one think the doors and windows are coming loose from their fastenings. Later on our coastal batteries joined in the game of keeping us awake, so we await with interest any news which may throw some light.

August 2nd 1944
Another restless night, heavy bombing, much rifle and machine gun rattle from a crowd doing their anti-invasion stuff around home, rounded off by more coast battery activity. BBC reports suggest the heavy bombing to be oil dumps at St Malo, whilst the coast guns probably opened up against Allied reinforcements which the Germans report are being landed south west of Avranches.

Telephones are again in operation between 8.00 a.m. and 8.00 p.m. but despite this sign the Germans regard the emergency as less urgent, they seem to be in a greater state of preparedness than usual, consequent no doubt on the fact every hour brings more complete isolation as the Yanks approach St. Malo.

August 3rd 1944

The 3rd successive, almost sleepless night – this time bombing on a super scale was wholly responsible.

I had a soul-satisfying row with an erstwhile friend whom I found to be supplying potatoes to the Germans (black market) – for once I can't remember anything I left unsaid that might have been included. Usually I think of all the remarks I might have made after the argument, not this time.

August 5th 1944

Perfect weather conditions, intermittent bombing and a situation for the occupying forces which the BBC describes as "delicate" and with cut off almost complete. 7 or 8 ships came in this morning, presumably from St. Malo. For several nights now a low flying plane, from the sound of it German, passed over and it is believed the mail for the troops is brought that way.

Later - I believe a small batch of US paratrooper prisoners, some wounded, were brought up by the boats this morning.

August 8th 1944

Perfect weather, except for a light haze. Activity over the holiday weekend around the district has been in an ever increasing crescendo. Confirmed by the BBC is a naval action between here and St. Malo early Sunday, of which we heard sundry bangs, without knowing what was happening. Throughout Sunday we heard sounds of gunfire and bombing intermittently, no doubt from St. Malo region. Yesterday (Monday) there was a considerable step up in air activity, and although the haze prevented us from seeing most of the planes (I only saw 13), many hundreds must have passed our way. There was one short burst of flak during the forenoon when some passed over the harbour area. During the afternoon three more crossed the island, and this was immediately followed by a rip-snorting explosion giving the impression of a bomb on the Island. I heard of none, so presume it was just a particularly heavy one somewhere in France, not connected with the planes. In the early evening 8 more passed in 2 wing tip to wing tip formations, and later 2 heavies circled St. Aubins Bay before disappearing. Our local light battery thought they were preparing to attack them, as did I, but they just went peacefully on. Throughout the evening, night, and this morning terrific bombing on the adjacent coasts shook the Island, partly explained by the BBC report of 1,000 heavies doing their stuff south of Caen. We heard of the ultimatum to the St. Malo garrison, but judging from the noise coming from that direction, it has not been accepted. It lends colour to the general expectation here, now we are completely surrounded, an ultimatum will be dropped here during the next few days – whether or not it will be accepted is another tale. It would be nice for if it was, but I can hardly imagine 4 years of occupation will end so tamely.

August 9th 1944

The considerable air traffic, with intermittent bombing, continues. One big machine, or a close formation of planes, came within range of the heavy batteries about 9.00 p.m. last night, and had about 50 rounds sent in its general direction. A hospital ship brought some 350 German wounded from St. Malo last night causing considerable activity amongst the ambulances. At 6.00 a.m. this morning there was another naval action quite close inshore along the south coast. I went to sleep last night with the sounds of the anti-invasion exercise being carried out in my ears, and half awakened by gun fire, thought in my comatose state the practise was still going on. Therefore I have to rely on 2nd hand, and conflicting reports, but it seems two ships were sunk and others damaged, whilst we lost an E boat. The action was fought so close in, houses along the coast to St. Brelades are said to have been damaged.

Later - I hear there are about 350 wounded in the General Hospital, plus many more in German hospitals at Mayfair and Merton Hotels and the Ladies College, and the town is crowded with less severely wounded, so several hundred must have been brought. The harbour is full of ships, and it is rumoured many troops have been brought from Guernsey owing to the more difficult food situation there. Another rumour insists Alderney is being evacuated. Certainly a quantity of big guns and ammo has arrived.

August 11th 1944

Once again I have to rely on other eyes for information a blazing ship appeared from the south about 2.00 p.m. yesterday, and sank before getting in; by the time I got to the coast road she had disappeared. Last night too, the coast road was the venue for many people watching large fires in St. Malo.

August 12th 1944

There were further strong noises from the direction of St. Malo and Dinard during the afternoon and evening, and a big pall of smoke, which must have risen to a considerable height to stand high above the horizon to us 40 miles away. Another disturbed night, with many planes passing and our own coast batteries again in action, no details yet.

There was a demonstration in town this morning, when two Yanks recently brought as prisoners were taken (under guard) to Roberts, the Germanite hairdresser. A crowd collected, and it looked as if the shop front would be pushed in. Local and German police were called, many names taken and people warned to attend at College House. Also in trouble are 3 youths (one a parson's son) who beat up an informer. Two US sailors' bodies have been washed ashore, presumably from the E boat lost this week, and are to be buried Tuesday at the Howard Davis Park cemetery. I have been given a version of that scrap – our E boats sank 2 ships and a barge, and one of the E boats, finding himself in a sinking condition, rammed and damaged another vessel. The German communiqué version is one of their vessels rammed and sank one of ours. If so, she must have done the ramming sideways, as one of their vessels is at present lying below the abattoirs with damage which would meet the case.

Later – No proof, but I have an idea the affair at Roberts shop was a hoax – I cannot imagine the Germans provoking the demonstrations they loathe by bringing US prisoners, still in uniform, through the main streets of the town, just to get their hair cut. One would expect the barber to be sent in to them. A yarn like that would spread quickly and collect a crowd, and mass auto suggestion would quickly provide many to testify to the report's truth.

August 14th 1944

A fairly quiet weekend but with more intermittent loud noises from St. Malo and Dinard, and smoke could again be seen yesterday. The hospital ship made another trip on Saturday, bringing more wounded from there. Our garrison are carrying on with their detailed preparations to fight it out here, including digging small pits in gardens and on street corners in town for snipers, and a group of about 9 searchlights have been tested the last night or two towards the north of the Island.

August 15th 1944

More bombing and gun fire during the night and this morning – it sounds as if the Yanks are fed up with playing around St. Malo, and are just flattening the place. One of the US wounded has died, and was buried this morning with the two bodies recovered over the weekend.

One already hears tales of reduced German rations. For weeks now they have had horse flesh, no butter (only lard), and 3½ lbs of bread a week. They have taken some of our stocks of butter, with the result the extra two ounces we had fortnightly to replace the minus meat ration is no longer available. A small ration of cheese has been issued this time in lieu, but we won't get that for many fortnights. No doubt we shall suffer other cuts, with all imports stopped, and the Germans will surely not allow our rations to be larger than theirs. I am indebted to the BBC for the information, opening the direct assault on the Channel Islands, the Rodney gave Alderney a 2½ hour bombardment with 16 inch guns on Saturday. Judging by current sounds, the dose is being repeated – it sounds as if Alderney has been pushed nearer to here – even in town one feels the tremors.

There are many of the less severely wounded German soldiers and scuttlers wandering loose about town, and I notice a big proportion of those with arm and hand injuries have them on the left side. Query – are these self imposed or deliberately sought to get out of the fight?

There have been several more wireless cases – knowing they can't be taken to gaol in France or Germany, many people have become less careful. For me, I am just dying for the time when I can take home the super big job I have bought –both that, and the small one which has been such a boon this past 12 months, are doubly valuable for having been pinched off the Germans, the latter by an ingenious piece of miscounting on the part of friend B. Small as it is, and badly treated in being kept outside in a hollow concrete block, it has been a fine little job, and it will be nice for the set and me when I can turn the volume control right up instead of, as now, keeping it just audible.

Completely isolated as we are, once again in a backwater, we are seeing little now. There is an occasional spasm of noises from St. Malo region, but we have seen no planes the past day or two. There seems to be a considerable relaxation in the military precautions. Holes are still being dug in odd places to accommodate snipers, but our friends no longer carry tin hat, gas mask (and extra filter), rifle and full equipment as they have since D Day, except on guard duty.

Many times in the past 4 years we heard the gas and electricity supplies will only last a few weeks but every time some of the necessary material for producing has come along just in time. Now it seems definite the gas supply will expire on September 2nd, and this time there can be no reprieve – except a change to Allied control in time for supplies of coal to come. Meanwhile arrangements for communal meals are being made. Sea water is again on sale for cooking purposes, to supplement the salt ration of one ounce a month, and is being used in making bread, to its detriment.

As I thought, no Americans were in Roberts Shop on Saturday – the whole thing was a hoax. 47 people had to appear at College House on Sunday, and from them 10 were selected to return on Monday, when they were fined 10 to 20 Marks, according to their incomes, the other 37 being lucky.

August 19th 1944

The Germans are commandeering 350 heavy old farm horses (believed for troop fodder), and lending as replacement a like number of their light draught horses. They have also taken 800 tons of our wheat harvest, their own stocks having suffered badly through being kept in tunnels with which they have honeycombed the place. I notice many new iron crosses about, particularly amongst the many scuttlers wandering around loose – I imagine the recipients to be émigrés from St. Malo. There is considerable banging going on now – gun fire, not bombs, and I don't think it is practise. These Islands being the only German occupied territory within earshot, it must be local, and I fancy our own coastal batteries have been helping with the noise.

August 21st 1944

Saturday's sundry noises were a daylight naval action. Jerry was taking advantage of poorer visibility to slip through a convoy from Guernsey or Alderney, and was unlucky. The Navy chimed in the whole time the convoy was coming around Grosnez until it got into St. Aubins and coastal batteries had one of the biggest 'dos'. Results are variously reported – on my way home from work, I saw two of their escort minesweepers tied abreast of each other, with a tug ahead towing at an angle, from which I deduce the steering and probably engines of one of them was damaged in the action. As they approached the pier, an increased amount of smoke was seen coming from the group, as though a fire had broken out.

The Germans, in commandeering local farm horses for sausage meat, are not replacing with smaller horses as I previously understood, but offering to hire one out to the farmers who lose their horse for an occasional day, if available.

August 23rd 1944

On Sunday there was more banging going on; it may be demolition in clearing docks at St. Malo. Four planes went across during the evening, but although not high there was no flak. I believe in Saturday's naval cum-coastal battery action there was an explosion at one of the guns firing from La Moye, causing several casualties amongst the crew and damage to neighbouring houses.

When the invasion took place, I confidently expected the Germans to leave these Islands before they were trapped, as they now are. I imagine it to be the result of an oversight on the part of the High Command in the panic of the few days after the landing, when it became apparent the BEF had come to stay. There seems no military, and little political reason for attempting to hold the Islands as isolated pockets. Even if they were putting up an aggressive defence, with an occasional raid on the French coast (they have the shipping here), it might make sense. They have adopted a completely passive 'wait for it' policy, this forgotten army, and yet signs point to them intending to put up a scrap for the place when the moment arrives.

There are many more troops here now than a month ago, brought from St. Malo and from the other Islands, as well as the scuttlers from the many ships in harbour. I even hear there are ships at St. Aubins, which would be used for the defence of the Islands. The figure of the total number of Germans here now, including wounded, is said to be in the region of 12,000 to 14,000. Assuming say 8,000 are available for fighting purposes, they could make a great nuisance of themselves to any landing force. I regard a seaborne landing as almost out of the question, with the natural defences of a rocky, dangerous coast, large rise and fall of tide, and well placed coastal defence positions. So I expect to see an airborne invasion sometime soon, preceded by an ultimatum. Many people here expect the Germans to be left here until the end of the war, but from a purely selfish point of view I hope not. It would mean considerable hardship in food and other essential items, which after 4 years, most of us are not in a position to withstand, plus the distinct possibility of a period when military discipline would cease to exist, and when the garrison would become merely armed bandits. It is all surmise but the question of what will happen to the Islands, and when, is uppermost in all our minds. I make no apology for Jersey there has been no emulation of the feats of the FFI. I fancy there would not have been many towns liberated in France by them if they had been policed at the rate of 200 to 300 to the square mile, as we are here.

August 26th 1944

Stories have been circulating, purporting to have come out of a recent meeting between States and German officials, it was the German intention to treat these Islands as model occupied territory, and to capitulate without subjecting them to the devastation of fighting. Now I get definite information from friend B, who has been told by Dr. Wolken, previously referred to, the Islands will be surrendered within 3 weeks; which would be nice from the point of view of all concerned.

There is little activity here now, except for the sounds of bombing, which would be from Brest, and if German reports are true, (they probably are this time) from the small island fortress off St. Malo still holding out. I am told the naval commander from St. Malo is here, and he often runs across to the isolated garrison at nights, taking water, food, and ammo. One must admit they and he are brave, if foolhardy, their courage deserving of a better cause. I also hear they are dismantling some at least of the armed escort minesweepers. It may be only those damaged are being so treated, though reports talk of all.

August 31st 1944

Heavy flak sent a few rounds after a group of planes flying at wave top height off the south coast about 5.30 p.m. yesterday, and it wasn't long before we heard bombing noises, so it would seem Cezembre (St. Malo) was again being attacked. During the forenoon, our coast batteries had a frantic few seconds, but I haven't been able to find out what the target was – probably the Navy came in further than usual.

SEPTEMBER 1944

September 1st 1944

Two editions of leaflets, printed in German, have been dropped, giving up to the minute news of the situation in France, pointing out the hopelessness of the situation. Countering this Allied propaganda, there have been meetings at the Forum, in an attempt one presumes to bolster morale.

September 2nd 1944

The States taking an unexpectedly firm tone in the present crisis gives some indication of our plight. In addition to rations, we are to receive the following items, supplies of which we presume will stay constant – 4¼ lbs bread, 7 ounces oat flour, 5 lbs potatoes, 3½ pints milk, a plentiful supply of vegetables (unrationed), and 4 ounces meat fortnightly. Even those who have supplemented rations on the black market are finding it increasingly difficult to get anything.

To make matters worse, gas ceases Monday. The fuel situation generally is about as bad as it can be. An instance of the devaluation of money in relation to fuel is a tender of £1,000 for timber to be demolished from a store at Commercial Buildings. Most of it is pretty ripe and it is computed it will cost the speculator £18 per ton.

We have all had occasion to criticise the States in their difficult task, but in this most difficult phase, surely the most ardent of the underground Jersey

Democrats will concede to the States firmness combined with diplomacy above criticism. On the subject of food, our final jam ration, 1lb about every 8 weeks, has been commandeered, as has a further quantity of wheat and oats.

As an experiment, electricity is being cut off for 3 evenings at 11.00 p.m. This will be rather awkward for the 'little man' – won't be able to hear the midnight news. All cooking by electricity is banned, to bring electricity users into line with gas consumers. Communal cooking starts Monday, but I can't see it being a great success. Under present conditions, one hot meal a day isn't much, with nothing to make suitable cold dishes for other meals. I am afraid most peoples' 'hot' meals won't burn them by the time they get them home from the bake house. Most people have exactly no fuel, there having been no ration during the summer months, and the ration for September won't help much – one hundredweight of wood and half a hundredweight of anthracite dust-cum-tar. As our States have pointed out to the German Authorities, it is indeed time this most lousy business came to an end – though their phraseology is less crude than mine.

September 6th 1944

A single big plane was greeted with heavy flak yesterday evening and it flew in the usual dignified way over the Island. A little later and again this morning, upwards of 50 planes were allowed to pass without interference, presumably from returning from tidying up at Brest.

More electricity restrictions – 'perms' are banned, as is the use of electricity for any purpose in a long list of specified businesses on Mondays, Wednesdays and Thursdays. No doubt in order the Germans may not be inconvenienced by the 11.00 p.m. cut off they have been commandeering 6 and 12 volt batteries.

September 7th 1944

Air activity continued throughout yesterday, with a constant stream passing back from Brest, all without flak opposition.

The new communal cooking is now in full swing. We are doing our entire ménage on a perforated bucket, relying on others' experience of this makeshift answer to the no-gas and no-fuel situation. The population were offered the choice of registering for meals at one of several restaurants still operating for one meal a day, forfeiting their meat ration and part of their potato ration. Except it works out dear (2/- to 2/6d for a small vegetarian meal), this arrangement is working well. The other alternative was to register for communal cooking at a bake house, some of which have been specially erected, to take one small dish per household either at midday or evening. One hears nothing but moans about this arrangement – meals completely uncooked or much overdone, or upset by unskilful handling. No doubt there will be improvement as experience is gained, though I cannot see the mass production arrangement working with such a motley collection of dishes. There has been a certain amount of moaning about the cut of gas, but nothing comparable with what might have been expected (and would have been justifiable). Revised electricity regulations – current is now to be cut off between midnight and 6.00 a.m. whilst refrigerators and all domestic appliances are banned – this to bring consumption within the capacity of the steam power house the Germans erected in St Peters Valley. Our own Queens Road station has only enough oil to run for 3 weeks, to be kept in case of breakdown of the steam plant.

September 9th 1944

More leaflets, booklets and dummy German money dropped last night – the latter a good facsimile on one side, whilst the other is used for propaganda.

September 11th 1944

Our German friends got into a panic yesterday morning, looking for paratroops suspected to have been dropped around St. Johns. I am told they have started a general house to house search for wireless sets. I am content, if they find my little man at home hidden in a dummy concrete block ostensibly supporting the meat safe, they deserve to catch me. It is a great consolation they can't take one away, and can only keep one in gaol a short time. The only snag is you lose your set. The two at the store have been transferred to a less obvious hiding place – in the grain. All this adds a spice of interest to life. If our friends had the sense to make the search a massive affair, and covered the Island in a day (they could with 17,000 troops available) they would catch a lot. As it is, everyone is forewarned, and it is only the foolish and unlucky who get caught. It may be they don't want to catch too many as the gaol is already overfull, just scare folk into not listening. Despite the fact the initial search is being made close to the store, I am not nearly as windy as I used to be when they caused these scares in the past.

There was another escape attempt and failure on Saturday night when two or more men tried to get away from Le Hocq on floats and were caught. Details are lacking, except the names of two are Le Sueur and Briard.

September 16th 1944

Leaflets continue to arrive every night with regularity. We hear occasional bombing from the direction of Brest, and had the pleasure of seeing 5 of our planes pass at about 3,000 feet on Thursday evening.

September 19th 1944

A young girl (Miss Turner) and a Dutchman got away on Saturday evening in broad daylight from Havre des Pas. I don't know whether they made it or not, but they certainly deserve success for their ingenuity in not using the usual 'hole in a corner' method. The search for radios seems to be going on continually, but they seem to select just a small group of houses here and there to search. I have not yet heard of anyone being caught, but that it easily explained. It is invariably known a day in advance where the selected area is. The news plane has become such a regular habit we listen for it every night, with its pop pop as the canisters of leaflets explode and scatter their contents.

September 20th 1944

There was another escape attempt last night. I gather 3 young men were picked up swimming in an exhausted condition near Le Hocq this morning. I imagine their float, or whatever they were using, capsized.

Guernsey's steam power plant was not finished before we got into a state of siege, so they do not need the 400 tons of steam coal taken there in readiness. It has been brought here, and the fuel oil we were holding for use at the Queens Road Power House has been sent there to keep their oil plant going. Barring breakdowns (a big possibility in a plant literally Jerry built) we are comparatively well off now for electricity, and can hold out till the New Year. One hears the Bailiff took advantage of the opportunity of the exchange to go to Guernsey to interview Major General Schmettow, Military Commandant of the Islands.

I just heard the girl Turner has been brought back after being at sea for nearly 3 days. I don't know whether the Dutchman was brought back with her. In one way it is foolish to try to get away – we have waited more than 4 years and there can't be so long to go now – surely not long enough to justify the great risks entailed in a crossing to France on a float. Given my own old canoe, suitable weather and the short run from Gorey, I wouldn't mind trying myself, but it seems most of the recent attempts are completely foolhardy. None of us are physically capable of standing the many hours of exposure and muscular effort necessary to paddle a minimum of 25 miles amongst fast running tides. In addition most of the recent attempts have been by those who lack the essential experience in handling this temperamental type of craft in an open sea, especially as the first part of the trip must be made in the dark through rock infested waters. On the other hand, I should like to know the powers were aware of the position in the Islands, both from a civil and military point of view. For instance, the BBC have several times mentioned the Islands as holding a division of troops, whereas I gather, there are 17,000 here, 6,500 in Guernsey and 3,500 in Alderney.

September 22nd 1944

There was considerable firing from the coast batteries last night. I imagine the Navy must have come in closer than usual. It is curious the mail plane, still as regular as ever, is never fired upon, although he never flies high and always comes around 10.00 p.m.

Friend B was searched again this morning. They say they know civilian sets are being repaired somewhere, but didn't suspect him. The search was cursory and they didn't notice many things which might have produced awkward questions.

September 26th 1944

Leaflets go on arriving nearly every night, and quite a few people have received short gaol sentences for having or distributing them.

It is generally believed 5 men got safely to France. Several people claim to have heard the report of their arrival on the French news.

September 28th 1944

It is rumoured an Allied officer went to Guernsey under a flag of truce during the early part of this week, and Schmettow refused to see him. Schmettow arrived in Jersey yesterday and is supposed to be in conference with local officials. It is also said no fishing boats are allowed out, and even the nocturnal patrols are now banned, following the decamping of some scuttlers in a patrol boat.

September 30th 1944

No leaflets have been dropped this week, which may be connected with the reported visit to Guernsey of the Allied Officer. This last is not confirmed, but I am told Major General Schmettow informed the States of his intention to defend the Islands to the end. When asked what would happen when food for the population ran out, he is supposed to have replied an appeal would have to be made to the Red Cross.

There have been two more escapes, one Thursday night, one last night, and as far as I know, both got clear of the Island. One lot of 5 went from L'Etacq in a boat with sail and two outboard motors, but I don't know details. I know of two more escapes pending, one for next week, and one for the following week. It is getting quite a regular traffic.

OCTOBER 1944

October 4th 1944

In addition to cutting supplies of electricity for 12 hours daily as per the new order, we have to contend with regular unintentional breaks, as a result of overloads and breakdowns.

We thought last night our mail plane had taken up its old round, when a plane came circling low. There were several sharp explosions in the air, accompanied by vivid flashes, much bigger affairs than the leaflet canister explosions, and there seem to be no leaflets about today. We wonder whether the plane came for the purpose of taking floodlight photographs.

October 5th 1944

I quote Mr. Eden's reply to a question in Parliament yesterday, vide the BBC:

"The garrisons in Jersey and Guernsey have been given the chance to surrender, but they have refused. There is nothing to show that they are not treating civilians properly".

Latest economy is water, now completely cut off except for short periods each morning, afternoon and evening, totalling 5½ hours daily.

October 10th 1944

A further group escaped on Sunday night from Rozel, an apparently impossible locality, but one hears they got over the difficulty of evading the guards by giving them passage to France. Another crowd went last night from Le Bourg, a more suitable spot, there being no German posts between Rocqueberg and La Rocque Point, the only fear being of patrols, whose heavy footsteps usually give away their approach. In general the German attitude to escapees now seems to be – go if you can, and to blazes with you. Certainly there have been none of the reprisals which might have been expected, even against the immediate relatives of those who have gone; and those intending to go make no secret of their intentions. I knew, for instance, several days before about Sunday's crowd, even where they were to leave from, and I know of at least two more batches intending to try this week, and others pending. I think almost everyone young enough has considered the pros and cons, but for me, I feel having waited for 4 years, it isn't worth taking the attendant risks for the sake of what might only be a few days. Foolish as it sounds, my self-imposed duties as historian of the Occupation have helped me in coming to that decision.

October 11th 1944

At least one more boat load made the attempt last night, but with the wind springing up early this morning, they made for the Island again. Approaching St. Catherine they were fired on, one of the crowd was killed and, I believe, another injured.

October 14th 1944

Further details of the above unfortunate incident show the 6 men put in to Anneport after their outboard motor broke down. They carried their gear up out of the boat, returned and got the motor, and were returning for the 3rd time to pull the boat high and dry when machine guns opened up. One, Machon, had most of his head shot away, whilst another suffered injury to his hand. One can attach no blame to the Germans, who might possibly have imagined it to be a small scale commando raid. Subsequent heavy weather, and maybe this distressing business, has deterred the several parties due to go since then.

The Gendarmerie have been having an 'anti black market' round up, and examining the parcels of everyone approaching town. As usual, the word went around quickly and I don't think they made very heavy hauls. I imagine it to be an attempt to stop civilians getting the extras, so they can have them. Their policy of cutting the rations of the troops and increasing their pay would surely point that way.

October 16th 1944

There appears to have been another panic last evening. The sirens sounded about 8.30 p.m. and all the Germans left cafes, pictures, Soldatenheims to rush to action stations. The 'all clear' went about 10.00 p.m. and it is rumoured the Navy and RAF were off the west coast in strength. There is no evidence of any action, and it may only have been a try out.

I think these last 3 months have been the worst of the whole Occupation. When the invasion came, especially as it was so close, we all thought it would only be a matter of a few weeks before we were relieved. Now we are in a state of complete siege, with a garrison showing no signs of any intention to surrender until forced to. We fully realise the natural and artificial defences of the Island would make it a difficult nut to crack – so difficult indeed it would seem to be hardly worth the Allies while to attempt it. So we are faced with a peculiarly lousy situation, with food becoming less, and with the next man's guess about the probabilities as good as one's own. It seems there are three possibilities and none of them good.

Firstly – an attempt to take the Islands by force. This would be expensive, with a strong and well entrenched garrison. The alternatives are the civilian population might be evacuated to France first – a big job, to shift 70,000 people – or, if left here, would suffer badly in the fighting.

Secondly - the Germans may surrender through food shortage, if the war goes on so long. By the time the German garrison are so short of food and medical supplies as to hoist the white flag, how many civilians will be interested? The Germans will certainly not go short whilst we have anything.

The last possibility is the war ending with the Germans still in control. Even that has disturbing possibilities. It is surely not unreasonable to expect rioting following such an event as the official capitulation, and it is difficult to know what an unarmed population could do against armed rioters.

In view of the appeal to the Protecting Power (Switzerland), it is possible, if no local invasion is intended, there may be supplies of food, soap and medical supplies, our primary needs, brought here. I am not sure I would whole heartedly welcome them. We should get all that arrived by such means, but it would absolve the Germans of all responsibility towards us.

It is therefore hardly surprising if these past months have been an increasing headache. Our prospects of release are as remote as 6 months back, whilst our position all round is infinitely worse. All our nerves have suffered considerably, and there is a pessimistic tendency showing through the Island. No one, even the many Germanites (and probably the Germans themselves) doubts the issue, but it appears certain we have to face a 5th and infinitely worse winter under occupation and siege.

October 19th 1944

The anti black market campaign was apparently the result of a misunderstanding between the German civil and military authorities. As many unrationed goods and genuine rations were confiscated in addition to black market stuff, the States are supposed to have protested. There was a notice in last night's paper defining black market and it is generally believed there will be no more of this general search business.

Probably because of the several escape attempts, the order allowing the use of a few lengths of beach for bathing is now cancelled. In the case of those wishing to go vraicing or limpeting, individual permission must be obtained from the Commander of the district.

I hear two Dutch barge skippers and two local men went on Saturday or Sunday night from Gorey and they can't have had a very smooth trip. I am also told, thanks to a local informer, several more fellows have been caught preparing a boat at St. Saviours for a future attempt.

Most farmers have received orders to plant no grain or potatoes for 1945. It seems the seed so saved will enable the Germans to hold out a week or two longer. They are drawing heavily from the 1944 harvest, which though a comparatively good one, cannot stand the strain for long. I have just received an order to supply them with 10 tons from wheat I am storing for the States, and wish I could get enough rat poison to dope it.

October 23rd 1944

After an unsuccessful attempt on Saturday night, from which they got safely ashore, a party of 5 men and a girl left from Pontac last night in a 14 foot boat. Another intending party were caught yesterday. They were preparing canoes for the trip, and there having been the usual lack of reticence about their intentions, someone must have split on them. In addition to canoes, two radio sets were found.

There have been persistent rumours during the past week about a possible exchange of the garrison here with a like number of British prisoners from Germany. Rumour, our old friend, has it the Germans are demanding to leave the Islands with their guns and full battle honours, whilst the British demand they be regarded as exchange prisoners, and so only able to carry their personal belongings. This may be far from the truth, but the yarn is so persistent, and comes from usually impeccable sources, there may well be something in the form of negotiations proceeding behind it all.

October 27th 1944

The passage of a plane on Tuesday over the Island was followed by a rumour (unconfirmed) Red Cross representations had arrived either here or in Guernsey to enquire into local conditions. This was the first plane to pass this way for some while, but we heard others during yesterday.

Five intending escapees were unlucky on Wednesday night, for their boat had disappeared when they went to get away. The Germans got there first. They were not caught.

It is reported one of the first batch who was caught and gaoled, named Le Sueur, made an excuse to be taken under guard from the gaol to his home. There he locked the guard in a room, made a getaway on a bicycle, and is said to have since stolen a boat and got clear. He at least is one of the few who have enough experience of boat work to stand a chance of arriving on the other side. In an attempt to stop this wholesale evacuation, the Germans have issued an order calling for boats of any description, including canoes and floats and outboard motors, to be declared.

On Wednesday evening the doors of the States buildings and the premises of many known local collaborators were daubed with tar. Windows were broken and tarred swastikas painted on the walls. A notice in tonight's paper threatens an increase in curfew hours if this is repeated.

There has been great activity in the store this weekend, Jerry having commandeered a lot of our wheat and oats, as well as some going for Guernsey's civilian requirements. Jerry's stuff was duly sabotaged, a more useful racket than tarring local houses.

The Germans, continuing their anti black market campaign, and acting on an anonymous letter, this week raided the house of Dr. Labesse, and the proceeds thereof are displayed in a shop window in King Street. Bacon and a ton of potatoes are included in the spoils, which says the notice in the window, is to be handed over to the Communal Kitchens.

October 31st 1944

Last evening a big plane criss-crossed the Island several times, flying low and with navigation and cabin lights on. The last time it passed, heavy and light AA guns opened up a furious barrage for a few minutes, where on the plane extinguished its lights and appeared to dive. I hear this morning it crashed into the sea off St. Ouens. This is the first time local batteries have been in action for many weeks.

Later - the plane crashed off Bouley Bay. One member of the crew (US Navy) was rescued, and 3 bodies were recovered out of 7. They are to be buried on Saturday.

NOVEMBER 1944

November 4th 1944

The burial of the US Naval Airmen (6 now recovered) has been postponed till Monday. Meanwhile attempts are being made to salvage the plane and recover the bodies of the remainder of the crew (said to be 11).

The first, but probably not the last, occupation murder occurred this week, when a man strangled his Germanite wife, now 5 months pregnant, before hanging himself.

Despite the States refusal in their memorandum to reduce the rations further to eke them out, our sugar has been cut from 3 ounces to 2. One hears there is prospect of a cut in butter, too, following on a fair size confiscation from local stocks.

November 7th 1944

There were only 6 US Airmen buried yesterday, and judging by the fact some were clad only in underclothes when found, the plane must have been in trouble before it was fired on, and the men getting ready to bail out into the sea.

Despite German threats, there have been several more instances of tar daubing. Also, 4 youngsters were caught by the Gendarmerie with a quantity of dynamic whilst preparing up the premises of R, one of the Arch Germanites, last week.

November 11th 1944

Major General Graf Von Schmettow again arrived from Guernsey on Wednesday, since when many conferences and meetings have been held – results unknown, but duly and variously detailed in many rumours. It is a fact they have sequestrated all stocks of grain in excess of civilian requirements to 31st January.

In anticipation of the usual Hitler radio speech on November 8th, it was at first arranged the electricity be on all day, but this was later cancelled. Before this date, it was said the German troops here would regard Hitler's non-appearance at the mike as proof of the suspected fact he was no longer in existence, but I have not yet heard what the reaction actually was.

November 13th 1944

Another batch of youngsters (8) got away over the weekend, including Constable Crill's son. We are in the midst of yet another panic, there being prospects friend

B's shop and stocks may be commandeered in view of his refusal to undertake radio work at the Standort Kommandantur. Ergo, much valuable, as well as a lot of illicit, material had to be hurriedly lifted.

It is rumoured about 1,000 scuttlers are gaoled in the Fort. Their offence is variously reported to be shooting 3 officers and selling arms and ammo to civilians. It sounds a bit farfetched, but seems generally accepted as truth.

Another rumour concerns the meetings last week between Schmettow and the States, it being said he advised them to write to the Protecting Power themselves about conditions here. Sugar and salt rations have ceased, and anaesthetics are now only being used in vitally urgent cases. In other minor operations, local anaesthetics are being used, which must be trying to the nerves of the patient.

November 14th 1944

In the words of the Evening Post – "We are officially informed of the following – In spite of strict prohibition, 4 islanders again tried to leave the island yesterday in order to avoid the common fate of the inhabitants. Their boat was driven ashore and dashed to pieces against the cliffs of the north coast. They themselves were drowned. The population will only have to put to the credit of such irresponsible persons if the occupying authorities are now forced to take stricter measures for the enforcement of their orders".

This is not the batch referred to yesterday, which apparently got clear. In addition to this there is at least one man and probably more now in gaol, caught whilst preparing or attempting to get away. I know of yet another boat now undergoing the finishing touches for an attempt to get clear.

With things as they are now, and prospects getting worse each week, it is not surprising many people are regarding the not inconsiderable risks of the passage to France as a lesser evil than holding on and sharing the 'common fate of the inhabitants'. I think the Germans chose a rather apt term. Even the most chicken hearted here would welcome some decisive action, however drastic, in preference to this worrying period of gradually increasing starvation – for it is surely coming down to that stage.

Arrangements have been made for a limited number of Red Cross messages to be sent from here each month, presumably by air to Germany and thence via the usual channels.

Another chap had a narrow escape this morning when the Gendarmerie collected him at his shop to search his house for a radio. A quick witted friend in the shop at the time cycled quickly to the man's house, and arrived sufficiently before the Gendarmerie's car to throw the set over the garden wall into the next garden, so nothing was found. It gives one a queer feeling in the stomach whenever anyone is caught for this or any other offence of which one has been guilty. You can't help thinking "There, but for the Grace of God, go I".

November 17th 1944

I gather the 4 intending evacuees who lost their lives did so through bad arrangements. They smuggled themselves aboard a boat at Gorey at low tide, and were unable to test whether the engine and equipment were in order. When the tide rose, they slipped their moorings and let the boat drift out, but when clear found the engine wouldn't start. Whether there were paddles aboard which got lost, or whether there were none, the boat was certainly out of control when they lost her. She was sunk in daylight and quite a few people saw her go. Amongst the 4 were a 19 year old and his wife. I don't think any of them had experience of boat work.

It is fairly certain quite a lot of the others (upwards of 100) who have succeeded in getting clear of here have not arrived safely the other side. The weather has been far from perfect since the craze started. In addition to the open sea journey, there are the perils of landing an open boat on an unknown and exposed coast.

Laundries are no longer able to take civilian work, and the mills are no longer allowed to grind the wheat which civilians have gleaned (or obtained by other methods less able to stand the light of investigation). The Germans have ordered all horse owners (who were allowed to keep a certain quota of their own growing of oats) to bring in half and it is understood a search of all farms is to be undertaken immediately. This is because an appeal to farmers to bring their stuff into town has failed. One hears, having run through all the horse flesh which can possibly be spared from the limited quantity available for civil and military transport, the Germans intend and will soon start taking our cattle for meat. As usual, they invoke International Law to stress their right. No account seems to be taken of the effect which the reduced milk supply will have when, after a certain amount of cattle have been slaughtered, it begins to make itself felt. I quote these small items as some indication of the reasons for our feeling of apprehension as to the future.

November 18th 1944

I had a look at the boat in which another crowd intend to decamp tonight. I reckon they must be nuts. The sea has not settled after a strong wind yesterday, and the fresh breeze still blowing is right in their teeth. The boat is a 10 foot dinghy, with trysail and outboard. It will surely give the wind a nice grip on the boat. Unless they change their minds, or are very skilful, I shall not be surprised to hear of yet another tragedy.

To keep down the load, there are now two half hour periods during the evening when electricity is switched off, and usually one or more during the morning, in addition to not infrequent breakdowns. Owing to fuel shortage, the majority of gas vehicles are to come off the road, and henceforth buses will only run on Tuesdays, Fridays and Saturdays.

November 23rd 1944

In the words of the official notice "As a result of negotiations instigated by the Occupying Authorities re: supplies for the civilian population, a delivery of medical supplies, soap and food parcels have been promised as a first measure". I greet the announcement with rather mixed feelings. It seems a certain indication we shall remain under German occupation until the end of the hostilities. But it surely does reduce the worries of all of us, especially those with invalids or children in their care. I notice most people seem to have great expectations of this traffic once it starts, each individual expecting supplies of those things he or she most needs. Some even hope for coal for gas and domestic purposes, forgetting, in the case of gas, it would not be possible to prevent the Germans from benefiting the same as civilians. On the whole whatever comes, for what we are about to receive we are truly thankful.

The escape venture referred to above has not yet taken place, having been twice postponed owing to unsuitable weather.

Coming back to the food parcels again, I venture to make two forecasts. Firstly it will drop the bottom out of the black market racket, and secondly more than a few of the parcels will be sold to Germans by some of those who prefer extra money (even marks) to being set free.

November 25th 1944

I think I might try to describe a typical day in our lives, with some of the restrictions and difficulties. There is no point in rising too early, for one cannot go out before curfew and for those who rely on gas, there is no light, and quite often no electricity. Having got over the irksome business of getting out of bed, we tackle morning ablutions, for most people soapless and not much better with ration soap. Breakfast is concocted on a wood fire and for most comprises of oat porridge and tea or coffee, both ersatz, (no bread, the ration won't allow it).

Assuming one's tyres have not deflated the cycle ride to work is accomplished with regard to the many regulations on the subject – in single file, both hands and feet in their appropriate places - should the Feldgendarmerie be looking. Having arrived at work (not infrequently the journey is completed on one's feet pushing a deflated and dejected looking cycle) one is faced with agreeably filling in the 3½ hours of the morning. Friends come in for a gossip on local and war news, and rumours are exchanged and duly disbelieved. If the weather is cold, one might find some work to do, there being no artificial heating. Customers are not infrequent, and sometimes one can even supply what they want, though more often it is a case of "sorry, none left". The morning, short in hours, but long enough, passes, and the awaited lunch time arrives. Cycling home one is greeted by a completely vegetarian meal. Potatoes, form the main basis, supported by such other vegetables as available. The only two methods of cooking it are the aforementioned wood fire, used with discretion owing to the difficulty and expense of getting wood, or the communal oven may be used, in which case there is a long trek to fetch the dinner, and when it arrives at the table it is not so warm. Following the vegetable concoction, the more fortunate may be treated to a flour and water pudding (the flour obtained either by gleaning or more probably black market) and, when available, seasoned with sugar beet syrup. One leaves home feeling very full up, and returns to work with some trepidation lest one's decrepit tyres should give up the ghost. Some have long since given up the struggle, and cycle on bare rims. After half an hour at 'work' one is feeling as if one hasn't eaten for a week, and goes for a walk to change library books and return visits to friends. The town atmosphere does nothing to relieve the depression. The only signs of activity are around vegetable shops with Germans as well as civilians anxious to buy vegetables to eke out rations. Even on the days they are open most other shops are empty and forlorn, staff standing about waiting for closing time. Windows almost without exception display such 2nd hand goods as no-one wants to buy, and look unattractive without artificial lighting in the half light of a winter afternoon. A few civilians wander about on like errands to one's own, but if they wish to observe another of the myriad of German regulations do not stand about in groups. Usually there are more German soldiers than civilians about, and occasionally one hears a party of them marching and singing. So the working day comes to an end. Home and a wait in the fading light until the electricity is switched on at six o'clock before one can have tea (less fortunate gas users would wait in vain, and must hurry through their meal in the half light). Tea, like dinner, is again based on the ever recurring spud. That over, one prepares for one's evening of work or amusement, intersected at least once by the half hour electricity cut off, while one twiddles one's thumbs and waits for lights to come on again. If one elects to go out for the evening, due care must be exercised ample time is allowed for getting home before 10.00 p.m. Should one 'miss the boat', and find insufficient time to get back, there is no way of satisfying German laws it being an offence to be out of doors after curfew, and another to sleep anywhere but in one's own home without a permit. And so to bed, with the same fed up feeling with which one started the day, the only consolation being we are one day nearer the end of this seemingly endless period of wasted life.

November 29th 1944

After two postponements, the escapees (3 young men) left at 4.00 a.m. yesterday from Fauvic. At 11.00 p.m. one came ashore in a car inner tube life belt at St. Catherine, the other two brothers (Larbalastier) are presumed lost. Whilst I am naturally sorry, my earlier remarks will show I am not surprised. Meanwhile, friend H is sweating lest the survivor reveal the fact the boat has been stored at his place for the past fortnight. It is said the Germans have already managed to elicit the name of the man who sold them the boat.

DECEMBER 1944

December 4th 1944

New electricity restrictions – now only switched on for a total of 7 ½ daily. Our own cut off periods at home are always between 7.00 p.m. and 9.30 p.m. so when you cut three half hour periods from that it rather cuts up the evening. The earlier and later periods are reserved for those town areas where the Germans need the light for their cinemas etc.

A sign of the times – regular mass attacks are being made on the trees of the Island, in defiance of all Jersey and German laws and in complete disregard of questions of ownership. Whole neighbourhoods declare war over a group of trees, and make havoc with saws and axes. It is only natural with the sole fuel ration for cooking and heating being only 1½ hundredweight of wood a month, and with the November ration not yet forthcoming, people are in dire need, and are acting accordingly. Don't tell me it isn't honest – the only honest folk in Jersey today are those who admit they are dishonest. It is easy to have scruples when, for a few shillings, you can buy the things you need, but a different matter when money won't buy it, and you and yours will suffer if they have to go without.

December 5th 1944

The mutli coloured pom poms had a short and concentrated show yesterday. I did not see the planes, but am told there were two rather high up, and another at roof top height, the latter having navigation lights on, as though looking to land. Although some of the many hundreds of shells burst close, they failed to get the plane, which shot off in a southerly direction at terrific speed. It was believed to be a Mosquito.

Following on the German search of the farms, they have started to collect the potatoes, grain and sugar beet, all of which they 'blocked', allowing only a small quantity for the farmers' own use. It is reported they intend to confiscate all fowls in excess of six.

December 9th 1944

Great excitement in town, it having been officially announced the Red Cross ship left Lisbon on Thursday en route for Jersey via Guernsey with essential food and medical supplies.

It is announced curfew is to be extended over the Christmas holidays but no mention has yet been made as to whether there will be a relaxation in lighting restrictions.

Milk rations are now reduced to three pints a week.

December 13th 1944

The RAF has been around the district several times during the last few days. Last night's BBC announcement our parcels will be leaving Lisbon in a few days does not fit in with the local official statement the vessel left last Thursday. No doubt future events will prove which is right.

December 16th 1944

Total extras for Christmas are a 4 ounce ration of ersatz coffee, with the concession the following week's meat ration can be drawn in advance. As it is now certain the Red Cross ship will not come in time for the parcels to be delivered before the holidays, it looks like being a very poor holiday.

December 18th 1944

My complaints about the lack of Christmas extras were a little premature – influenced no doubt by the non arrival of Red Cross supplies, a last minute notice announces the issue of a tiny tin of tunny fish this week.

Nearly 30 young men have been arrested during the past few days for having possession of arms and ammunition. As usual in cases like this, reliable details are difficult to get.

Latest information is our Red Cross ship, the 'Vega', left Lisbon on the 20th with 1,000 tons, and is due in Guernsey on Christmas Day. Without the help she is bringing, this will surely be the poorest Christmas we have ever spent (or ever hope to). It will be the first time since the Occupation we have no black market meat – every other year I have handled a pig (or half a pig). The cheapest price this year is 14 marks (30/-) a lb and it is being sold even higher. With the store just about defunct and no commission this 3rd successive year, it seems rather more than I can afford to pay. I have no doubt our bellies will be filled, albeit of stodgy commonplace flour and water compounds and vegetables, and I look forward to quite an ambitious round of festivities over the holidays. It is only fair to mention you should not think us worse off than we really are, and we have got a skin and bone cockerel through the good offices of one of the circle of friends. There are extensions of electricity throughout the holidays, though the arrangements are too complicated to detail. Suffice to say, barring break downs or overload cut offs, we shall hear the King's speech.

The Germans have been carrying out a house to house search this morning in our district, but fortunately they worked away from us. I have a feeling the business is quite unofficial, and is an attempt by some unit to secure Christmas rations at our expense. I hear they have been sequestrating such items as fowls ready for cooking and other food stuffs.

December 30th 1944

Further information on the subject of the fore mentioned search is it was carried out by the scuttlers looking for fishing tackle with which to augment their own meagre rations. Apparently they found it apt to improve the occasion by taking possession of the grub nearest to hand.

The Red Cross ship is definitely due here this evening, having been in Guernsey for a day or two. The Bailiff has been to Guernsey for consultation with the Guernsey Bailiff, Schmettow and the Swiss International Red Cross representatives, and is returning with the ship. The Germans are taking elaborate precautions against the possibility of the parcels being looted en route or in storage. Naturally these parcels and their contents (as yet unknown) are the chief topic of conversation these days.

The buses cease running today, though it is hoped to run a bus on each route every Saturday for a week or two – reason being the shortage of fuel for gas producer vehicles.

It has been my habit since I started this Occupation manual to indulge in a little hoping at each year's end that the next year may be the last under such conditions. But surely I am not being unduly optimistic in not only hoping but expecting 1945 will be our last year of Occupation – and indeed not too much of that will have vanished into the past before we are free. I am afraid if by some queer mischance we should have to endure beyond the end of 1945, there would be a whole lot of the population who would not be there to welcome the end. Indeed it is time something drastic happened – mentally and physically we are coming to the end of our tether.

Anyway, welcome 1945 – may it bring release and relief.

1945

JANUARY 1945

January 3rd 1945

The 'Vega' has duly arrived and finished discharging yesterday, and the first issue of parcels is being made to the shops now. She brought sufficient parcels for more than one issue, plus soap, salt, medical supplies, and a small quantity of cigarettes. All except the salt is the gift of the Canadian and New Zealand Red Cross, and whilst the parcels vary a little, the following list of contents will give some idea:-

6 ounces chocolate, 20 ounces of biscuits, 5 ounces of sardines, 20 ounces milk powder, 6 ounces prunes, 4 ounces tea, 10 ounces salmon, 14 ounces corned beef, 8 ounces raisins, 6 ounces sugar, 4 ounces cheese, 16 ounces marmalade, 20 ounces butter, 13 ounces ham, 3 ounces soap, 1 ounce pepper or salt.

There are a limited number of invalids' parcels, containing such things as Horlicks, Ovaltine, creamed milk and some baby's' layettes, the gift of the wife of the British Ambassador to Portugal. The total brought here is about 450 tons.

It is intended this ship be permanently on the job of looking after the Islands, and she will take about a month to make the round trip. The first issue of parcels is being made at once, and the next will be made when it is known definitely the 'Vega' has left Portugal on her next trip. It is hoped on her next trip she will bring, in addition to a batch of parcels, flour and essential clothing, particularly footwear for manual workers. Tentative proposals for the future include voluntary evacuation of such invalids in need of treatment which cannot be given locally and the establishment of a news service between here and England, probably on the lines of field postcards. There have been conferences held between the States, German officials and International Red Cross representatives regarding the future needs of the Island, and the urgent question of fuel has been brought up. With no gas, no coal, electric supply limited to a few days, and even wood becoming difficult to get owing to transport difficulties, this is indeed a vexed question. It has been suggested the best means is for the Red Cross to send gas coal, which after the gas has been extracted, might supply coke for household fuel, but one snag I foresee is the difficulty of ensuring the gas is used only for civilian needs. No doubt that factor has not been overlooked.

Our gratitude for this practical help in our great emergency, which will save the health of many and the lives of more than a few, is limitless, and a fund is being opened as a small measure of our appreciation for the Red Cross. It is no exaggeration to say the Red Cross saved the lives of our unfortunate friends who were deported to Germany, so we have double reason to thank them.

Cases of people dropping dead are almost a daily occurrence, and are by no means confined to elderly folk - a sign of the times and food conditions. Another less tragic one is the complete lack of restraint, even in company, of breaking wind. It is really funny how people, who 5 years ago would not have dreamt of making rude noises in public, now do so without blush or apology. We shall surely have to mend our ways, or our friends in England will not want to acknowledge us.

In order to eke out electricity, it is to be available from 4¼ hours daily because of overload cut offs – by this economy, it should last till mid February.

January 8th 1945
One of three Allied fighters was shot down by local flak yesterday afternoon around five. The pilot bailed out – his fate is unknown and his machine crashed near St. Brelades Church.

I thought today's activity around town by big groups of patrols, stopping people for identity cards, might be connected with the possibility of other parachute troops landing from the plane. Our friends are always quick to suspect that sort of thing. Today's paper, however, reports two Yankee prisoners have escaped and are at large.

One of the first results of the Red Cross parcels is – no meat ration last weekend. Although we were amongst the unlucky ones whose parcels contained no soap, and although we have not yet sampled all the good things therein, we have seen enough of them to appreciate how really wonderful they are. Still to come are a small separate issue of soap, cigarettes and salt.

Later - Yesterday's air mishap was to a US fighter and the pilot is in hospital with a slight injury to his foot. The plane is a burnt out wreck on the headland off St. Brelades Church.

January 11th 1945
No definite information yet about the escaped prisoners, though it is believed one of them has been caught. In the search for them in the vicinity of the Fort, several radios were unearthed, thus increasing the prison waiting lists. Speaking to a chap already on the waiting list to be sentenced, I remarked the worst part was losing the set, but he tells me he has four others planted. Originally he was questioned on suspicion of having carted a boat for one of the escape groups, but they were unable to pin anything on him. (He tells me he did the job).

Latest German orders insist anyone who has a stock of more than a certain quantity of tinned goods and flour should hand over the excess to their less fortunate neighbours. This order is made as an excuse to justify the searches of houses. Another order calls for the immediate destruction of any dogs in excess of one per household, to conserve the food stocks of the 'fortress', and I also hear the States have been ordered to issue no further butter ration. Guernsey's plight seems worse than ours, 3 lbs bread, 3 lbs potatoes, and 2¼ pints skimmed milk weekly, and in addition root vegetables are rationed. One does not need a big appetite to be hungry on that ration in this cold weather.

These new electricity restrictions are a pest, and news is scarce as a result. With no light in the morning, and sunrise after 9.00 a.m. it isn't so good, whilst at night there are usually 3 half hour periods without light out of the 4 hours when the current is switched on. The periods almost always correspond with news times. Even people who have been using batteries to supplement lighting during these cut off periods are not so lucky now, as batteries cannot be charged, whilst many businesses are finding it difficult to carry on without light and power all day. In collaboration with the rest of the gang, I have been busy of late devising and fixing a water wheel to meet the needs of battery charging. It looks as if it will work, though it has caused us many a headache. I have been glad of something to take my mind off the state of the business, now nearly defunct.

January 13th 1945

A US flying boat skirted the south and east coast on Thursday afternoon, so low its markings were clearly visible. Local flak merchants got excited, and threw up just about everything bar Gorey Castle. During an artillery practise on Monday, a direct hit was secured on a house near Grouville Church. The house was damaged, but the occupants had a lucky escape.

January 15th 1945

Taking the good things first - the issue of cigarettes, salt and soap from the Red Cross cargo are being distributed this week and next. Now the not so good:- as a corollary to the Red Cross supplies, and by order of the Fortress Commandant, the 4 ounce meat ration is to be issued fortnightly, whilst the 2 ounce butter ration has joined the sugar in the 'no longers'. Milk is available only 4 days a week, making the adult ration 2 pints, whilst the electric supply is now rationed down to 1 unit a week. Not that everyone will take much notice, with the juice only on for 2½ hours a day and the use of all power banned. As the supply will only last a week or two, the threat of cutting off offenders doesn't work so well.

The wood racket goes on. Several empty houses in town have been broken into and completely gutted of all wood and it isn't advisable to leave any sort of wood lying around loose. People have even lost their garden gates and fences. On Sunday, a crowd of a hundred or more people descended like locusts on the trees in the Lower Park. (It is curious how, once someone starts in a district, everyone joins in until the area is completely denuded). The States officials and the German College House crowd, from the Bailiff and Civil Commandant downwards, took a hand in things, and as a result the culprits had to appear at College House and be reprimanded. It seems clear the Germans attach the blame on the States for not providing a proper fuel ration – this winter, the ordinary household's ration has been 2½ hundredweight total – and no issue for January; colder weather has brought considerable hardship. Remember this 2½ hundredweight of wood in three months of winter is the only fuel available for heating and cooking.

Our 'public utility' services are a joke. Water is cut off at 7.00 p.m. every night to conserve the pumping fuel, gas just doesn't exist, and electricity will possibly last for 3 weeks at the rate of 2½ hours light a day. Transport is provided by a bus on each route on Saturdays. You have to queue for hours ahead and it cannot pick up passengers en route. The latest victim of 'fortress economy' is the telephone service. All except essential numbers have been cut off without warning.

January 20th 1945

As expected following the official interest in the wood raids, new orders promise severe penalties for the illicit felling of trees. It would appear from the order and from what was told to the people who were reprimanded for last Sunday's affair, it is the Germans' intention to avoid the need for a repetition by seeing the population gets a regular monthly ration.

January 27th 1945

Following the official warning the fuel for the St. Peters Power Station would cease, the electricity supply came to an end Thursday night. I gather it is not the German intention to include themselves in this go without business. They have been laying power lines from the Old Queens Road plant to their most important places, with the idea of using the balance of fuel oil, held in reserve against a breakdown of the other plant, for themselves. The Power Station employees are refusing to work if the supply is confined to the Germans and it is said there would be enough to run for a while at 1½ to 2 hours a night. That I gather is how matters stand at the moment. Moi meme, I am as selfish as the Germans, and am using an acetylene table lamp, nicely decorated with eagle and swastika, and duly filled with German carbide.

A similar situation exists at the Evening Post which ceases publication tonight till further notice. The Germans want the staff to continue to produce only the Deutsche Ingelzeitung, and they refuse.

FEBRUARY 1945

February 3rd 1945

The electricity situation has resolved itself into the Germans taking over the Queens Road plant for their use, and running lines to the premises they want supplied. The Evening Post is being published 3 days a week.

The 2nd batch of Red Cross parcels is being issued on Tuesday and Wednesday, but there is no news of the arrival of further supplies, now well overdue. Rumour is busy about it, but I can get no definite information on the supposed statement we are to get no more. This is variously credited to Eden and Churchill. The reason is supposed to be the interception of a ship taking grain and potatoes from here to St. Nazaire. If it be true no more supplies are to be sent here because it is giving the Germans the chance to take everything except Red Cross stuff, it is a little late to think about it now. The Germans started taking as soon as there was mention of outside help, and have now taken as nearly all as is possible. For instance, for the next two weeks the basic (maximum) ration of bread is 2 lbs, then no more, thanks to German confiscation of grain. The potato ration is not yet reduced, but we are eating those stood for seed for 1945, so it doesn't look as if they will last long. The Germans have, of course, had a go at the spuds. The sole ration from the grocers is seven ounces oat flour and probably only for a week or so. The meat at four ounces fortnightly looks as if it could carry on, provided there is no wholesale sequestration. Extra to the rations there are only vegetables and a walk through the markets this morning revealed nothing but swedes, carrots, a few leeks and a few small cabbages. So what we have to live on for a week would hardly keep a cat. It makes me laugh to compare our menu with that which the unemployed in the distressed areas had before the war, and which was described as malnutrition. The death role over this period is heavy indeed. The cold spell, though not so severe as England, combined with extreme shortage of food and fuel, has taken off a whole lot of elderly people, as well as more than a few young ones. I can see that soon no one will be able to do an ordinary day's work, and many people have to go to bed immediately after their scanty tea through lack of light or firing.

One bright spot to report is two American prisoners who escaped on January 8th, after living on a boat at Gorey for 3 days, got away to France a fortnight ago. Their action in going straight to the closest point, and their general arrangements point to outside help, and the yarn a German naval and military officer went with them may be true.

February 10th 1945

The 'Vega' is due to start unloading here Monday. She is apparently only bringing parcels, though rumour insists another ship is on the way with flour.

Another attempt at escape was made 10 days ago by some US prisoners, as a result of which they have been deprived of the weekly batch of food sent in by the local population. Seems funny, we are near starvation, and yet people are able to send in quantities of food for the US prisoners.

Rumour (busy this week) has it several ships left here last weekend by night carrying volunteer troops to help the garrison at St. Nazaire. For some time we have been wondering why the Germans were busy working on some of their ships. Amongst the obvious alterations they made was to shorten the masts. The sequel apparently came last Wednesday, when there was a type of Commando raid from here at Granville. There is no official confirmation of this, but it does seem to be definite. There are some wounded in the Merton as a result, and one of the barges went aground at La Rocque on the way back. Maybe more details will be forthcoming.

February 17th 1945

The 'Vega' duly arrived here on Tuesday, and was discharged by Thursday. She had been delayed by a fortnight in Lisbon dry dock for repairs. She has again brought a double issue of parcels, a few medical stores, a little tobacco, some leather goods (probably for repairs), parcels for the US prisoners and one or two items of clothing, possibly for the Algerian prisoners. There was a little trouble about her discharge as local crane drivers had refused to load a ship with swedes for the Guernsey garrison, so the Germans would not allow them to work the 'Vega'. The first day German crane drivers were on the job, but were so dangerous at their unusual task the local crane drivers were brought back.

Official comment on this 'Vega' shipment is that "for some unexplained reason" the British Red Cross would not allow the flour which is in Lisbon to be brought by this 2nd cargo. The Vega is going straight back to fetch it and should be here again about mid March.

In view of the bread shortage, there is to be another issue of parcels next week. I made a mistake in saying 'shortage'. The bread entirely finishes today. Meat is being issued weekly instead of fortnightly until supplies of flour arrive, and for the next week at least there is to be a double ration of potatoes.

Buses have completely stopped running, and mail is only being delivered thrice weekly. Schools are only opened in the mornings, and there is a lot of talk about reducing working hours still further. Also all football is stopped.

In mentioning all our shortcomings, it is only fair to mention it is mostly not as bad as it sounds. In common with those who are able and willing, one succeeds in some measure in avoiding the worst consequences. Officially, for instance, there is no light, but most people have tackled that problem one way or another if only by buying candles at 9/6d each or more. The fuel problem is more urgent, and if tackled with cash, devilish expensive. Most people have to buy tomato chips at exorbitant rates and it seems to work out at over 5/- per day for kindling. Matches are 3/2d per box, black market. If one has to rely on black market for logs, they will cost anything up to £30 a ton. I bought a tree of about a ton, sacrificing my years wood ration, and with much hard labour have considerably more fuel in hand than if I relied on the almost nonexistent ration. On top of this we still have a little of the coal I got hold of last year (pinched from Jerry), so by present day standards we rank in the plutocratic class. The same applies in other directions. Some of the flour (also pinched from Jerry) is being used for bread making by a good baker – you take your own flour and he does the rest, but it is all quite illicit. Just before the Red Cross parcels arrived, we exchanged 1lb of our pre-war tea for 60 lbs of beans (dried), and a useful food reserve. Since the parcels came the value of tea has gone down very sharply. Thus do we manage.

February 23rd 1945

Most of the parcels issued this time were Canadian, but the whole of the next issue will be New Zealand, which we are due to get on Monday week. There was even less soap in the parcels than usual and no other soap was sent. The leather sent was sufficient for about 200 pairs of soles, but 40,000 of us urgently need soles, in fact new footwear. I do not possess anything which will keep my feet dry on wet days. There is sufficient salt for a 6 ounce issue. I still await news of the amount of tobacco and cigarettes, but I hear the medical supplies are again disappointing. From what the Bailiff told people, there seems to be ample stuff in Lisbon, but the shortage is shipping.

2,000 Red Cross messages came by the 'Vega', but here too we were not so lucky. By the same opportunity news came of the safe arrival in England of several friends repatriated through ill health from the internment camps in Germany. Messages are now being accepted from England via the 'Vega' on her next trip.

Said to be a protest against civilians getting Red Cross supplies whilst they, the occupying forces, get nothing, the German scuttlers had a night out on Wednesday. Judging by results, there must have been several hundred engaged working on an organised basis, for they painted black swastikas on almost every building in or around town. Most places had many 'crooked crosses' and there has been some frantic work trying to clean the mess. We were lucky at the store, the premises each side being adorned within a few inches of our place. The local police came across groups of the artists, but found it useless to protest. Quite a number are supposed to have been arrested either by the patrols or gendarmerie.

February 24th 1945

In mentioning some of the difficulties which I have been able to overcome, I didn't mention one which is beyond me. Tobacco is now terribly scarce, and the best price I have been quoted is 130 marks per lb, which I just won't afford. However, an issue of Red Cross is being made next Saturday of 5 cigarettes or 2 ounces of tobacco for all adults, which will ease the situation somewhat.

The medical supplies seem to have been most inaptly chosen and included slimming tablets and purgatives neither of which are needed in Jersey after 4½ years of vegetable diet.

MARCH 1945

March 3rd 1945

It is generally reported Schmettow, the Military Commandant, Heider, the Civil Commandant, and Baron Von Helldorff, another big noise, have all resigned for health reasons – a peculiar coincidence. Command has been taken over by a very Nazi Admiral, who came here some months ago to enquire into the food situation of the troops. Probably as a result, the clocks were last night advanced an hour, so we are once again on Double Summer Time. With no light, this isn't a bad idea, though it was done very precipitately, and being done on a day when no paper was issued, there were many people in the country who did not know about it.

The 4th issue of parcels is being made early next week, and we welcome the news the 'Vega' is once again on her way, bringing flour we hope. There have been reports of another ship to supplement the 'Vega', which we hope is true, for that ship will hardly be able to keep us going on the 800 tons she can carry every 5 weeks or so.

The town this morning was decorated with several Vs and red, white and blue signs, which I take to be the work of locals. One hears the Bailiff has protested about the swastikas painted by the scuttlers. As a result local employees of the OT building firms have been busy chipping the paint from house walls.

The advent of the new Nazi Commandant may quite easily precipitate trouble, especially if he starts to handle affairs with traditional Nazi ruthlessness.

In 1942 I reported Spanish OT workers were eating raw roots and digging up seed potatoes to eat. In 1943 it was the Russians. In 1945 it is the Germans who are hungry enough to eat raw swedes, and who, when they see a farmer has planted potatoes, come along and rake out the seed for food. What a change.

March 7th 1945

At 11.30 this morning, there was an almighty bang, the blast from which shattered shop windows in town. It came from the Palace Hotel, now well ablaze, with sundry minor explosions still coming from it. My theory is, it was a mistimed time bomb, possibly intended to go off tonight. If it was part of the general scheme of things, I am afraid it will expose the whole plot and wreck any chance of success the revolution might have had. One hears there are many casualties, but it is impossible just now to get reliable information, more especially as the whole neighbourhood has been cleared for fear of further explosions.

We have had our New Zealand parcels, and the following is a sample of the contents. One tin jam, 1 lb butter, 15 ounces cheese, four ounces tea, one tin condensed milk, one tin coffee, one tin lamb and peas, one tin corned mutton, 1 lb of sugar, eight ounces sultanas. The parcel was about the same size as the Canadian (10 lbs).

Our new Commandant's name is supposed to be Huffmeier, Vice Admiral.

March 10th 1945

Not much detail is forthcoming about the Palace Hotel affair. The place was completely burnt out, and the explosions went on until after 8.00 p.m. the blast shattering shop windows as far afield as Bath Street, Georgetown and St. Lukes. There was a certain amount of superficial damage to surrounding houses, but there seems to be no serious casualties amongst civilians outside the hotel. The most reliable source I have found says 28 bodies were recovered and others amongst the many injured will die. I think an estimate of 30 killed and 30 seriously injured would be a conservative one. This may include civilian personnel working in the hotel. It seems generally agreed it was the work of the underground movement, possibly as proof of its power to those troops still vacillating, or another account says a big lunch was being held there at noon, officials from the Guernsey garrison having come over for a conference. It is all guess work and it is doubtful whether the truth will ever be known.

At 10.30 the same night there was another fire in a shed on the OT dump at Clifton Park Estate, but I think this was the work of some opportunist saboteur, not a planned job. The fire destroyed one hut, but did not spread, being quickly put out.

Our next spot of bother, which made it look as if the expected riots were getting under way, was yesterday at 5.30 a.m. when we were awakened by more heavy explosions and much rumbling. The BBC report is of a Commando raid on Granville, probably from the Channel Islands, with casualties on both sides. To enlarge on that from this side of the ditch, there is the following data and a whole host of rumour which I prefer to ignore.

The German ships were observed raising steam the previous evening, the ones which had masts cut. At 5.30 a.m. yesterday there was the aforementioned banging and rumbling which lasted 30 minutes, including firing from the batteries at St. Martins. Later in the morning, the ships reached harbour, amongst them a small collier, believed the 'Asquith' under tow. Adding 2 and 2, it seems the collier must have been hit and disabled, and must have been taking German prisoners to England on her return trip from France. The Germans managed to rescue somewhere in the region of a 100 prisoners, all neatly marked POW and not looking so cheerful – who would, knowing they have to be taken prisoner again, and meanwhile going short of grub. Our friends also brought back other prisoners; I believe a dozen, which would include the crew of the collier. Judging by the activity of the ambulances there were quite a number of wounded amongst the Germans.

The 'Vega' duly arrived here from Guernsey yesterday afternoon, and is now discharging her cargo, which, according to the BBC, includes flour, parcels, yeast, salt, soap and petrol for ambulances.

Later - I have been given a feasible account of events at the Palace, according to which there was an accident during a lecture on explosives. Treating the resultant fire with water, it spread to the next room where explosives were stored, hence the big bang.

It is noteworthy how completely unkempt the German soldiers are now. They are clean neither in person nor clothing, and a high proportion has boils and skin troubles. In view of the fact their main diet is reputed to be swedes and sugar beet pulp, this is hardly surprising. A whole lot of civilian dogs are constantly being reported missing, and we imagine this is where the meat ration comes in.

March 14th 1945

A fact not mentioned in the Communiqué is the Germans lost one of their ships. The interesting aftermath was the investiture held since; the men taking part were presented with an Iron Cross of whichever class their rank earned them, a packet of 20 cigarettes and a pot of sugar beet syrup. One wonders which reward was the most valued.

March 17th 1945

The ration of bread was being issued almost as soon as 'Vega' was discharged. We are getting 4 lbs for adults, 3 lbs pounds for juveniles and 1½ lbs for infants and are paying at the rate of 6d for 2 lbs. I gather the Red Cross have bought the flour and brought it here on our behalf, and it is not a Red Cross gift. We are still just as grateful, especially after 3 breadless weeks. 'Vega' left again on the 15th, after having spent a few days idle here. Rumour is rampant about the reasons behind the delay, but it seems probable the 15th was the date agreed by the German and British. She must have had a slight leak for about 1,000 parcels were damaged by bilge water. It may sound ungracious, after all the good the Red Cross and 'Vega' have done here, but we honestly need an additional ship, especially if the clothing and other stuff mentioned in Parliament is to be brought. Believe me we need it. I do not have a pair of shoes which are watertight, and I am well shod compared to many. But the 'Vega' can only do the round trip in a month, and can only bring enough flour for a month, plus one issue of parcels and a few small sundries. Even if one assumes that to be enough for us to manage on, it allows no margin for a delay in the ship's arrival. Had we a month's stock, the case would be different, but without another ship, shipment of clothing, footwear or coal will mean our going short of bread and parcels.

A further 1,700 letters from England and some from the German internment camps, came by the 'Vega'.

With the advent of this very white Red Cross bread, the double ration of potatoes has ceased, and there is no meat ration this week.

Nine months ago we all felt the end was near. Now it once again looks endless, especially as I hear our new Commandant, Vice Admiral Huffmeier, mentioned in his first order on the day of taking over command here, he had personally promised Hitler to fight to the end no matter what happened – inferring he would fight on even if the official war ended. The Germans are planting potatoes for this summer and cutting down trees ready for next winter, and asking farmers to grow tobacco, which won't be ready till September, for them. We don't really believe they will be anywhere near here next winter, but I still can't foresee how or when the end will come. It is getting badly on everyone's nerves. Granted we did do wrong in electing to stay here in 1940, we are surely being punished for our sins. It is so ironic to have been so near relief and missed it, to be able to see the coastline of now friendly France. I could not analyse my feelings, bitter as they are, except by reiterating I am fed up. Everything one does is an effort and I don't seem able to take an intelligent interest in anything. I don't seem able to maintain interest in plans and preparations for much needed resuscitation of the business after the war. Probably as a result of the food, one's brain seems to work much slower and one just drifts through the day, doing little or nothing, and yet finding the time short. I can only imagine most of us spend a big proportion of one's time in mooning.

Another result of the arrival of bread supplies is postal deliveries are now made daily instead of thrice weekly, and children will shortly go to school in the afternoons as well as the mornings.

March 19th 1945

Early last evening, there was another fire, accompanied by more explosions, this time at a garage in New St. Johns Road which the Germans had been using as a repair depot for guns. It was completely burnt out, but as far as I know there were no casualties, and the damage amongst surrounding civilian property was confined to broken windows.

Leaflets are being issued by underground Germans. It emphasises the Nazi intention of holding on to these fortress islands even after Germany itself is beaten.

Red Cross soap and salt are being issued this week; the former to women and children only, at the rate of 2½d per four ounces. Salt is for everyone, 6 ounces for 2½d. This principle of charging for the stuff and passing the proceeds to the Red Cross fund has also been adopted in the case of medical supplies, which chemists are handling gratis.

March 24th 1945

Just over a week ago, a high up Nazi General came here from Germany; whether over or under Admiral Huffmeier, or whether merely here temporarily in an overseeing capacity is not known. His name is said to be Wolfe, and rumour has already put forward an unsuccessful attempt on his life.

There has been a considerable amount of distant rumbling going on these days, reminiscent of the preparations for D Day. We can't fathom out what it is all about, unless the Yanks are undertaking demolitions in the neighbouring ports. Also one or two local bangs are without explanation and some continual air activity which we assume to be general reconnaissance following the Granville raid.

March 31st 1945

The 5th issue of parcels was made on Tuesday 27th, Canadian again, and we are getting ten more cigarettes each today (male adults only).

The position on paying for Red Cross supplies has been made a little clearer. The parcels and some other items are the gift of the International Red Cross. There are some things, which are supplied by the British Government, who have asked an account be kept of any moneys received against these goods. Hence is the principle of making a charge against some things and not others.

There have been no signs of activity on the part of the German underground movement, though the High Command have deemed it necessary to put over one or two 'pep' talks at the Forum. I spoke to 3 tank corps men this morning and after they told me the current BBC news, I realised it would only be a matter of days before Germany was finished. I asked about the fighting on here afterwards. They promptly told me that when the war in Germany ended, they won't 'work' any more – and added they were not the only 3 who thought that way.

I have another of my famous prophecies to make – this time a long term one. With her potato and tomato exports gone, and probably no income from English residents, Jersey will certainly find herself in a pretty poor way when this is over and we have had the chance to settle down. I can see no alternative except that the Island's population will reduce itself, being tempted away by work elsewhere, until it gets down to the 10/20,000 region. The Island may be able to support such a population but I cannot see it reaching nearly 60,000 as before. From a general point of view, I won't call the idea so good, and it makes one think whether the Island will be a good place to go on trying to get a living. If one has to go elsewhere, better go first than last.

APRIL 1945

April 7th 1945

This has been one of the quietest weeks of the 240 weeks of the Occupation. The only report is the arrival in Guernsey of the 'Vega' on Thursday with flour and food parcels, and it is due in here tomorrow (Sunday).

Despite the fact all the news indicates the end is very near, and it won't be long before we are free, I and many others have got into a terribly apathetic frame of mind about it. I just can't be bothered doing any sort of planning or making any preparations. I can't even get excited at the fact the day for which we have waited nearly 5 years is near, and can't imagine myself getting excited when it does arrive. This last 6 months have been just too much for us. Had it not been for the Red Cross supplies, I am afraid we would have suffered as much physically as we have mentally. I only hope when it does end, we shall be able to recover our mental energy and enthusiasm, for under peace time conditions we should just get no place as we are now.

After foreswearing the things, I have at last joined the swelling ranks of those enjoying the tribulations of radio reception via the crystal, and now twiddle the cat's whisker in the best traditions of 20 odd years ago. Hitherto, I have left the things alone, for I just couldn't find the patience to twiddle, but I should just hate to have to rely on the garbled 2nd hand accounts of that broadcast for which we have waited nearly 5 years, and which surely must be coming soon.

To-day's press contains a notice by the Fortress Commandant that from 8.00 p.m. armed patrols will be about, with orders to shoot straight at anyone seen robbing, or apparently intending to rob from fields or greenhouses. During the day, anyone found so doing will be shot at, unless they immediately respond to challenge. This order is directed more against marauding Germans than civilians, for we are now comparatively well fed – certainly better than before Christmas, whereas the Germans are much worse off. Their idea of fruit is raw swedes, or the stumps of cauliflowers, and their jam is cooked swede or turnips with the coloured water cum-saccharine sold locally as cordial. Stinging nettles are another regular item on their menu – cooked, of course. Being a German soldier in the siege of the Islands is far from being fun.

April 10th 1945

The RAF (or Yanks) passed this way on Saturday evening and again at 8.30 a.m. today, each time being greeted by a short burst of flak.

The Vega is now discharging her cargo of flour, parcels, sugar, salt, soap, seeds, yeast, flints, candles, paraffin, medical supplies, leather for repairs, working boots and textiles (clothing). I do know tobacco is not included and there are not enough parcels for a complete issue. That can be made up by the 'overs' from previous cargoes.

There are unconfirmed reports of two escape attempts. One, believed unsuccessful, from Bonne Nuit by a solitary man, he being forced ashore at La Saline after being fired on. The other was by a party of fishermen who had undertaken to fish for the Germans, and who took advantage of misty weather to get clear. No further detail is yet forthcoming.

April 16th 1945

The 'Vega' left again yesterday morning, and the 6th issue of parcels is being made tomorrow. It will be the last until she again arrives here, so there is at least 4 weeks to wait for the next lot – a long time, since we now rely so utterly on the parcels. Without this Red Cross help we would surely be in a bad way. The 'Vega' again brought about 1,800 messages from England. It seems they can't get more than this number censored at a time.

April 20th 1945

The RAF were around on Wednesday (19th) just after dark, dropping a succession of vivid flares which suggested photographs were being taken of the harbour area, curious there was no flak response.

Owing to the fuel shortage, there has been a considerable modification of the communal cooking arrangements and the communal feeding centres only serve hot soup, other restaurants being closed. I spent another day yesterday felling trees, having wangled the necessary permit, but it is mighty hard work.

The Germans did us a better turn than they knew when they cut off the telephone service, the receivers making useful headphones for crystal sets. The lack of headphones was one of the chief snags before. It is no exaggeration to say there are many hundreds in service.

The following Red Cross supplies are being issued next week. A ¼lb household soap to adults, one tablet toilet soap to all, one candle per head, one box matches per head, 6 ounces of salt per head and 8 ounces sugar all round.

April 20th 1945

The potato ration for next week is 1 lb per head, thereafter ceasing completely. In lieu thereof, we are to have an extra 1 lb of bread. There is some argument going on between the local and German officials about the milk supply. The latter have, it seems, for some time been trying to commandeer the entire milk supply for themselves, which would be a mighty bad thing for us. Another economy under German orders is water – the main supply is now cut off except for 3 spells of 1½ hours each day, and its use for anything but essential purposes is forbidden.

April 28th 1945

There was a report last week of the shooting of an officer concerned with the underground movement. Another rumour fixes the date of the rising as next Saturday, May 5th, but at the present pace of events, it may be it will not be necessary.

The milk situation is at the moment no worse than threats of dire retribution to any farmer who fails to send into town the whole of his milk production, and any rounds man caught issuing more than the bare ration. We had an extra milkless day last Sunday, but I don't think that is supposed to be regular. Farmers are allowed to keep ½ a pint per head, with no milkless days, but in order to do so must forego their meat ration. The food situation now is just about at its worst, and the markets can offer nothing more sustaining than flowers and tobacco plants. It surely won't be long now, so why worry.

The Germans had a spasm of moving around here, and have taken other houses all over the place, after summarily evicting the occupants. Some people have suffered their 2nd and 3rd evictions in this good cause. The shifting around of troops is possibly an attempt to split any groups formed ready for the long promised rising, said rising, according to rumour, being due to start on May 1st or 5th.

Explosions on Sunday are explained by a press report of a German commando raid on Cherbourg, presumably from Alderney, followed by shelling from Alderney of targets spotted by the Commando Unit. The report states 'some' of the unit evaded the enemy and managed to get back, so it may be imagined casualties were not light.

MAY 1945

May 5th 1945

There is a great air of expectancy here, this being the day various rumours have fixed for the capitulation of the Islands. The rumours are borne out by the passage of two small patrol boats in the direction of St. Malo on Wednesday forenoon, returning later, and this has been followed by the clearing of the Airport and of some of the minefields on Grouville common. Yesterday in town several thousands of Union Jacks put aside for this occasion nearly 5 years ago, were brought out by the shops and sold. Combined with the general war news, this optimism seems not unjustified. Unfortunately it is pouring with rain and visibility is bad, which might interfere with an airborne Allied occupation. It may be a symbol, being the direct antithesis of the cloudless and hot day which greeted the Germans when first they came.

Dealing briefly with other events of the week - The Red Cross seeds have been issued, a small charge being made, and the reconditioned Army boots are starting to be issued today (price 32/-). I pity the many hundreds of men now standing outside boot shops waiting for theirs in the teeming rain, probably almost all in leaky boots. Moi meme, I am having a pair put by, and so can avoid the wait. A limited quantity of women and children's footwear is to be issued on special permits only, as is the various assortment of new and second hand clothing. The 'Vega' is again in Guernsey, right up to schedule this time, a good job, as our need is even greater than usual.

May 7th 1944

Yesterday's premature excitement continued throughout the day. Many hundreds of people gathered in the Royal Square hoping to hear the rumoured proclamation by the Bailiff, and there were some minor incidents when some of the less tactful flaunted Union Jacks under the noses of the not too happy Germans – foolish, as the Germans were still armed. One must admit as individuals, they have been well behaved. It was noteworthy all the scuttlers had been disarmed and no official notice was taken of the failure of many of the troops to give the Nazi salute. On Sunday most of the troops seemed confined to their billets, and as a whole they and the civil population have behaved with admirable restraint. Smoke of the Navy was noticed during the afternoon and again this morning between the Island and Les Minquiers. There seems no doubt the surrender of the Islands is already arranged. Rumour insists Colonel Voisin of the Militia is now in the Island, and telephones and electricity will be going again tomorrow. A misinterpretation of yesterday's official radio statement of the impending laying down of arms in Norway and the Channel Islands caused many people to think the end had already come. We have had many false alarms before, but this time, thanks be, it is the real thing, the time we have waited for so long. I must admit I cannot get as enthusiastic and excited about it as I would have expected, and as I would have been had it come last summer. This last 8 or 9 months have rather made it an anti climax. We have already started getting our own and other people's radio sets out ready for service again, I am looking forward to hearing properly the small radio which was such a good friend to us while we had the mains. Although I could no doubt sell it for a good price, we have a really great affection for it, and it will remain in the family.

May 8th 1945

VE Day in England, but what here? Verey lights were being flashed last night from the high points of the Island, and from midnight to 12.30 a.m. the harbour was flood lit by several searchlights, so I waited hopefully for the British troops who did not come. This morning the Germans are all running around busily, and those who had put up flags are asked to take them in until 3.00 p.m. We had ours out first thing, but I don't know yet whether the gentle hint is being dropped in the country as well as the town. We are in a state of suspended animation, with the war finished and yet we are still occupied. The Bailiff has asked the public to maintain their calm and dignity during these difficult days, adding he is in constant touch with the Admiral commanding the Islands, and will inform the public of any change in the military situation at the earliest moment.

Later - One hears the Bailiff is to speak at 3.00 p.m. and to again hoist the flag of the Island and a British destroyer will come in this afternoon. The Vega is in St. Aubins Bay and coming in this afternoon.

May 11th 1945

Much has happened since my last entry, so I must endeavour to keep things in chronological order. I can only remember one day of such excitement, though of a different sort – the evacuation of 1940, and I can only remember one such volte face on a town in a single day – London 5 years ago when people there realised there was a war on. But the change and excitement on VE Day here surpassed everything believable. But there, I must go back further to keep things in order. The destroyers 'Bulldog' and 'Beagle' arrived off Guernsey on the 8th and made rendezvous with a German naval officer who was under the impression he could parley for an armistice. Being quickly disillusioned, he returned to shore, meanwhile having requested the destroyers withdraw from the coastal waters – failure to do so would be regarded as a provocative act and under the threat of the coastal batteries, the destroyers withdrew. They came up again at nightfall, and from midnight onwards awaited the German plenipotentiary. Eventually the unconditional surrender of the Islands was signed by Major General Heine at 7.14 a.m. on the 9th, 17 hours after the ceasefire. The 'Bulldog' stayed in

Guernsey and the 'Beagle' came and lay off Jersey. A few naval ratings came ashore, followed later by a small batch of Tommies, all looking wonderfully fit and cheerful to our eyes. It made us realise how much most people here had suffered physically and were showing in their faces, when comparing them with these men. The whole Island had downed tools without ceremony on the afternoon of the 8th, and had the whole place decorated in a short while. I think the best part of the population had gathered on the piers – the first time they had been allowed there for 5 years. The welcome given to these first British troops to arrive was delirious and hysterical. I must admit that I, who before could not get excited about it all, really felt the thrill of that first sight of our boys. They included some 30 Islanders. I was lucky enough to be on the Albert Pier having a look at the 'Vega', now discharging, when they came ashore. In the words of Colonel Robinson, commanding the Unit, progress was at the rate of 100 yards an hour, but the troops took their boisterous reception cheerfully, and shook hands and signed autographs ad lib. I think they were made to realise just how much their arrival meant to us. Eventually the Unit arrived at the Pomme D'Or Hotel, now to be British HQ instead of German Naval HQ. The German scuttlers were bundled out in short time, without undue politeness, and the Island was taken over. Colonel Robinson impressed everyone as being a MAN, and a very loveable one. I shall be surprised if, before many days, the Island doesn't almost worship him. His men don't seem to like Germans, and bully them around in a way to bring admiration in the eyes of a Prussian officer. In addition to the many flags, bunting and favours, many pre-war fireworks came to light (literally) and helped the jollifications. Nearly everyone who had car or motorbike left got petrol from who knows what sources and went joy riding. Radios blared from open windows, so the less fortunate might share with those who had the courage to keep their sets. Even I, who was in on the racket, never realised how many there were. I nearly forgot to mention the electric mains were got going very quickly, and the telephones department asked ear pieces be returned from use on crystal sets to their legitimate use so as to get the phones working again.

Description of the scenes is impossible – in my mind is a kaleidoscope of impressions – a lorry load of released Russian prisoners, driven by a German, singing heartily. Released US prisoners happily signing autographs at the Ommaroo Hotel, their new quarters. A dejected looking scuttler trying to push a wheelbarrow loaded with ammo through the dense crowds to the assembly dumps. German ships in the harbour painted with the white cross of surrender we found so galling in 1940. Our troops on the veranda of the Pomme D'Or, throwing cigarettes, chocolate and razor blades to a surging mass of people. Everywhere were groups of about 50 people, and in the middle of each was a soldier or sailor doing his best to answer the many questions, shake the many hands, kiss the many babies and sign the many books thrust at him. There was plenty of pilfering – the Masonic Temple where radio sets had been stored was broken open and many went, and I saw two men aboard one of the German assault craft dismantle and take away a complete gyroscopic compass. I myself got a German automatic as a souvenir. No attempt was made to take the Germans prisoner – indeed it would have been impossible with the handful of men to handle 15,000 prisoners. Instead, they were ordered to take their arms to various depots, over which they had to guard at first. Then they were ordered clear of the harbours, and later clear of the town and precincts. The general scheme is to herd them into one quarter of the Island. Many of them were quite pleased when the end came, no doubt looking forward to a quiet time in a camp, but they mostly look less contented now. I must admit they have kept their tempers very well under most trying conditions, especially when people were flaunting flags under their noses before the Islands were surrendered. There were one or two minor incidents, but not what might have been. Indeed, even hating them as I do, I must say the behaviour of the individual German soldier throughout the whole Occupation has been good. Several of the more prominent Germanites have sought police protection and are now in gaol, though their premises have been smashed up. Others have received attention already and been rather damaged. The rest have heard many rude remarks, and must be rather apprehensive.

Yesterday (Thursday) was another holiday, and was marked by an address in the Square by Colonel Robinson. The Guard of Honour of Tommies was headed by the band of the local Boys Brigade, which had been practising during the Occupation for this day, and led by Colonel Robinson, Captain H. Le Brocq leading the Jersey contingent, and Lieutenant Colonel Taylor who is in charge of civil affairs during the transitional period.

Today is normally a working day, but there is yet another holiday declared for tomorrow (Saturday). It is funny getting back into old habits again. One still has a tendency to take precautions when discussing the news, or go fumbling in the dark instead of switching on the light. If anyone is walking in the road after curfew, one's ears prick up, thinking it to be a German patrol. Curfew, black out and all other restrictions are disregarded. It is fortunate there is little or no drink available – up to date, with the exception of the justifiable assaults on Germanites, the civil population has behaved with great restraint, considering their overwhelming joy.

I forgot to mention we had two squadrons of Mustangs and some medium bombers doing formation flying over the Island during the days, no doubt as a threat to any attempt at insurrection, especially in view of the laxity in signing up the surrender. I have this afternoon had the pleasure of walking all over the Airport, which for five years has been banned to us. Great fun to go pushing past the Germans as if they didn't exist – they do, and are busy scrubbing and clearing up the buildings, even though there is no British guard. The Germans are obeying orders and making all the necessary preparations for their own incarceration in St. Peters Barracks. Minesweeping has been going on since yesterday, and there are frequent loud explosions. One hears Wolfe and other heads of the German Secret Police have been caught – they tried to fade into ordinary prisoners by getting into uniform, but it didn't work. They will have awkward questions to answer.

May 14th 1945

Weekend news is of the arrival of a veritable armada of ships of all types, mostly too big to bring into harbour. Some 2,000 troops and huge quantities of cargo have been pouring ashore, the latter being brought ashore in 'Dukws', the new amphibious craft. Tank landing craft are also being used, being backed up against the sea wall at West Park and discharged directly onto lorries. It's altogether a good piece of organisation.

Things are getting back to something nearer normal. We are back at work again, there seems to be a skeleton bus service running, and we are back on the left of the road.

Preparations for our release were made in England some two months ago, since when the whole shooting match has been standing by. There have been several changes of mind, especially during the last month, as to when, but I gather it would have been done on this spring tide whether the war had ended or not. It is said it would have been a bloody business for all parties, the Islands being amongst the most strongly fortified in the world. It appears Vice Admiral Huffmeier wanted to hold out despite the end of the war, but was overruled by his other officers. This intention of his is the probable reason why the surrender was not signed until seven hours after the cease fire. We are safely out of the mess this time, and grateful to be so without demolitions and so forth. Altogether Jersey has had wonderful luck.

Arrangements have been made for us to send messages to England on a special type of field postcard. I would mention, from the outset, it has been the apparent intention of the British Authorities to help and be decent to the civil population. Even the Red Leafs are putting themselves out to be helpful – and our joy riders must be a confounded nuisance to them.

I had the pleasure, so long awaited, of having the motorbike back on the road, having managed to secure a gallon of juice by underground methods.

May 16th 1945

Herbert Morrison, the Home Secretary, Lord Munster and other Home Office Officials have been in the Islands enquiring into local conditions and needs. Morrison made a fine speech in the Square yesterday just before returning to England.

Marks are being exchanged at the rate of 9.36 to the £ (full value) and cease to be legal tender after Friday, so there is a rush on the banks.

It appears there was a small scale commando raid at Trinity on Boxing Day 1943, when four British soldiers knocked up a farmer for particulars. Until now, he has kept mum about it, or he would have had a bad time from the Germans.

The discharge of supplies and the taking away of German prisoners continue at high speed, and there are few, if any, areas of the Island where Germans are still at large. There are still some about, mostly engaged in clearing up the premises they have made such a filthy mess of during their occupation. Believe me, with their filthy habits they surely have made some mess, as well as badly knocking about the premises.

May 19th 1945

The mails started running yesterday. Telegrams are also being accepted, but with only one line open it is slow. It surely is nice to once again get in touch with old friends. The money exchange has been extended to Wednesday 23rd, it being impossible to get it done in three days as planned.

We are getting 4 ounces tea, 8 ounces soap and 30 cigarettes this week, plus chocolate for the children, all the gift of the British Government. Next week starts a general increase in our ordering quota, such items as lard, margarine, sugar etc. being available in the shops. Ship after ship is being discharged here, bringing food, clothing, coal, etc. and the Army and Navy are busy. Up to date the British control a coastal belt, and are herding the Germans into the centre of the Island, taking away large batches of prisoners each day. Newly arrived servicemen are amused at our various ersatz devices, especially at the substitute cycle tyres.

May 25th 1945

Rations are now on a more generous scale than at any time for more than five years, being larger than those operating now in England as a chance to us to make up what we have been lacking. Potatoes are once again on the board (unrationed) and bread ceases to be rationed next week. Newspapers and mail arrive every day, and in general things are rapidly getting to something like normal. We are still, for the time being, under military government, but in rather difference form than we have known. Most of the prisoners have been taken away, though I hear some 150 Germans are missing and believed to have been supplied with civvy clothes by their Jerry bags. A few have already been caught, but meanwhile the troops carry their arms all the time. There is a rumour some of the Nazi crowd in Guernsey hid like this, complete with arms, and caused trouble. Some of the more inconvenient of the German structures are already being demolished.

There is still no news of many of the political prisoners taken away from here by the Germans. One man, Le Druillenec, taken for sheltering an escaped Russian at St. Ouens, is said to have been brought to England from Belsen horror camp. The lady taken at the same time (Mrs. Gould) is missing. Some of the escaped Russians have been telling their stories to the paper, and it is surprising to me how many of them got away, and with the aid of local people, stayed hidden.

Documentary films are already being shown here. A parade of troops and vehicles was held yesterday, but generally things are quiet. I, like many others, have plenty of correspondence to attend to, picking up the threads of the past five years.

The Islands had a special broadcast all to themselves on Tuesday (22nd), comprising messages from evacuees to England and introduced by Mr. Morrison.

JUNE 1945

June 2nd 1945

We have had oranges this week, the first for five years, and the first which some of the younger children have ever seen. Things are straightening out at high speed now, and the military are no longer carrying arms. The only Germans now remaining are those kept for various chores – clearing out billets, shovelling coal and so forth – it's so nice to see them.

Nearly all shops have sacked their Jerry bag employees, and they and men who were working for the Germans are having great difficulty in getting employment. The States Labour Department, acting on instructions from the military, have refused to take them on; which is as it should be.

We have the King and Queen coming to see us on Wednesday, hence another holiday. They are flying here, with fighter escort, and their Rolls Royce has already arrived. The troops are grousing – like soldiers of all generations, they hate parades.

We are told there is the equivalent of a year's clothes rations on the English basis here for us, in addition to a quantity of clothing brought by the Red Cross and now being issued. So altogether we are doing fine, and there is an air of real busyness about the town.

June 8th 1945

After a 24 hour postponement owing to bad flying conditions, their Majesties came yesterday in the cruiser 'Jamaica', with an escort of four destroyers. They arrived at 11.00 a.m. and left by air for Guernsey at 3.00 p.m. with an escort of fighters (two squadron). They had royal weather and a right royal reception, making a short tour of the Island before the King and the Bailiff exchanged speeches at the Royal Court. The event was the subject of a recording by Howard Marshall, broadcast in the one o'clock news today. There seems to have been few days during the past month when we haven't appeared in the news.

June 12th 1945

The good work of rehabilitation goes on apace. The gas services are once again working, and we had our first dust collection for nine months. The 'Vega' came in again last weekend, with flour, clothing and a few parcels, probably her last trip. As from June 22nd commercial shipments to the islands are permitted. Also, a new Lieutenant Governor has been appointed for Jersey – Major General Hyland. We are getting back on the rails far quicker than I imagined possible. There is an utterly different atmosphere in town these days. Gone are the lethargic days of yore, with everyone meandering about. Now, everyone goes about with a purpose, and there is a general air of happiness. On the other side of the picture, we have learnt of the deaths of quite a few of the unfortunate local people who, for some minor offence or other, got taken to German prison camps. Methinks I have been taking even bigger risks than I knew at the time, for many of them were being punished for 'crimes' less than my own budget of undetected offences.

June 25th 1945

The need, the time and the paper for continuing my long diary are all rapidly expiring. Things are getting better all the time, and the Navy will shortly be leaving us, whilst the Army's 90 days are already well advanced, though I think it is intended to leave a garrison here afterwards. A petition has been presented to the States, calling for an enquiry into all cases of collaboration with the Germans, even including those who cohabited or even had them in their homes. The latter crimes are so widespread it is hardly possible to punish offenders. For one thing it would draw a lot of undesirable attention to its extent, and would tend to brand the whole Island in the eyes of the world. Moi meme, I think it sufficient if they are ostracised until the time when the majority of them will leave the Island. The plane service is again running, and the first mail boat comes in tomorrow. It is easy enough to get away, but owing to returning evacuees, not so easy to get back, hence I have to wait for my long promised business trip.

From the papers and the more easily available radio news, it seems there has been less general change in England than I expected, and certainly less than during the last War. Even the change in the value of money is less than I thought.

And so, failing any outstanding news in the near future, I close my book of words. Writing has been a comfort to me for these five long years, and I have enjoyed it.

We have much to be grateful for. We have come through a very trying experience with comparatively little loss, with our health unimpaired, and as far as I am concerned, with a future ahead. Please God, however, there will never again be such a time. Certainly the worst aspect of the whole show has been the mental strain and the uncertainty. We have been in the unfortunate position of not being able to tell the whole truth even to one's most intimate friends.

I have made little mention of my mother throughout, but in closing it is only fair and proper to mention that she has done more than her share in making life bearable for us both. The shortage of fuel, food and clothing has reacted more heavily on the women than on men, but in our little household things have run much more smoothly than in most, thanks to her infinite capacity for making the best of things.

Glossary

AA	Anti aircraft
ARP	Air Raid Precuation
BEF	British Expeditionary Force
Befehlshaber	Military Commandant
Bekanntrachung	Public announcement
Communiqué	Brief report or statement
Constable	Head of one of Jersey's 12 parishes
Dogs Nest	Reef of rocks
Evening Post E.P.	Jersey evening paper
Feldgendarmerie	Field Gendarmerie
Feldkommandant	Field Commander
Feldkommandantur	Field Command
FFI	French Forces of the Interior (Resistance)
Flaming Onions	Flares from anti-aircraft gun
Flying Pencil	Dornier Do 17, German light bomber
Fritz	Nickname for German troops
Hun	German
HE	High Explosive
Inselzeitung	German newspaper
Jerry	Nickname for Germans
Kriegsmarine	Navy of Nazi Germany
Kultur	Nazi Germany culture held to be superior
Messerchmitt (ME)	German aircraft
Oberleitnant	Senior Lieutenant
Organisation Todt O.T.	German workforce of slave and forced labourers
Platzkommandant	Area Commander
Platzkommandantur	Area Command
Pompom	British quick firing gun
POW	Prisoner of War
Quisling	Collaborator of enemy occupying force
RAF	Royal Air Force
Soldatenheim	Institution for relaxation of troops
Standort Kommandant	Town station
Star shells	Projectile for illumination
States	States of Jersey (local government)
US	United States
Verboten	Forbidden
Vraicing	Collecting seaweed for fertiliser
Wehrmacht	Unified army forces of Nazi Germany